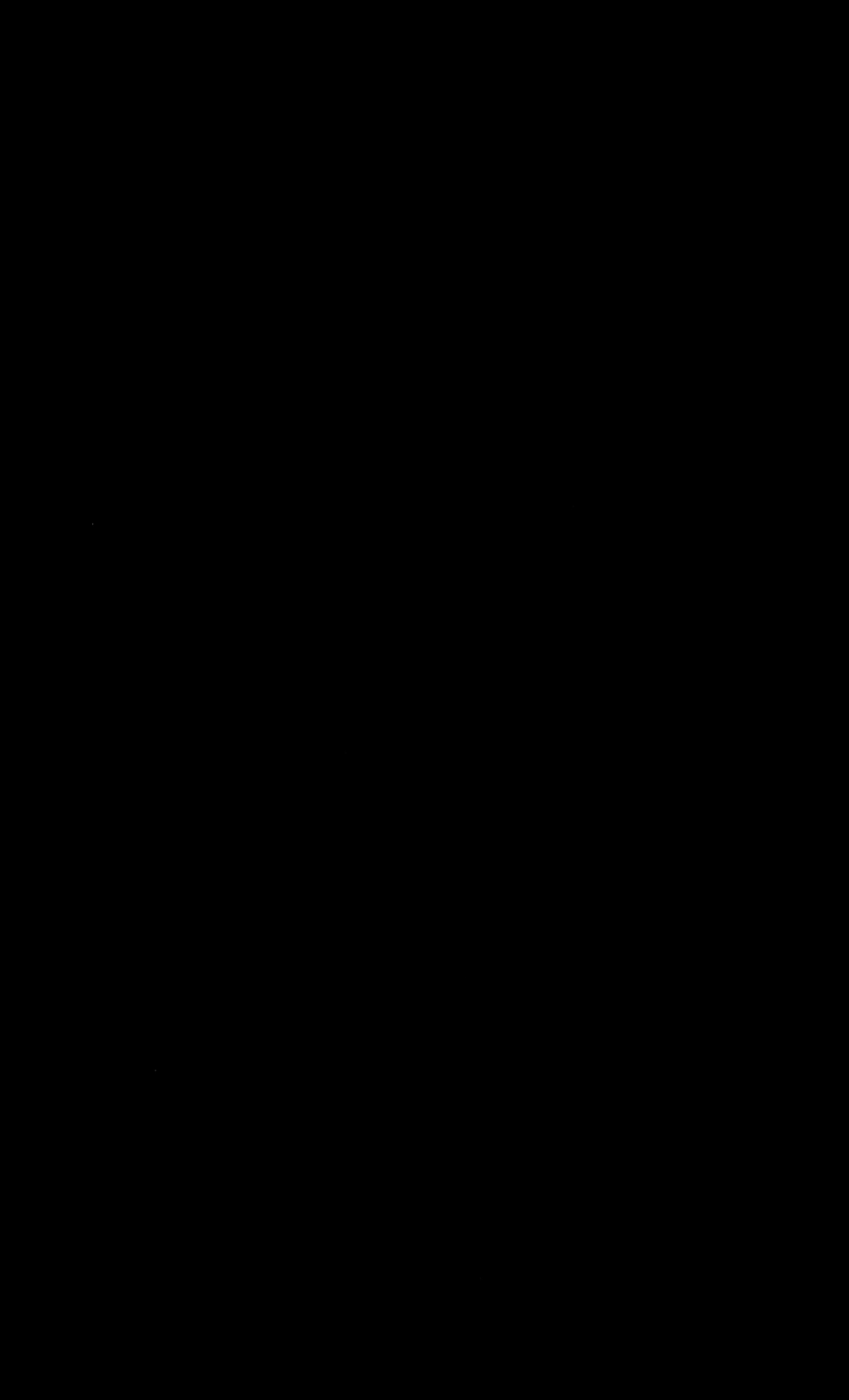

FIFTY YEARS OF BANGLADESH-INDIA RELATIONS
Issues, Challenges and Possibilities

FIFTY YEARS OF BANGLADESH-INDIA RELATIONS

Issues, Challenges and Possibilities

Md. Shariful Islam

PENTAGON PRESS LLP

Fifty Years of Bangladesh-India Relations: Issues, Challenges and Possibilities
Md. Shariful Islam

ISBN 978-93-90095-29-2

First Published in 2021

Copyright © RESERVED

All rights reserved. No part of this publication may be reproduced, stored in a retrieval system, or transmitted in any form or by any means, electronic, mechanical, photocopying, recording or otherwise, without the prior written permission of the Publisher.

Disclaimer: The views and opinions expressed in the book are the individual assertion of the Authors. The Publisher does not take any responsibility for the same in any manner whatsoever. The same shall solely be the responsibility of the Authors.

Published by
PENTAGON PRESS LLP
206, Peacock Lane, Shahpur Jat,
New Delhi-110049
Phones: 011-64706243, 26491568
Telefax: 011-26490600
email: rajan@pentagonpress.in
website: www.pentagonpress.in

Printed at Aegean Offset Printers, Greater Noida, U.P.

Contents

	Preface	ix
1.	**Introduction**	1
	Historical Background of Bangladesh-India Relations	7
	India's Role in the 1971 War	8
	Organisation of the Book	11
2.	**Narratives on Political and Diplomatic Relations**	16
	Introduction	16
	Evolving Political and Diplomatic Ties	18
	Relations between 1972 and August 1975	18
	Relations between post-August 1975 and 1990	22
	Relations between 1991 and 1995	24
	Bangladesh-India Relations (1996-2000)	26
	Relations between 2001 and 2008	27
	Bangladesh-India Relations (2009-present)	29
	Critical Engagement	38
	Conclusion	40
3.	**Emerging Trends in Development Partnership**	45
	Introduction	45
	Understanding Development Partnership	47
	Major Dimensions in Development Partnership	48
	Trade	48
	Institutional/Instrumental Development	49
	Changing Volume of Trade	51
	Bangladesh's Imports of Services: Health and Education Sector in Focus	53
	Investment	55
	Special Investment Zones	56
	Energy Cooperation	57
	Challenges	59
	Policy Imperatives	62
	Conclusion	63

4.	**Understanding Security Cooperation**	66
	Introduction	66
	Conceptualising Security Cooperation	69
	Major Areas of Security Cooperation	70
	Narratives on Military Cooperation	71
	Cooperation on Combating Terrorism	73
	Maritime Cooperation	75
	Cooperation in the Area of Cyber Security	77
	Cooperation within Indian Ocean Regional Institutions	77
	Conclusion	78
5.	**Border Issue: Challenges and Responses**	82
	Introduction	82
	Theorising Borders	84
	Historicising Bangladesh-India Border	85
	Challenges	87
	Border Killings	87
	Smuggling	89
	Women and Children Trafficking	93
	Border Tensions	93
	What can be Done?	94
	Promoting Border Cooperation	94
	Ensuring Strong Commitment	94
	Promoting Awareness	95
	Conclusion	95
6.	**Understanding Water Sharing Disputes**	99
	Introduction	100
	A Brief Historical Account	101
	Teesta Water Sharing	103
	Why has Bangladesh-India Water Sharing Dispute not been Resolved yet?	104
	Lack of India's Interest	104
	Lack of Information/Knowledge of Water	106
	Domestic Politics	106
	Creating Narratives of Water as 'Scarce' Resource and Rivers as National	107
	Policy Imperatives	108
	Still, Hope Exists	108
	Addressing Domestic Politics	108
	Hydro-diplomacy Pedagogy and Water Cooperation	109
	Promoting Joint Research	110
	Constructive Role of Academics and Media	110
	Is Statist Approach Enough?	110
	Conclusion	111
7.	**Narratives on Connectivity**	114
	Introduction	114
	Conceptualising Connectivity	116

	Dimensions of Connectivity	117
	Physical Connectivity: Connectivity by Road	117
	Connectivity through Waterways	120
	Connectivity at Sub-Regional Level	122
	BBIN Motor Vehicles Agreement	122
	Implications	123
	Challenges	125
	Domestic Politics	125
	Poor Infrastructure	126
	Lack of Political Will	126
	Conclusion	127
8.	**Unfolding the Role of Civil Society**	130
	Introduction	130
	Understanding Civil Society	131
	Civil Society and Bangladesh-India Relations	132
	Role of the Media	133
	Role of the Indian Media	134
	Role of Bangladeshi Media	139
	Role of Scholars and Scholarship	142
	Role of Business Lobby Groups and Others	145
	Role of Think Tanks	146
	Conclusion	149
9.	**China Factor in Bangladesh-India Ties**	153
	Introduction	153
	Contemporary Developments in Bangladesh-China Relations	155
	Chinese Investments in Bangladesh	157
	Defence Cooperation	157
	India's Concerns and Responses	158
	Bangladesh's Response	161
	Conclusion	162
10.	**COVID-19, Post-COVID-19 World and Bangladesh-India Cooperation**	166
	Introduction	166
	Implications of COVID-19 on Foreign Policy	167
	Impact on State Behaviour	167
	COVID-19 and Bangladesh-India Ties	170
	Post-COVID-19 World and Bangladesh-India Cooperation	172
	Conclusion	175
11.	**Looking Ahead: Strengthening the Partnership**	178
	Index	185

Preface

This intellectually stimulating book examines the key issues, challenges and possibilities in Bangladesh-India relations in the last fifty years. The Bangladesh-India partnership has become a textbook case of (ideal) ties in South Asia and beyond. From mistrust and a lower level of engagement, the Bangladesh-India relationship has grown into a development partnership. The outcome of Bangladesh-India ties profoundly impacts millions of people in these two countries and in the region of South Asia and beyond. Consequently, nurturing the warmth in Bangladesh-India partnership becomes essential. One can cite the example of how Bangladesh-India cooperation brings benefits to the people of Northeast India or Bangladeshi medical aspirants.

Bangladesh-India cooperation in connectivity, trade and investment has transformed the lives of tens of thousands of people across the borders. For instance, billions of dollars of bilateral trade create benefits through creating direct and indirect employment opportunities, ensuring the balance in the supply chain. Increased economic cooperation between Bangladesh and India is likely to improve the economic growth of these two countries. Consequently, increased economic growth will be imperative to increase the national budget in the social sectors, e.g., education, health and social safety net programmes that directly affect millions of the poor in these two countries. Also, harnessing the untapped potentials in bilateral investment becomes essential to ensuring the welfare and well-being of the people. Thus, from both the state and people perspectives, improved Bangladesh-India relations matter a lot.

While teaching Bangladesh-India relations to my undergraduate students in the International Relations Department at the University of Rajshahi, I found no scholarly book available covering contemporary Bangladesh-India relations. Therefore, I decided to write a book on the subject. Besides, India's Prime Minister Narendra Modi's 2015 Bangladesh visit elevated Bangladesh-India relations in a new height which also inspired me to author the book. I started writing this book in 2015. Consequently, the current shape of the book is a result of five years of research. One of the key aims of writing it is to place the issues, challenges and possibilities in Bangladesh-India relations before readers so that everyone concerned becomes well-informed about the necessity of having an improved Bangladesh-India partnership and thus play their respective roles for deepening bilateral ties. This book provides a knowledge base on Bangladesh-India relations.

This book will be useful to graduate students of International Relations and Political Science, to academics, researchers, and policymakers working on Bangladesh-India relations, Bangladesh foreign policy, and India's foreign policy in particular, and South Asia in general. It will be distinctive in itself as there is no book available focusing on contemporary Bangladesh-India relations. It covers significant issues in contemporary Bangladesh-India ties, including security, border management, water cooperation, and connectivity.

I am deeply thankful to Pentagon Press, New Delhi, India for keeping faith with the book project's idea. Pentagon and its production management have extended excellent support in the process of editorial work. Special thanks go to Mr. Rajan Arya from Pentagon Press for his generous cooperation throughout the publishing of this book.

I dedicate this book to the millions of poverty-stricken people in Bangladesh and India who can be immensely benefitted from better and improved Bangladesh-India relations based on mutual interest, respect and reciprocity. I sincerely acknowledge with gratitude the contribution of my family members (particularly my daughter Eelma Sharif Samata, son Shabib Ibn Sharif, and their mother Jannat Ara Tithy, for their sacrifices and loving support in this endeavour), friends (especially Sariful Islam from South Asian University), and colleagues and students at the Department of International Relations at Rajshahi University to finish the manuscript. I am also grateful to Professor Dr. Delwar Hossain,

Department of International Relations, University of Dhaka; Professor Dr. Md. Abul Kashem, Department of History, University of Rajshahi, Bangladesh; Professor Dr. Sanjay Chaturvedi, Department of International Relations, South Asian University, New Delhi; and Professor Dr. Kavita Sharma, former President of South Asian University; Mr. Abdullah al-Modabber, Assistant Librarian, South Asian University, New Delhi, India; and to all my teachers for their continuous support in all of my intellectual pursuits including this one. Finally, I take full responsibility for any error or omission whatsoever in the book.

Rajshahi, Bangladesh **Md. Shariful Islam**

1

INTRODUCTION

The year 2021 marks 50 years of Bangladesh-India relations. Though formal relations at the diplomatic and political level began in December 1971 through India's recognition of Bangladesh, one can note that Bangladesh-India relations started in March 1971 through India's help to the Liberation War of Bangladesh. Thus, it is timely to review the partnership's progress and identify the challenges and possibilities for continued and enhanced cooperation. Studying Bangladesh-India relations becomes important from political, economic, strategic, and socio-cultural perspectives. In fact, the nature and scope of the Bangladesh-India partnership impact millions of people of these two nations, in the region of South Asia and beyond. One can also argue that Bangladesh and India are two crucial regional powers in South Asia that can contribute immensely to the discourse of peace, security, and prosperity at bilateral, regional, and global scales. Against this backdrop, this book examines a few key questions, i.e., Why do Bangladesh-India relations matter for 165 million Bangladeshis and 1.3 billion Indians? What factors have accounted for the development of Bangladesh-India relations over the last 50 years? What are the challenges and possibilities to move Bangladesh-India ties forward?

Existing literature suggests that there are some issues in Bangladesh-India relations which are widely studied while some issues are poorly studied. For instance, there is much scholarship available on India's role and foreign policy in the 1971 War of Bangladesh (i.e., Azad, 2006; 2008; Basu & Datta, 2007; Dixit, 1999; Kumar, 1972; Rama, 1978; Sharma 1978), on the economic aspects, problems of refugees and minorities and Farakka barrage disputes (i.e., Bindra, 1982; Hossain, 1981; Saha, 2000; Singh, 1987; Haidar, 2005; Nair, 2008) in Bangladesh-India relations. On the other hand, there is a paucity of scholarship on the issues of connectivity, security dimension, development partnership, role of civil society, China factor, and bilateral relations in the post-pandemic era which merits serious attention. There is no scholarly book available that covers comprehensive and contemporary Bangladesh-India relations. Consequently, this book fills the existing knowledge gap.

In addition, the findings of this book will provide critical insights to the policymakers in deepening Bangladesh-India relations. Also, one can look at the policy relevance of the book by looking at the question of why do Bangladesh-India relations matter? The book argues that seven specific factors make Bangladesh-India relations necessary. **First,** one can look at the relevance of geography behind having a stronger Bangladesh-India partnership. In fact, neighbours matter in the context of security, development, peace, and prosperity. Concerning the importance of neighbours, the former Indian Union Finance Minister Pranab Mukherjee once said, 'You can change your friends, but you cannot change your neighbours, so it is better to live in peace' (Dutta, 2010). In the case of Bangladesh-India relations, it is argued that 'Geography dictates that the destinies of India and Bangladesh are, and will always remain, inextricably intertwined' (Sikri, 2009, p.58). Thus, it is suggested that 'The imperatives of geography and interdependence demand that the two countries should work together' (IDSA Task Force, 2011, p.11).

In fact, the peaceful, cooperative and friendly ties between two neighbours—Bangladesh and India—impacted the economy, security and development of both of these countries which resulted in increased welfare and the well-being of the people of these two countries. Besides, the peaceful shared past can also be looked at to have close ties between Bangladesh and India. Both of them had experienced two hundred years of British colonialism and exploitation. This shared history also inspires them to work together for shared development. In fact, there are many cultural similarities including language, food, music, sports and literature between Bangladesh and some states of India, including West Bengal. K.A.S. Murshid (2011, p.43) states, 'India deserves special attention given its proximity and a shared history, culture and geography'. Thus, a shared past, geographical proximity, and cultural affinity need to work as a significant catalyst for improved Bangladesh-India relations.

Second, both Bangladesh and India need each other for their mutual interest, whether in the context of security, economy or people-to-people contacts. Being surrounded on three sides by India and having lots of dimensions in the bilateral ties, India matters to Bangladesh and vice versa. In fact, in the foreign policy discourse of Bangladesh, 'India factor', or 'India-locked' are dominant keywords (Ahmed, 2008; Hassan, 1984; Hussain, 1989; Iftekharuzzaman, 1984). Therefore, it is argued that 'India remains, and will continue to remain, the central concern in the minds of Bangladesh's elites' (Hassan, 1984, p.44). On the contrary, from the Indian side, it is argued that 'Bangladesh is not just another neighbour of India. For India, Bangladesh will always remain very special for a number of reasons' (Sikri, 2009, p.58). One can also note that during his 2015 Dhaka visit, Indian Prime Minister Narendra Modi said that 'Bangladesh is "not merely a neighbour" but a nation with which India shares enduring links' which also signifies the importance of Bangladesh to India and vice versa. The *Dhaka Tribune*, in an editorial, for instance, notes that 'Good relations with India are imperative to the future economic development of Bangladesh' (*Dhaka Tribune* Editorial, 2017). The newspaper again writes that 'For Bangladesh, staying on the path to sustainable development involves fostering a strong partnership with neighbouring India' (2019). Bangladesh is also a crucial country for India. Kanti Bajpai (2011) writes about the importance of Bangladesh to India from the security, economic, water sharing and climate change perspectives. In fact, friendly neighbours play a crucial role in shared prosperity and development. *The Indian Express* in an editorial shows the importance of Bangladesh for India's economy and energy security and identifies Bangladesh as the 'best maritime gateway for India's Northeast' (*The Indian Express* Editorial, 2008). During Sheikh Hasina's 2017 India visit, it was argued that 'a stronger, stable and prosperous Bangladesh is in India's long-term interests' (*Hindustan Times* Editorial, 2017). Consequently, it is argued that 'Deepening ties...are important for both nations. Delhi must not let domestic political rhetoric derail diplomatic gains' (*The Indian Express* Editorial, 2020). Thus, whether one likes it or not, nurturing the Bangladesh-India partnership becomes essential for their mutual interest and shared prosperity.

Third, since no state is self-dependent in this world, they need to depend on each other. Thus, free trade becomes essential. It is widely believed that trade leads to interdependence, more communications or interactions, which results in peace and decreases the likelihood of conflicts. In addition, Sèna Kimm Gnangnon (2018) studies the impact of multilateral trade liberalisation on the economic growth rate by using a dataset comprising 150 countries over the period between 1995 and 2015. Gnangnon finds that there is a 'strong positive impact' of trade liberation on the economic growth of the countries. Control over trade is also seen as one of the key features of 'political contestation and dominance' (Koshy, 1999, p.15). In fact, trade constitutes an essential component in Bangladesh-India relations. For a long time, India was the largest trading partner of Bangladesh. One can argue that the increased volume of trade and commerce between Bangladesh and India impact people, the business community, and the state. In the fiscal year 2018-19, Bangladesh's imports from India stood at US$ 9.21 billion while exports to India were worth US$ 1.04 billion which touched upon every aspect of human life (Ministry of External Affairs, 2020, p.42). Trade has also impacted positively to lift tens of thousands of people in these countries out of poverty. Therefore, it is crucial to take into account the benefits of forging Bangladesh-India economic cooperation.

Fourth, there is increased tourism and medical tourism in Bangladesh-India relations. Notably, India receives its highest number of tourists and medical tourists from Bangladesh. On the one hand, for millions of Bangladeshi tourism lovers, India is the first and favourite destination. On the other hand, for tens of thousands of Bangladeshi people who cannot afford the medical expenses of Europe or Singapore, India becomes the first destination for medical treatments. For instance, one should note that in 2019, the number of visas issued by India to Bangladeshi citizens crossed the mark of 1.5 million where most of them were tourist and medical visas. Many Bangladeshi patients received treatment from Indian hospitals at a reasonable cost and recovered. A healthy person becomes an asset for any country and the family. This medical tourism also helps the Indian economy. Notably, many Indian people are involved in the process of tourism, including medical tourism, which also creates income opportunities for them. One can cite that even during the pandemic time, in October 2020, Kolkata's hotel and restaurant owners met with the West Bengal Tourism Minister Indranil Sen and sought his help to persuade the federal Indian government to resume issuing tourist visas for Bangladeshis which implies a strong political economy involved in the tourism sector of Bangladesh-India relations (*The Daily Star*, 2020).

Fifth, Bangladesh-India relations also matter from a geopolitical and geostrategic perspective. In fact, the location of Bangladesh made the country geo-strategically crucial for India and other extra-regional powers. Notably, Bangladesh is the key country for India's Look East Policy. It is argued that 'India's goal is not just to connect a remote, neglected, poor and discontented but resource-rich part to the rest of the country. It is in fact eyeing direct connectivity with south-east Asia and China using the north-eastern states, via Bangladesh' (Murshid, 2011, p.44). *The Hindu* defines Bangladesh as India's 'key strategic partner in South Asia to promote growth and contain terrorism' (*The Hindu* Editorial, 2017). The geostrategic significance of Bangladesh to India is also reflected in another editorial of *the Hindu* (*The Hindu* Editorial, 2015). It is also argued that Bangladesh and India, 'till date, have failed to secure the potential benefits of their ties since cooperation has been directly proportional to politics. It's time Bangladesh's strategic location catapulted sustainable growth for the eastern reaches of the subcontinent' (*The Indian Express* Editorial, 2010). Thus, it becomes crucial to work for regional peace and stability utilising the geopolitical and geostrategic importance of Bangladesh. In this regard, the active, visionary and constructive leadership and role of India becomes essential.

Sixth, in the post-COVID-19 world, there is a possibility of returning protectionism and decreased cooperation. In such a scenario, Bangladesh-India cooperation at the bilateral, regional, and global scales on the issues of mutual concern will bring benefits to the people of these two countries and beyond. It is argued that 'Bangladesh's economic growth can accelerate regional integration in the eastern subcontinent. Instead of merely praying for the revival of SAARC, Delhi could usefully focus on promoting regionalism among Bangladesh, Bhutan, India and Nepal' (Mohan, 2020). It is, therefore, forging India-Bangladesh partnership in the post-COVID-19 world in the areas of free trade, global health governance, global peace, and stability will be imperative.

Finally, the noble laureate Rabindranath Tagore had dreamt of Bangladesh as *'Sonar Bangla'* (golden land) which is found in the composition of the National Anthem of Bangladesh. The founding father of the country, Bangabandhu Sheikh Mujibur Rahman, also wanted to make Bangladesh *'Sonar Bangla'*. During the initial years of Bangladesh, many identified the country as a 'test case of development', or as a 'bottomless basket'. In 2020, the country is identified as a 'development miracle' by many. In fact, Bangladesh is a rising economic power with immense potentials. C. Raja Mohan, for instance, writes that 'rapid and sustained economic growth in Bangladesh has begun to alter the world's mental maps of the subcontinent. Over the last five decades and more, South Asia, for most purposes, has meant India and Pakistan. The economic rise of Bangladesh is changing some of that' (Mohan, 2020). Mohan (2020) further writes that 'the economic rise of Bangladesh could boost India's national plans to accelerate the development of its eastern and north-eastern states'. Behind the success story of Bangladesh, the role of the development partners, including India, has been crucial. On the other hand, India aspires to be a great power. If these two countries continue to cooperate based on mutual interest and reciprocity, it will be imperative to achieve economic advancement and the people's well-being. Thus, it can be argued that improved Bangladesh-India relations will bring benefits not only to the 165 million people of Bangladesh and 1.3 billion people of India but also to the region of South Asia as a whole and beyond.

Therefore, both from theoretical and policy perspectives, this book merits serious attention. This is the motivation to write this book because it will be imperative to raise Bangladesh-India relations to a new height based on mutual trust, interest, and reciprocity.

After analysing the book's rationale, this introductory chapter provides a background on the emergence of Bangladesh and the historical background of Bangladesh-India relations through looking at the role of India in the 1971 Liberation War of Bangladesh. Finally, this chapter briefly discusses the organisation of the book.

Historical Background of Bangladesh-India Relations

One needs to understand the emergence of Bangladesh and the historical background of Bangladesh-India relations to understand the emerging trends of the partnership. Bangladesh was earlier known as East Bengal up to 1956. Then, East Pakistan was adopted in the Pakistan Constitution of 1956. It is also argued that East Bengal was a geographic term while East Pakistan is a political term. In fact, East and West Pakistan were apart from each other geographically. There was no direct land communication between them. But since East Pakistan was a Muslim majority region, it was added to West Pakistan during the 1947 Partition of the subcontinent. West Pakistan exploited East Pakistan as its colony (Kalam, 1996; Singh, 1987). It is ironic for East Pakistan that it was exploited 200 years by the British and then 25 years by the West Pakistanis. Though East Pakistan was the key source of foreign exchange earnings for Pakistan, foreign exchange was used for the industrial development of West Pakistan. Notably, 80 per cent of foreign imports connected with industrialisation was utilised in West Pakistan. Thus, East Pakistan was severely discriminated with regard to the allocation of foreign exchanges (Singh, 1987, p.6). It is noted that 'there was a steady outflow of East Bengal resources to West Pakistan, making East Bengal even poorer than it was at the time of the emergence of Pakistan' (Singh, 1987, p.8).

Additionally, the constitutional provisions, the military, and the judiciary all worked for the centre, West Pakistan. Despite being 55 per cent of the population in East Pakistan, all senior military members of the administration were West Pakistanis while 87 per cent of the senior officers in the Central services were from West Pakistan in 1960 (cited in Appadorai and Rajan, 1985, p.101). The resources of East Pakistan were used to serve the interests and needs of the people of West Pakistan. Singh (1987, p.6) noted that 'in the income and production of the country, East Pakistan never got its due share'. East Pakistan was a colony for West Pakistan for 25 years. It is also noted that 'the central government controlled imports and exports in such a way that East Bengal was forced to buy commodities from West Pakistan at high prices' (Singh, 1987, p.6). On the contrary, the West Pakistani business community never paid a fair price to the East Pakistani jute farmers. West Pakistan also imposed restrictions on East Bengal's trade with the neighbouring Indian states. Thus, forging economic ties between East Bengal and Indian states was structurally prevented. There were decades-long inherent grievances among the East Pakistan people against West Pakistan due to its political, economic, cultural, social, and structural exploitation of East Pakistan which led to the independence movement/Liberation War in Bangladesh.

India's Role in the 1971 War

To understand Bangladesh-India relations, one needs to look at the role of India in the 1971 Liberation War of Bangladesh, which led to the emergence of Bangladesh as a sovereign nation-state. On the midnight of 25 March 1971, Pakistani military forces invaded East-Pakistan and committed massive atrocities on a large scale like crimes against humanity, war crimes, and genocide which lasted more than nine months. It is estimated that around 60,000 people were killed on that single night (Kabir, 1999). This war led three million innocent civilians of the then East Pakistan to death including intellectuals, politicians, academics, students and 2.5 million Bengali women who were raped during these few months by the Pakistani military (Ministry of Liberation War Affairs, n.d.). Over 10 million people were deported to India, causing them brutal persecution. These perpetrators burnt and destroyed thousands of localities in rural and urban areas of East Pakistan (present Bangladesh).

The Indian government and its people contributed significantly to the emergence of Bangladesh. Notably, 1,661 Indian soldiers sacrificed their lives for the Liberation of Bangladesh (Ali, 2018). Bangladesh's former High Commissioner to India, Syed Muazzem Ali, writes, 'The emotional bonds stemming from the invaluable contributions of the government and people of India during the Liberation War remain a dominant factor in Bangladesh's political, cultural and social wave. The spirit of comradeship of 1971 remains the foundation stone of the two countries' ties' (Ali, 2018, p.529). Against the backdrop of West Pakistan's invasion in East Pakistan, on March 26, 1971, a sovereign, independent People's Republic of Bangladesh was proclaimed, and a government with Sheikh Mujibur Rahman as its head was established. On April 24, 1971, the acting President of Bangladesh, Syed Nazrul Islam, sent a letter to the President of India seeking Indian recognition of Bangladesh.

India provided full support, i.e., moral, and material (military), to the people of Bangladesh in their Liberation War of 1971. When 10 million people from East Pakistan took shelter in different states of India, including West Bengal, the people of those states wholeheartedly supported them.

On March 30, 1971, both the Houses of the Indian Parliament unanimously adopted a resolution extending the support and sympathy of the people and Government of India to the independence struggle of East Pakistan. India's diplomacy was revolving around mobilising world opinion against the killings and destruction in East Pakistan, and to persuade the nations in the world including the major powers for a political solution of the East Pakistan crisis. In fact, India was the first country to tell the international community through the United Nations on 1 April 1971 that 'the scale of human suffering in East Bengal is such that it ceases to be a matter of domestic concern for Pakistan alone' (Bhattacharya, 1985, p.45). In June 1971, the External Affairs Minister of India, S. Swaran Singh, visited Moscow, Bonn, Paris, Ottawa, New York, Washington D.C., and London to tell the world about the prevailing situation in East Pakistan to raise world public opinion on the issue (Kumar, 1972, p.491). It is also worthy to note that thirteen ministerial delegations visited 70 countries to explain the 1971 crisis and its consequences for India (Appadorai and Rajan, 1985, p.103).

Additionally, on September 27, 1971, India's External Affairs Minister called upon the United Nations and all other international organisations to convince them about the political settlement between the military regimes of West Pakistan and the already elected members of East Pakistan (Singh, 1987, p.22). The Minister also urged all the countries to tell West Pakistan to stop their military atrocities over East Pakistan and sought a political solution. At the end of September, the Prime Minister of India, Indira Gandhi, visited the Soviet Union, which was crucial to take her decisions regarding the East Pakistan situation (Kumar, 1972). In fact, Indira Gandhi was not satisfied seeing the response from the international community. Speaking at a luncheon in Moscow on September 28, Indira Gandhi said:

> The international response has fallen short of the scale which a grim tragedy of this magnitude demands... The growing agony of the people of East Bengal does not seem to have moved many Governments. Our restraint has been appreciated only in words. The basic issues involved and the real threat to peace and stability in Asia are being largely ignored (cited in Kumar, 1972, pp.495-96).

Indira Gandhi also visited some Western European countries and the USA while the External Affairs Minister visited Germany, France, Canada, the USA and the UK to draw their attention and seek support for a political solution to the 1971 Liberation War of Bangladesh. India played a crucial role to internationalise the 1971 crisis.

On December 4, 1971, a Joint Letter from President Syed Nazrul Islam and Prime Minister Tajuddin Ahmed of Bangladesh was sent to the Prime Minister of India, Indira Gandhi, repeating the request for recognition of Bangladesh. In response, on December 6, 1971, Indira Gandhi stated in the Indian Parliament that:

> The valiant struggle of the people of Bangladesh in the face of tremendous odds has opened a new chapter of heroism in the history of freedom movements. I am glad to inform the House that in the light of the existing situation and in response to the repeated requests of the Government of Bangladesh, the Government of India have, after the most careful consideration, decided to grant recognition to the *Gana Prajatantri Bangladesh*. It is our hope that with the passage of time more nations will grant recognition and that the *Gana Prajatantri Bangladesh* will soon form part of the family of nations (Bhasin, 2003, pp.8-9).

Thus, after Bhutan, on the same day of December 6, 1971, India recognised Bangladesh as a sovereign and independent state. One can question why did India help Bangladesh in its independence movement in 1971? To answer this question, Partha S. Ghosh (1989, p.61), a former Professor of International Studies at Jawaharlal Nehru University, writes:

> India's interest in the Bangladesh war was primarily politico-strategic. India and Pakistan have been locked in a conflictual relationship even since the partition of the subcontinent. The two wars they fought (1947 and 1965) changed neither the power balance nor the political equation. Therefore, the political turmoil in East Pakistan in 1970-71 which culminated in a civil war was for India a golden opportunity to dismember its enemy. India's military intervention on behalf of the Bangladeshi freedom fighters was indeed motivated by this resolve.

Nalini Kant Jha and Bibhuti Bhusan Biswas (2012, p.187) maintain that 'One of the important objectives of India's support to Bangladesh's liberation struggle was to overcome geo-strategic weakness *vis-a-vis* Pakistan'. It is also argued that '[t]he defeat and dismemberment of Pakistan had made India the undisputed preeminent nation in the subcontinent' (Ghosh, 1989, p.65). One can debate on India's geostrategic, political, economic, or humanitarian reasons, but India's contribution to the Liberation War of Bangladesh was inevitable and is always acknowledged both by the government and people of Bangladesh. Bangladesh has conferred the 'Bangladesh Freedom Honour' on July 25, 2011, on former Indian Premier Indira Gandhi for her unparalleled support and contributions to Bangladesh's Liberation War in 1971. In addition, Bangladesh also honoured 226 Indians for their crucial support to the Liberation War under the Sheikh Hasina regime.

Organisation of the Book

The book has 11 chapters, including Introduction and Conclusion. The Introductory chapter focused on the emergence of Bangladesh and thus the historical background of Bangladesh-India relations. The necessity of improved Bangladesh-India relations is also highlighted in this chapter.

Chapter 2 focuses on the political and diplomatic narratives in Bangladesh-India relations. It shows the emerging trends in the political and diplomatic ties, which is the foundation of Bangladesh-India relations.

Chapter 3 focuses on the emerging development partnership between Bangladesh and India. It argues that development partnership has been a new defining characteristic in Bangladesh-India relations. Increasing trade, investment and energy cooperation are hallmarks in this partnership. This development partnership has become an example for many in the world. The chapter also concentrates on the challenges and possibilities in the partnership.

Chapter 4 concentrates on the security dimension in Bangladesh-India relations. This chapter investigates: What factors define the security partnership between Bangladesh and India? The chapter argues that from traditional trade and aid dimensions, Bangladesh-India relations have turned into security and strategic partnerships. Increased military cooperation, cooperation over fighting terrorism and increased maritime cooperation defines the current security and strategic partnership. It is also argued that strong Bangladesh-India security cooperation is in the interest of not only these countries but also of the region.

Chapter 5 focuses on Bangladesh-India border cooperation and challenges. Bangladesh and India share 4,096 km of land borders. This border demarcation and governance issue has always been a matter of discussion and debate in Bangladesh-India relations. Though the Land Boundary Agreement has been ratified, tensions still remain on the Bangladesh-India border including cross-border terrorism, smuggling, and border killing. The chapter argues that this long border can be turned into possibilities for the people of these countries. Against this backdrop, the chapter tries to understand: What is a border? How can one understand the Bangladesh-India border both historically and theoretically? What kind of challenges are there in Bangladesh-India border management on the ground? How can the Bangladesh-India border be turned into greater possibilities instead of conflicts or tensions?

Chapter 6 discusses Bangladesh-India water cooperation and challenges. Why have Bangladesh-India water-sharing disputes not been resolved yet? How can they be resolved? The chapter investigates these questions. Bangladesh and India share 54 transnational rivers. Being an upper riparian country, India diverts water depriving Bangladesh of its legitimate rights of a fair share of water. Also, there is only one water-sharing agreement, i.e., Ganga Water Sharing Treaty. It came into being in 1996, and it is only for 30 years. So, nobody knows what will happen after 30 years. Though there was much expectation in 2011 about the Teesta Water Sharing Treaty during Manmohan Singh's visit in Bangladesh, at the last hour, it did not happen due to the strong opposition of Mamata Banerjee. Notably, Teesta is the fourth largest transboundary river of Bangladesh for irrigation and fishing. Negotiations on Teesta water sharing have been going on since 1983. India is not showing standard (expected) behaviour with Bangladesh concerning water sharing. Consequently, tens of thousands of Bangladeshi farmers and fishermen are suffering from extreme water scarcity. In this context, the chapter will look at the possibilities of resolving Bangladesh-India water sharing disputes.

Chapter 7 analyses the recent hallmark development in Bangladesh-India relations: the connectivity. After two decades, Dhaka-Kolkata direct bus service began in 1999, which created the foundation in building connectivity in Bangladesh-India relations. In addition, direct train service has also added a new impetus in promoting Bangladesh-India connectivity. The chapter argues that growing Bangladesh-India connectivity fosters people-to-people contacts and greater cultural intimacy.

Chapter 8 discusses the role of civil society in either deepening or disrupting Bangladesh-India relations. The chapter argues that the role of the media, academics, think tanks and lobby groups are vital for the promotion of Bangladesh-India relations. The chapter also discusses the limitations of civil society.

Chapter 9 focuses on the China factor in Bangladesh-India relations. It is widely believed and discussed that the China factor is emerging as a significant determinant of Bangladesh-India relations. It is argued that the growing hostility between China and India and its regional and global implications may shape the contours of Bangladesh-India relations. It is in this perspective that Bangladesh-India ties are examined in this chapter.

Chapter 10 tries to map Bangladesh-India relations in the post-COVID-19 world. It is argued in the post-COVID-19 era, the world might experience protectionism and the rise of populism in some parts. In this context, the chapter argues that there is no alternative to promoting Bangladesh-India cooperation at the bilateral, regional and global levels on issues of health cooperation/governance, free trade, regional cooperation, and climate change.

Chapter 11 concludes that Bangladesh-India relations are critical not only for bilateral partnership and peace but also for regional stability and development in South Asia. It is also a critical factor for peace and stability in the Bay of Bengal and the western part of Southeast Asia. In fact, Bangladesh and India need each other for ensuring peace, prosperity, security and development. Many believe that from the Indian side, there is an absence of reciprocity which needs to be addressed. In fact, back in 2011, it was argued that 'India will need to redouble its efforts to deliver on its obligations so that the Bangladeshi side remains confident about India's continuing interest in strengthening and cementing of bilateral ties' (IDSA Task Force, 2011, p.13). This book proposes the same argument in the case of India's role in deepening Bangladesh-India relations. In fact, it also suggests that both countries need to view the other as central to their efforts to meet the developmental, security, and emerging health challenges in the post-pandemic world.

REFERENCES

Ahmed, K.U. (2008). *Bangladesh and its Neighbours*. Dhaka: Asiatic Society of Bangladesh.

Ali, S.M. (2018). The current and future state of India–Bangladesh relations. *Strategic Analysis*, 42 (5), pp. 529–537.

Appadorai, A. & Rajan, M.S. (1985). *India's Foreign Policy and Relations*. New Delhi: South Asian Publishers Private Ltd.

Azad, S. (2006). *Contribution of India in the War of Liberation of Bangladesh*. New Delhi: Bookwell.

Azad, S. (2008). *Role of Indian People in the Liberation War of Bangladesh*. New Delhi: Bookwell.

Bajpai, K. (2011, September 17). Why Bangladesh should matter to us. *Times of India*. Retrieved from https://timesofindia.indiatimes.com/edit-page/Why-Bangladesh-should-matter-to-us/articleshow/10009443.cms

Basu, S. & Datta, D. (2007). India-Bangladesh trade relations: Problem of bilateral deficit. *Indian Economic Review*, 42 (1), pp. 111-129.

Bhasin, A.S. (2003). *India-Bangladesh relations documents-1971-2002*, Volume 1. New Delhi: Geetika Publishers.

Bhattacharya, V. (1985). India and Bangladesh. *India Quarterly*, 41 (1), pp. 44-52.

Bindra, S.S. (1982). *Indo-Bangladesh Relations*. New Delhi: Deep & Deep Publications.

Dhaka Tribune Editorial (2017, April 7). More than neighbours. Retrieved from https://www.dhakatribune.com/opinion/editorial/2017/04/07/more-than-neighbours

Dhaka Tribune Editorial (2019, October 4). A friend and a neighbour. Retrieved from https://www.dhakatribune.com/opinion/editorial/2019/10/04/a-friend-and-a-neighbour

Dixit, J.N. (1999). *Liberation and Beyond: Indo-Bangladesh Relations*. Delhi: Konark Publishers Pvt. Ltd.

Dutta, I. (2010, January 1). You can change your friends but not neighbours: Pranab. *The Hindu*. Retrieved from https://www.thehindu.com/news/national/other-states/You-can-change-your-friends-but-not-neighbours-Pranab/article16835208.ece

Ghosh, P.S. (1989). *Cooperation and Conflict in South Asia*. New Delhi: Manohar Publications.

Gnangnon, S.K. (2018). Multilateral trade liberalisation and economic growth, *Journal of Economic Integration*, 33 (2), pp. 1261-1301.

Haidar, S. (Ed.) (2005). *India-Bangladesh: Strengthening the Partnership*. Chandigarh: Centre for Research in Rural and Industrial Development.

Hassan, S. (1984). The India factor in the foreign policy of Bangladesh. In M.G. Kabir and S. Hassan (Eds.), *Issues and Challenges facing Bangladesh Foreign Policy* (pp. 44-61). Dhaka: Bangladesh Society of International Studies.

Hossain, I. (1981). Bangladesh-India relations: Issues and problems. *Asian Survey*, 21 (11), 1115-1128.

Hussain, A. (1989). The Bangladesh-India relations, 1972-75: Seeds of future discord. In M. Ahmad, & A. Kalam (Eds.), *Bangladesh Foreign Relations: Changes and Directions* (pp. 9-19). Dhaka: University Press Limited.

IDSA Task Force (2011). *India-Bangladesh Relations: Towards Convergence*. IDSA: New Delhi.

Iftekharuzzaman (1984). The India doctrine: Relevance for Bangladesh. In M.G. Kabir & S. Hassan (Eds.), *Issues and Challenges facing Bangladesh Foreign Policy* (pp.18-

43). Dhaka: Bangladesh Society of International Studies.
Jha, N.K. & Biswas, B.B. (2012). India-Bangladesh relations: Constraints and prospects. In N.K. Jha & S. Shukla (Eds.), *India's Foreign Policy: Emerging Challenges* (pp. 187-195). New Delhi: Pentagon Press.
Kabir, S. (1999). Introduction. In Shahriar Kabir (Ed.), *Tormenting Seventy One* (pp. 2-7), Dhaka: Nirmul Committee.
Kalam, A. (Ed.). (1996). *Bangladesh: Internal Dynamics and External Linkages*. Dhaka: UPL.
Koshy, S. (1999). From Cold War to Trade War: Neocolonialism and Human Rights. *Social Text*, 58, pp. 1-32.
Kumar, S. (1972). The evolution of India's policy towards Bangladesh in 1971. *Asian Survey*, pp. 488-498. Retrieved from http://online.ucpress.edu/as/article-pdf/15/6/488/66978/2643261.pdf
Ministry of External Affairs, Government of India (2020). Ministry of External Affairs Annual Report 2019-20, New Delhi: Policy Planning and Research Division, Ministry of External Affairs.
Ministry of Liberation War Affairs (n.d.). Retrieved from http://www.molwa.gov.bd/history.php
Mohan, C.R. (2020, October 20). Explained ideas: Five main strategic implications of Bangladesh's economic rise. *The Indian Express*. Retrieved from https://indianexpress.com/article/explained/india-bangladesh-per-capita-gdp-c-raja-mohan-6799038/
Murshid, K.A.S. (2011). Transit and Trans-shipment: Strategic considerations for Bangladesh and India. *Economic and Political Weekly*, 46 (17), pp. 43-51.
Nair, P.S. (2008). *Indo-Bangladesh Relations*. New Delhi: A.P.H. Publishing Corporation.
Rama, S. (1978). *Role of India in Bangladesh Independence Movement*. Madras: The city Printing Works.
Saha, R. (2000). *India-Bangladesh Relations*. Kolkata: Minerva Associates.
Sharma, S.R. (1978). *Bangladesh Crisis and Indian Foreign Policy*. New Delhi: Young Asia Publications.
Sikri, R. (2009). *Challenge and Strategy: Rethinking India's Foreign Policy*. New Delhi: Sage.
Singh, K. (1987). *India and Bangladesh*. Delhi: Anmol Publications.
The Daily Star (2020, October 15). Kolkata hotel and restaurant owners want visas for Bangladeshi tourists.
The Hindu Editorial (2015, June 8). Modi's day in Dhaka. Retrieved from https://www.thehindu.com/opinion/editorial/modis-day-in-dhaka/article7291974.ece?homepage=true
The Hindu Editorial (2017, April 10). Building bridges. Retrieved from https://www.thehindubusinessline.com/opinion/editorial/building-bridges/article21957367.ece1
The Indian Express Editorial (2008, December 31). Dhaka, a new year. Retrieved from archive.indianexpress.com/news/dhaka-a-new-year/404724/0
The Indian Express Editorial (2010, January 12). Railroading ties. Retrieved from http://archive.indianexpress.com/news/railroading-ties/566341/0
The Indian Express Editorial (2020, December 19). A friend indeed. Retrieved from https://indianexpress.com/article/opinion/editorials/india-bangladesh-relations-narendra-modi-sheikh-hasina-7110534/
Hindustan Times Editorial (2017, April 6). India must go the extra mile for Sheikh Hasina to strengthen ties with Bangladesh. Retrieved from https://www.hindustantimes.com/editorials/india-must-go-the-extra-mile-for-sheikh-hasina-to-strengthen-ties-with-bangladesh/story-cwjxa8iEidvl2oA7Zxt7bO.html

2

NARRATIVES ON POLITICAL AND DIPLOMATIC RELATIONS

ABSTRACT

How can one understand the historicity of Bangladesh-India relations? This chapter investigates this question by looking at the political and diplomatic dimensions. It argues that one needs to understand the historicity in Bangladesh-India relations to understand the present contours, and to move the ties forward. Also, political and diplomatic dimensions work as foundations for other dimensions in the bilateral ties. It is argued that there are ups and downs, accusations and counter-accusations, claims and counter-claims and mutual interdependence in Bangladesh-India relations throughout the decades. It is suggested that for their mutual interest, it becomes essential to nurture warm political and diplomatic relations.

Keywords: *Bangladesh-India relations, political dimension, diplomatic dimension.*

Introduction

Political relations work as the foundation and driver for other dimensions in Bangladesh-India ties. It is argued that 'In inter-country relationships all over the world, economic and political relations are intertwined. Close or strong economic relationships, including trade and economic cooperation between countries, have often been propelled by the prevailing close political relations or by a desire to strengthen future political relations' (Islam, 2004, p.4069) which implies the significance of political ties. Additionally, Jyoti Prakash Dutta notes that 'it is the mutual trust and friendly political relations of the two countries [Bangladesh-India] that will ultimately decide the future course of all initiatives taken for reinforcing cooperation' (Dutta, 2005, p.50). Due to India's direct contribution to the emergence of Bangladesh and given the interests of both countries, Bangladesh-India enjoyed warm relations since the very beginning of their partnership. But in the post-August 1975 era, Bangladesh-India relations experienced ups and downs. In order to deepen the relations, Bangladesh and India also developed institutional mechanisms like Joint Rivers Commission (JRC), Joint Economic Commission (JEC), Joint Boundary Working Groups, and Home Secretary-level talks over time which resulted in better Bangladesh-India ties.

Suhasini Haidar, the Diplomatic Editor of *The Hindu*, points out the survey result conducted by *The Hindu* and The Centre for the Study of Developing Societies (CSDS) in India back in 2003. According to that survey, Bangladesh was the least trusted country in the region. In 2013, they did another study on the question of which country India trusts the most. The answer came out: Bangladesh. Forty-eight per cent voted for Bangladesh, which was the highest figure, even higher than the USA or Russia. This was because of the changing political attitude in Dhaka and New Delhi, which resulted in the growing Bangladesh-India partnership. Haidar points out that 'Today the India-Bangladesh relationship is seen as a template for other countries in the region' (*The Daily Star*, 2016). In order to understand this development, one needs to look at the historicity of Bangladesh-India relations by looking at the political and diplomatic dimensions. In fact, one needs to understand the historicity in Bangladesh-India relations to understand the present contours, and to move the ties forward. In addition, the political and diplomatic dimensions work as foundations for other dimensions in the bilateral ties. It is argued that there are ups and downs, accusations and counter-accusations, claims and counter-claims, trust and mistrust, and mutual interdependence in Bangladesh-India relations throughout the decades which defines the nature and scope of Bangladesh-India relations to a larger extent which impacts the lives of the people across boundaries.

This chapter is divided into four sections, including the introduction.

The second section discusses the evolving nature of Bangladesh-India political and diplomatic relations over the last 50 years. The third section critically analyses the ties while the final section concentrates on the concluding remarks.

Evolving Political and Diplomatic Ties

Relations between 1972 and August 1975

Though Bangladesh and India share deep historical, cultural, and social affiliations, they could not harness the untapped potential of their ties for a long time. Given India's support in Bangladesh's Liberation War, and friendly regimes in Dhaka and New Delhi, Bangladesh-India relations was going well during the regime of Bangabandhu Sheikh Mujibur Rahman in Bangladesh and Indira Gandhi in India. For instance, between 1972 and 1974, Bangladesh and India signed 13 agreements on several subjects including trade, telecommunications, oil, culture, passport and visa. In fact, given India's contributions in the Liberation War of Bangladesh, and the geographical reality, Bangladesh maintained close relations with India during the Bangabandhu period. Craig Baxter (1997, p.145) observes that 'it is not surprising that Bangladesh's most important relations in the international system are with India'. And indeed maintaining good relations with India was 'a cardinal principle of Bangladesh's foreign policy' during the Bangabandhu regime (Jahan, 1973, p.209).

Bangladesh Foreign Minister Abdus Samad Azad paid an official visit in India between January 5 and 9 in 1972. It was his first visit abroad as the Foreign Minister of Bangladesh which symbolised the importance that Bangladesh attached to India under the Bangabandhu regime. During the visit, the Foreign Minister acknowledged and appreciated the contribution of the Indian government and its people to the emergence of Bangladesh as a sovereign nation-state. In economic and political issues of mutual concern were discussed. More specifically, the vast destruction and devastation caused by the West Pakistan martial law regime and thus the necessity of the reconstruction of Bangladesh and the Indian role in this regard was discussed. The Government of India assured the Bangladesh delegation of all cooperation in the reconstruction process of Bangladesh. India also assured Bangladesh to address the shortages of essential commodities and supplies, caused by the devastation of the War. Bangladesh sought India's cooperation in getting the United Nations membership and the membership of other international and regional financial institutions. It is also worthy to note that both sides agreed to deepen Bangladesh-India relations based on 'respect for sovereignty and territorial integrity of all states, non-interference in each other's affairs, and equality and mutual benefit'. Both sides also agreed to work closely for stability, progress, peace and prosperity in the region.

After his release from a Pakistan prison on January 8, 1972, Bangabandhu went to London on the same day and held a press conference. On the way from London to Dhaka on January 10, he made a short trip to New Delhi. Mujib was wholeheartedly welcomed by the President, Prime Minister and the people of India. During the reception at Palam Airport, New Delhi, Indian President, V.V. Giri noted that:

> You [Bangabandhu] are the embodiment of the undying spirit of suffering and sacrifice in the cause of human liberty and human freedom. The emergence of independent Bangladesh is itself a unique event in the annals of democratic movements in world history. You have truly been acclaimed the Father of the new nation, Bangladesh. The trust and devotion of the 75 million people of Bangladesh reposed in you have led to the birth of *Sonar Bangla*, and we have no doubt that it will come to occupy a place of pride in the comity of nations (Trivedi, 1999, p.54).

In reply to President V.V. Giri's Address of Welcome, Bangabandhu acknowledged the role and sacrifice of India in the Liberation War of Bangladesh. For Bangabandhu,

> I have decided to stop over in this historic capital [New Delhi] of your great country on my way back to Bangladesh. For this is the least I can do to pay personal tribute to the best friends of my people, the people of India and this government under the leadership of your magnificent Prime Minister, Mrs. Indira Gandhi. She is not only a leader of men, but also of humankind. You all have worked so untiringly and sacrificed so gallantly in making this journey possible—this journey from darkness to light, from captivity to freedom, from desolation to hope (Trivedi, 1999, p.56).

On the invitation of the Government of India, Bangabandhu Sheikh Mujibur Rahman, the Prime Minister of Bangladesh, paid an official visit to India from February 6 to 8, 1972. Notably, as Prime Minister, it was Bangabandhu's first visit outside his country which demonstrated the importance that Bangladesh attached to India under the Bangabandhu regime. Consequently, in 1972, Bangladesh and India signed six Agreements on broader issue areas, i.e., Treaty of Friendship and Peace, Trade Agreement, Agreement on Cultural Cooperation, Agreement on Crude Oil, Passport and Visa, and Telecommunication. These treaties acted as building blocks in Bangladesh-India relations in the latter days. Among these, the Treaty of Friendship and Peace was for 25 years, which has been both appreciated and criticised by different corners of society in Bangladesh. Article 8 of the Agreement reads that 'the High Contracting Parties solemnly declare that it shall not enter into or participate in any military alliance directed against the other party and shall not allow the use of its territory for committing any act that may cause military damage to or constitute a threat to the security of the other high contracting party'. Ghosh (1989, p.65) writes that this 'actually foreclosed its [Bangladesh's] option to register extra-regional support to counterbalance India's superiority. As for India, it did not need any extra-regional support to establish its pre-eminence in the region in the aftermath of the Bangladesh war'. According to S.M. Ali, there was no preparation for, nor even pre-knowledge of, the signing of the Treaty among officials handling foreign affairs in Dhaka. This gave the impression that the Treaty had been forced upon Bangladesh (cited in Ghosh, 1989, p.66). This book argues that the Treaty was a necessity for Bangladesh, considering the geopolitical and economic realities of Bangladesh of that time.

After the independence of Bangladesh in March 1972, Indira Gandhi visited Bangladesh, which also underscored the importance that India attached to Bangladesh. On 17 March 1972, she addressed a public rally at Suhrawardy Udyan in Dhaka. In her speech, she praised the freedom fighters of Bangladesh and noted that 'I have come here today to pay homage to those millions who have sacrificed their lives and to the young and old who have borne arms to liberate their country. I salute the gallant men who have fought this battle, for it is their sacrifice and courage that has brought you freedom' (Bhattacharya, 1985, p.46). However, Bangladesh's relations with India expanded in multifaceted ways/dimensions. For instance, in 1973, Bangladesh and India signed four agreements on joint power coordination, telecommunication, atomic energy, and trade. In 1974, agreements on the land boundary, letter post, letters and boxes were also signed which signifies the importance that both Dhaka and New Delhi attached to their bilateral ties.

However, there was some dissatisfaction in Bangladesh over India's policies during even the Bangabandhu regime (Ahmed, 2008). For instance, regarding the land boundary agreement of May 16, 1974, while Bangladesh implemented the agreement immediately by handing over 'South Berubari' to India, 'the Indian government had not honoured its agreement to perpetually lease out "Tin Bigha" (15,130 sq. metres) to Bangladesh'. It is argued that 'India's protracted delay in handing over the "Tin Bigha" corridor not only created mistrust in the public mind, but also caused an anti-Indian feeling among the people of Bangladesh' (Ahmed, 2008, p.28). In addition, in the land boundary agreement, it was agreed that the enclaves would be handed over to the respective sides which was not respected by India (Banerjee, 2001). Another irritating issue during the Sheikh Mujibur Rahman regime was the water sharing dispute with India. Bangladesh's stand was that the country 'must get an adequate supply of water from the Ganges' (Maniruzzaman, 1975, p.127). Between April 1972 and January 1974, several official and ministerial level discussions failed to resolve the Ganga water sharing issue. Later, it was decided that the issue would be discussed at the Prime Ministerial level. Consequently, the May Summit between Bangabandhu Sheikh Mujibur Rahman and Indira Gandhi also failed to settle the issue though they agreed to resolve the issue with understanding 'so that the interests of both the countries are reconciled and difficulties removed in a spirit of friendship and cooperation' (Maniruzzaman, 1975, p.127). The issue of water sharing remained unresolved during the Bangabandhu regime.

To emancipate the people of Bangladesh from hunger and poverty, along with India, the Mujib regime realised the importance of maintaining good relations with the Muslim countries, China, and European and North American countries which displeased India. For instance, it is also argued that 'India did not like Mujib's rather quick rapprochement with Pakistan and other Islamic countries' (Ahmed, 2008, p.28) which also impacted India's relations with Bangladesh a bit as India was sensitive to Pakistan and China. It is also pertinent to note that a section of people in Bangladesh, particularly the radical parties, spread anti-India propaganda during the Mujib regime. It was said that the Awami League government was a 'subaltern to Indian interests' and that the sovereignty of Bangladesh was undermined due to the close ties with India. Against such claims, it is argued that 'Sheikh Mujibur Rahman was remarkably astute in manipulating the opportunities accruing from that relationship, and on balance, he was equally adept at influencing concessions from Mrs. Gandhi. Mujib was relatively successful in upholding Bangladesh's sovereign prerogatives' (Hassan, 1989, p.45).

Relations between post-August 1975 and 1990
On August 15, 1975, Bangabandhu and his family members (except Sheikh Hasina and Sheikh Rehana who were staying abroad at that time) were assassinated, which ended the golden chapter in Bangladesh-India relations (Chakma, 2015; Maniruzzaman, 1976; Pant, 2007). It is argued that 'with the exception of a brief period in the immediate aftermath of the liberation of Bangladesh in 1971, bilateral relations have been marred by mistrust, disharmony, and suspicion' (Malone, 2011, p.112). In the post-Mujib era, Bangladesh experienced several coups which created political instability in the country. Military regimes in Bangladesh in the post-August-1975 era established close ties with Pakistan, China and other Muslim countries while distanced from India (Maniruzzaman, 1976). It is also worthy to note that most of the army personnel were anti-Indian as they thought that the Indian Army had 'just walked into Bangladesh, when we had already finished the job' and robbed the glory of liberating Bangladesh (Maniruzzaman, 1976, p.122). The Bangladesh Army personnel were also dissatisfied with India as the Indian Army, before withdrawing from Bangladesh, 'took to India the vast amount of arms and ammunition left by the surrendering Pakistan Army and kept the nascent Bangladesh Army virtually disarmed' (Maniruzzaman, 1977, pp.191-192). It is also argued that to justify their military regimes and to divert the people's attention from the democratic process, an 'anti-India' sentiment was created and nurtured in the post-August-1975 era.

Harsh V. Pant points out that 'Opposing India became the most effective way of burnishing one's nationalist credentials in Bangladesh, and political parties, with the possible exception of the Awami League, made full use of this tactic' (Pant, 2007, 233). It is also argued that 'under the military rule of General Ziaur Rahman and General H.M. Ershad, India was figured as the hegemon, and the bogey of an Indian threat was used to rebuild the Islamic Bangladeshi identity viewing India not as a liberator but as a hegemonic "big brother"' (Majumder, 2014, p.333). Kalyani Shankar observes that 'despite India's role in the liberation struggle, the relationship between India and Bangladesh does not remain as strong as it should have been. While there was a brief honeymoon period soon after the liberation from 1971-73, things began to sour afterwards' (Shankar, 2017, p.161). On December 1, 1976, General Zia told the nation that 'I can assure you that today we are not alone or friendless. I want to tell every one that we do not want friendship at the cost of our independence, sovereignty and integrity' (cited in Maniruzzaman, 1977, p.194). Here, General Zia indirectly indicated India as a threat to Bangladesh's independence, sovereignty and integrity. Similarly, General Ershad defined India as an adversarial country to Bangladesh. In an interview to *Jane's Defence Weekly*, Ershad described India as the 'only adversary and possible source of threat' to Bangladesh (cited in Muni, 2009, p.75). In fact, Muni (2009, p.76) contends that 'It may be useful to recall that when General Ershad came to power in 1982, there was a tacit Indian backing for him'. But due to General Ershad's policies, i.e., supporting riots against the Hindu community in Bangladesh to secure support from Islamist parties and constituencies and allowing the use of Bangladesh soil as sanctuaries of the insurgent groups of Northeast India distanced India from Ershad (Muni, 2009, p.76). Consequently, India supported the pro-democracy agitation against General Ershad (Muni, 2009, p.75). The then Indian Ambassador in Bangladesh, Krishnan Srinivasan, in his memoirs noted that 'We had urged Hasina to concur with the rest of the joint opposition in rejecting participation in any future election under Ershad, and we helped to promote student unity' (Cited in Muni, 2009, pp.75-76). Muni (2009, p.76) argues that 'support for democracy in Bangladesh converged with India's perceived political and strategic interests'. S.D. Muni, in his book, *India's Foreign Policy: The Democracy Dimension* concludes that 'When the democracy factor coincided with strategic interests, Nehru's successors were prepared and capable of going to any extent, even waging a war and exercising overt economic pressures. Mrs. Gandhi's involvement in Bangladesh's war of liberation that also resulted in the break-up of Pakistan may be recalled here' (Muni, 2009, p.85).

It is also worthy to note that issues like the water dispute especially sharing of Ganga waters, maritime dispute, land boundary dispute, and disputes over the Muhurir Char and Purbasha Island in the Bay of Bengal had seriously undermined friendly relations between Bangladesh and India. In addition, India completed construction of the Farakka Barrage in April 1975, which 'became the focus of worsening relations between the two countries on a wider front' (Brichieri-Colombi and Bradnock, 2003, p.50). In fact, the Farakka Barrage created huge negative impacts on Bangladesh agriculture, fishing, and environment. This created negative perceptions about India in the public and political discourse of Bangladesh. To counteract India, military regimes in Bangladesh improved relations with China, Pakistan and Middle East countries (Maniruzzaman, 1977; Rashiduzzaman, 1978). Since February 1976, China officially condemned India's attitude to Bangladesh's Ganga river water and border disputes with India. It is also worthy to note that China provided full support to take up the Farakka issue at the United Nations (Maniruzzaman, 1977, p.194). Against such a backdrop, a strong anti-India sentiment is manifest in Bangladesh politics (Hossain, 1981; Bindra, 1984; Singh, 1987; Pant, 2011). In fact, Bangladesh-India relationship was in a terrible shape between 1980 and 1995. For instance, one can note that after signing the Trade Agreement in 1980, there was no single agreement until 1996 when the Ganges Water Sharing Treaty was signed.

Relations between 1991 and 1995

The world witnessed the fall of General Ershad in December 1990 due to the popular uprisings. In 1991, Bangladesh conducted a 'free and fair' election in which the Bangladesh Nationalist Party (BNP) under Begum Khaleda Zia came to power. The Khaleda Zia regime faced several challenges domestically, i.e., the Chakma insurgency problem in the Chattogram Hill Tracts in which the political elites in Dhaka believed that India had sponsored the insurgency. It is also widely accepted that 'the insurgents used Indian territory as a sanctuary' from which they attacked Bangladesh border security personnel and terrorized the civilian population (Khan, 1993, p.154). In May 1992, Khaleda Zia paid an official visit to India seeking India's help to address the Chakma insurgency problem, water sharing issue and border disputes but without much success. Instead, India raised the plight of the Chakmas of Bangladesh in the international community. As a result, in early 1993, the USA sent a delegation to the Bangladesh government asking for the resolution of the insurgency problem. Later, Khaleda Zia's Communications Minister, Colonel Oli Ahmed, was invited by New Delhi to discuss the Chakma issue. The bilateral ties were further complicated when Khaleda Zia raised the international Ganga water sharing issue while addressing the United Nations General Assembly in September 1993 (Khan, 1994). In addition, the election of Bangladesh to the SAARC presidency in 1993 also complicated Bangladesh-India relations (Khan, 1994). Bangladesh tried to arrange multilateral talks between India, Bangladesh, Nepal and a possible fourth country as a mediator to resolve the water-sharing problem with India by using the platform of SAARC.

Political relations between Bangladesh and India began to improve in 1994. In that year, several rounds of tripartite talks were held among the nine-member parliamentary standing committee on CHT, Indian representatives and the Parbattya Chattagram Jana Sanghati Samity leaders. As a result, a settlement was reached on return of the Chakma refugees from Tripura and Arunachal who had taken shelter there. The repatriation began in February 1994, which continued throughout the year (Hossain, 1995). It is also worthy to note that the Indian government was interested in repatriating the Chakma refugees as local tensions arose between the local people of Tripura and Arunachal and the Chakma refugees (Hossain, 1995). Several legislators from the Northeastern states of India even threatened to resign from Parliament if their demand for 'removal of the Chakmas was not met in 1995' (Hossain, 1996, p.202).

The improvement of political ties continued in 1995. As chairperson of the South Asian Association for Regional Cooperation (SAARC), Khaleda Zia visited New Delhi in 1995 and inaugurated the SAARC standing committee meeting where she also discussed bilateral and regional issues with the Indian Prime Minister, P.V. Narasimha Rao. Notably, Bangladesh and India tried to resolve many of their unresolved issues through a 'package deal' in which 'India would supply water from the Ganga as required by Bangladesh while Bangladesh would permit a road transit facility enabling India to improve communications with its northeastern states' (Hossain, 1996, p.202).

Bangladesh-India Relations (1996-2000)

In 1996, the Awami League, led by Sheikh Hasina, came to power in Bangladesh after twenty years 'in the wilderness' (Kochanek, 1997, p.136) making it imperative to improve Bangladesh-India relations. The Awami League government took a number of initiatives to increase the image of Bangladesh in the international arena, to improve bilateral ties with its immediate neighbours including India, to attract foreign direct investment focusing on economic diplomacy, to improve regionalism and sub-regionalism, and to promote new forms of multilateral relations (Kochanek, 1997; 1998). According to Stanley A. Kochanek (1997, p.142), the top most priority was 'improving relations with India in an effort to settle outstanding differences over water, transit, and trade'. It is also worthy to note that one of the election manifestos of Sheikh Hasina was that if elected she would bring waters from the Ganga to Bangladesh. Thus, immediately after the victory, in June 1996, the Sheikh Hasina government began negotiations with the new United Front government in India. As a sign of positive gesture, India dropped its earlier condition of sharing Ganga waters with the transit rights to Northeastern states of India. In early December 1996, a series of ministerial meetings was held in Dhaka, Kolkata and New Delhi which culminated in the signing of the Ganga water-sharing treaty for 30 years during Sheikh Hasina's visit to India.

The Awami League government was also successful in peace talks designed to end the Chattogram Hill Tracts (CHT) insurgency and to repatriate some 30,000 to 40,000 Chakma refugees living in the Northeastern states of India. On December 2, 1997, the CHT Accord was signed to end the 25 years of insurgency and repression in the southeastern part of Bangladesh and to restore peace there. The Indian Prime Minister, Atal Bihari Vajpayee, who took office on March 19, 1998, 'inherited a tension-free Indo-Bangladesh relation except for minor differences on some bilateral issues' (Singh, 2010, p.265). In this context, the Prime Minister of Bangladesh, Sheikh Hasina, expected that 'we have no doubt that as neighbours, we too will immensely benefit from your (Vajpayee's) acumen and your leadership in our common cause to further strengthen and consolidate our bilateral relations' (Singh, 2010, p.265). Notably, Hasina paid an official visit to New Delhi in June 1998 and discussed a wide range of issues of mutual interest with Vajpayee to promote

Bangladesh-India relations. Rajkumar Singh observes that 'the visit had an added importance because it was the first tour by a foreign dignitary after India exploded its nuclear device on May 11 and 13. It was significant that despite the fact that she is representing a Muslim majority neighbour, she restrained herself and accepted the sovereign right of India to take appropriate measures based on its own security perceptions' (Singh, 2010, p.266). Vajpayee visited Bangladesh in June 1999 to inaugurate the bus service from Kolkata to Dhaka. This was a big step to improve people-to-people contacts between the two countries. During the Hasina regime, India expressed an interest to buy Bangladesh's gas reserves and to use Chattogram and Mongla ports for its northeastern region. However, the Awami League government did not show enough interest in exporting gas to India. Also, border smuggling and intermittent border clashes often made newspaper headlines. Notably, during the summer of 2000, India unilaterally decided to expel as many as 1,000 Bangladeshis and sent them back to Bangladesh. Bangladesh only raised soft objections to India's 'push-in' activities (Rashiduzzaman, 2001).

Under Sheikh Hasina's leadership, Bangladesh joined the economic bloc of the Bangladesh, India, Sri Lanka, and Thailand Economic Cooperation (BISTEC) group. Notably, Bangladesh also entered a new sub-group comprising Bangladesh, Nepal, Bhutan and the seven federal states of northeast India which implied Bangladesh's interest to take Bangladesh-India relations to a new height expanding at the sub-regional and regional scale.

Relations between 2001 and 2008
In the October 2001, the Bangladesh Nationalist Party (BNP) under Khaleda Zia and its three coalition partners won the election. Historically, the BNP uses anti-Indian rhetoric to secure popular support. However, in its 2001 election campaign, the BNP did not use any anti-Indian card. And after it came to power, India also did not show any negative feelings toward the new government under Khaleda Zia. Bangladesh also showed a positive gesture to improve Bangladesh's relations with India. For instance, on November 17, 2001, the new Foreign Minister of Bangladesh, Morshed Khan, said that there is no serious problem about gas export to and transit facilities with India (Rashiduzzaman, 2002, p.190). It is noted that the *Dainik Inquilab* did not like the 'business-like' approach of the

BNP to the Bangladesh-India relations (cited in Rashiduzzaman, 2002, p.190). However, in 2002, Bangladesh's relations with Pakistan improved while ties with India 'hit their lowest point in decades' (Jahan, 2003, p.222). In January 2002, there was a bomb attack on the American Centre in Kolkata. India blamed Bangladesh-based Islamist groups for the attack. India also alleged that Bangladesh under the BNP was providing bases and training to the Northeast Indian insurgents. Another incident is that on November 7, 2002, Indian Deputy Prime Minister L.K. Advani publicly stated that with the change of government in Bangladesh, Pakistani military intelligence, the ISI, and al-Qaeda activists had increased their activities in Bangladesh (Jahan, 2003, p.229). These incidents deteriorated Bangladesh's relations with India in 2002. However, the issues of water and trade dominated the discussions of Bangladesh-India relations in 2003. Notably, Bangladesh 'stalled' on transit and transhipment issues with India.

In September 2004, Bangladesh Foreign Minister, Morshed Khan, alleged that India was harbouring anti-Bangladesh militants and criticised India's unfair trade barriers to Bangladesh (Riaz, 2005). Additionally, the Foreign Minister also criticised the Indian Prime Minister for calling Sheikh Hasina after the August assassination attempt which displeased India. Such remarks and criticism negatively impacted Bangladesh-India relations. Bangladesh-India relations deteriorated further in 2005. Border clashes at times escalated seriously. India opposed joining the SAARC Summit in February which disappointed Dhaka. The proposed Indian river-linking projects dominated the media and public discourse in 2005. Besides, in August 2005, there were countrywide bomb blasts which deteriorated Bangladesh's image globally. Bangladesh blamed India for such coordinated attacks (Riaz, 2006). The global media regularly covered the deteriorating human rights situation in Bangladesh and the rise of Islamic militancy under the BNP regime. For such negative media coverage, the BNP regime also blamed India (Riaz, 2006). In March 2006, Bangladesh Prime Minister Begum Khaleda Zia visited India where she had extensive discussions with the Indian Prime Minister Manmohan Singh and other senior officials on a range of issues including security, trade and water issues. The visit resulted in the signing of two agreements, i.e., Revised Trade Agreement and the Agreement for Mutual Cooperation between India and Bangladesh for Preventing Illicit Trafficking in Narcotic

Drugs and Psychotropic Substances. Except for these two agreements, Bangladesh-India relations did not improve much between 2001 and 2006 under the BNP regime. Accusations, counter-accusations, mutual suspicions dominated the policy and public discourse in Bangladesh's ties with India between 2001 and 2006.

Bangladesh-India ties deepened substantially during the caretaker government regime in Bangladesh between November 2006 and November 2008. Bangladesh chief advisor Fakhruddin Ahmed visited India in April 2007 to attend the 14th SAARC Summit in New Delhi. The army chief, Moen U Ahmad, visited India. In 2007, Bangladesh and India signed both bilateral and multilateral agreements to strengthen their counterterrorism cooperation. For the first time in history, the Bangladesh military invited Indian soldiers who had participated in the 1971 Liberation War of Bangladesh to celebrate victory day. The India-Bangladesh Chamber of Commerce and Industry was established in 2007 to facilitate Bangladesh-India trade.

Bangladesh-India Relations (2009-present)
Bangladesh-India relations improved substantially after Sheikh Hasina came to power in December 2008. In the *2009-2010 Annual Report of Ministry of External Affairs*, India, it is noted that 'Bilateral relations between India and Bangladesh acquired new momentum, following the formation of the Grand Alliance government, led by Prime Minister Sheikh Hasina in January 2009. India continued to engage the Government of Bangladesh on all important bilateral issues' (Ministry of External Affairs, 2010, p.2). In February 2009, Indian External Affairs Minister Pranab Mukherjee visited Bangladesh which was the first high-level visit from the Indian side to Bangladesh after Sheikh Hasina took office. This visit resulted in two crucial agreements, i.e., Trade Agreement; and Bilateral Investment Promotion and Protection Agreement. One of the notable developments was the visit of Sheikh Hasina to New Delhi in January 2010. A Joint Communiqué was issued outlining the significant areas of cooperation. Among them, infrastructural development in Bangladesh, i.e., the construction of the Agartala-Akhaura rail link, mutual consent on using Chattogram and Mongla ports and the Indian US$ 1 billion line of credit to support infrastructural development were notable. In addition, India also agreed to provide 250 MW of power to Bangladesh to address its

energy insecurity. A number of important agreements were signed, i.e., Agreement on Mutual Legal Assistance in Criminal Matters, Agreement on Combating International Terrorism, Organised Crime and Illicit Drug Trafficking and Agreement on Transfer of Sentenced Persons. An MoU on Cultural Exchange and Cooperation in Power Sector was also signed that bears significance in boosting Bangladesh-India relations. But the implementation of these aspirations was minimal from the Indian side. In this regard, Mihir S. Sharma (2011) writes:

> Since Sheikh Hasina's landmark visit to India in January 2010, an enormous amount of nothing has been achieved. India demonstrated not urgency, but its exact opposite. For each item, it appeared that the Bangladeshi side created the foundations for further cooperation, making what was already agreed-on happen. And, each time, the Indian side failed to reciprocate or did so with sloth and delay. India postponed boundary discussions for almost a year after Hasina's visit, for example. As for trade and transit issues, India's attitude has been abysmal. When Bangladesh's Commerce Minister snapped, after meeting Anand Sharma, that the concessions being offered were 'peanuts', his departure from normal diplomatic protocol was understandable. Sharma had just implied that a minor hike in Bangladesh's textile quota was a giant favour. It wasn't a fraction of what Bangladesh had a right to expect.

There were regular high-level visits and close contacts between Bangladesh and India in 2011. The most notable one was the visit of Indian Prime Minister Manmohan Singh to Bangladesh in September 2011. The visit was a milestone in Bangladesh-India relations as it resulted in several important agreements and MoUs, i.e., Framework Agreement on Cooperation for Development; Protocol to the Agreement Concerning the Demarcation of the Land Boundary between India and Bangladesh and Related Matters; Addendum to the Memorandum of Understanding (MoU) between India and Bangladesh to Facilitate Overland Transit Traffic between Bangladesh and Nepal. Furthermore, an MoU on Renewable Energy Cooperation; MoU on Conservation of the Sundarbans; MoU on Cooperation in the Field of Fisheries; MoU on Mutual Broadcast of Television Programmes; MoU between Jawaharlal Nehru University and Dhaka University; MoU on Academic Cooperation between National Institute of Fashion Technology, India, and BGMEA Institute of Fashion and Technology, Bangladesh, were notable.

Sonia Gandhi, the President of Indian National Congress, visited Dhaka in July 2011 to receive the Bangladesh Freedom Honour conferred on Indira Gandhi for her contributions to the Liberation War of Bangladesh in 1971. It is also pertinent to note that Sheikh Hasina visited Agartala in January 2012. She was conferred an honorary D.Litt. degree by the Central Tripura University. Jatiya Party President H.M. Ershad also visited India in August 2012. Bangladesh opposition leader Begum Khaleda Zia visited India from October 28 to November 3, 2012. Additionally, on March 3, 2013, Pranab Mukherjee, as the President of India, first visited Bangladesh, which also signifies the importance of Dhaka-Delhi ties. In fact, V.V. Giri was the last Indian president to visit Bangladesh in 1974. In an interview with *Samakal*, Mukherjee discussed different pressing issues like terrorism, water sharing, sub-regional cooperation. He argues that though India-Bangladesh relations have improved in many dimensions, still there are untapped potentials. He pointed out that Bangladesh-India has started cooperation in many new sectors including energy, education, environment, telecommunication, cooperation at the sub-regional level which are impacting the lives of millions (*The Daily Samakal*, 2013). After a gap of 42 years, Bangladesh President Mohammad Abdul Hamid also visited India in 2014. In the *2013-2014 Annual Report of Ministry of External Affairs*, it is noted that '[t]he visit of the Bangladesh President contributed to further strengthening and expanding the close bilateral relations between our two countries' (2014, p.2). In June 2014, as India's External Affairs Minister, Sushma Swaraj first visited Bangladesh, which also implies the importance that the new Narendra Modi government attached to improve Bangladesh-India ties. During her visit, Sushma contended that for a stable, secured, and prosperous South Asia, building an India-Bangladesh sustainable partnership was essential. She also claimed that India is committed to resolve the Teesta water-sharing dispute and to implement the 1974 land boundary protocol (*The Daily Prothom Alo*, 2014).

Indian Prime Minister Narendra Modi visited Bangladesh in June 2015 which was another milestone in the development of Bangladesh-India relations as 22 agreements/MoUs were signed. Among them were Exchange of Instrument of Ratification of the 1974 Land Boundary Agreement and its Protocol of 2011; Exchange of Letters between the Two Foreign Secretaries on Modalities for Implementation of the 1974 Land Boundary Agreement and its Protocol of 2011; Agreement on Coastal

Shipping; Renewal of the Bilateral Trade Agreement; the Protocol on Inland Waterways, Transit and Trade, and the Cultural Exchange Programme; MoU on the establishment of Indian SEZ (Special Economic Zone) in Bangladesh; MoU for extending a new Indian line of credit of US$ 2 billion to Bangladesh; MoU on prevention of human trafficking; MoU on Prevention of Smuggling and Circulation of Fake Currency Notes; MoU in the Field of Blue Economy and Maritime Cooperation in the Bay of Bengal and the Indian Ocean Region, etc. Narendra Modi's visit and its outcome was a milestone in Bangladesh-India relations. It is argued that though Bangladesh and India enjoy warm ties when the Awami League and the Congress remain in power, Narendra Modi proved the opposite resolving the longstanding disputes with Bangladesh, i.e., land boundary dispute and maritime delimitation dispute (Kashem & Islam, 2016). The Bangladesh Prime Minister also visited India in August 2015 to attend the funeral of Indian President Pranab Mukherjee's wife. Modi and Hasina discussed the progress of LBA implementation and the prospects of regional connectivity along with other common issues of interest to both.

In fact, the increasing number of high-level visits between Bangladesh and India impacted positively to deepen Bangladesh-India relations in multifaceted areas ranging from addressing terrorism to promoting the blue economy. In the *2016-2017 Annual Report of the Indian Ministry of External Affairs*, it is noted that 'The spate of regular high-level visits and exchanges kept the bilateral relations between the two countries on a high trajectory' (Ministry of External Affairs, 2017, p.4). In July 2016 Asaduzzaman Khan, Home Minister of Bangladesh, visited India during which an amendment to the Extradition Treaty was signed. In fact, being neighbouring countries, this Treaty is significant for both countries. In the same month, the Railway Minister of Bangladesh, Md. Mazibul Hoque, visited Agartala for laying the foundation stone of a new rail link connecting Bangladesh with Tripura. If implemented, it will be imperative to deepen ties between Tripura and Bangladesh.

Sheikh Hasina visited India in October 2016 for the BRICS-BIMSTEC Outreach Summit in Goa. In the following month, Indian Defence Minister Shri Manohar Parrikar visited Bangladesh which was the first-ever visit to Bangladesh since 1971 by an Indian Defence Minister. This also implies the strategic importance in Bangladesh-India relations. During her second visit in Dhaka, the former Indian External Affairs Minister, Sushma Swaraj notes:

> India attaches the utmost importance to its relations with Bangladesh. Our partnership today touches upon virtually all areas of human endeavour. Our relations are based on fraternal ties and are reflective of an all-encompassing partnership based on sovereignty, equality, trust and understanding that goes far beyond a strategic partnership (Ministry of External Affairs of India, October 22, 2017).

In May 2018, Sheikh Hasina visited West Bengal to inaugurate 'Bangladesh Bhavan'. It has been built on the Visva Bharati campus which was inaugurated by Indian Prime Minister Narendra Modi, Bangladesh Prime Minister Sheikh Hasina and West Bengal Chief Minister Mamata Banerjee. The Bhavan has been established to promote cultural cooperation between India and Bangladesh. During the inauguration ceremony, Narendra Modi contended that 'Relations between India and Bangladesh have entered a golden phase. In the last few years, rail and road connectivity between the countries has improved a lot. Complicated issues related to the land boundary and coastal boundary, which seemed impossible to solve at one point of time, were finally resolved' (Chowdhury, 2018). *The Daily Janakantha* (2018), in its editorial, contends that the Bhavan will work as a bridge to cement Bangladesh-India relations in cultural, educational, and intellectual dimensions.

Mamata Banerjee also expressed interest to set-up Bangabandhu Bhavan in the near future. She points out that 'We have already set-up Kazi Nazrul University. We renamed Andal Airport after Nazrul Islam. We will also set-up a Bangabandhu Bhavan' (Chowdhury, 2018). These are, in fact, good gestures and will contribute to accelerating socio-cultural relations between these two countries in the days to come. Given the growing ties, according to the *Economic Times*, Bangladesh-India relations is enjoying the 'golden period' in history (*Economic Times*, 2018). Among the contemporary developments, the daily (*Economic Times*) writes, 'Mention may also be made of the ongoing construction of 1320 MW Rampal coal-fired power plant, training of 4000 Bangladeshi officials in India from 2015 to date, training of 1500 Bangladeshi judicial officers in India, and a nearly three-fold increase in number of Indian visas to

Bangladeshi nationals from nearly 5 lakh in 2015 to 14 lakh in 2017' (*Economic Times*, 2018).

In the case of the political and diplomatic dimensions of Bangladesh-India relations, the role of the Indian states has been increasingly important. Shankar finds that 'West Bengal and the Northeast have four important concerns pertaining to the Bangladesh policy of the Government of India. It is about land, water, connectivity and security on the border' (Shankar, 2017, p.163). For instance, the then Foreign Minister I.K. Gujral was able to convince the then West Bengal Chief Minister Jyoti Basu 'to clinch the Farakka Treaty in 1996' (Shankar, 2017, p.163). Rajkumar Singh maintains that 'Jyoti Basu, played a very active and positive role in the negotiations and provisions have been made to take care that neither Bangladesh nor India or more precisely West Bengal is at a disadvantage' (Singh, 2011, p.284). On the contrary, due to the opposition to the current West Bengal Chief Minister Mamata Banerjee, Bangladesh-India could not sign the Teesta water treaty which was an expected deal in 2011 and 2015.

Indian Foreign Secretary Shri Vijay Gokhale paid his first official visit to Bangladesh from 8 to 10 April, 2018 which resulted in six Memorandums of Understanding on the Construction of the India-Bangladesh Friendship Pipeline between Siliguri (in India) and Parbatipur (in Bangladesh), on Cooperation between Prasar Bharati and Bangladesh Betar, on Cooperation regarding Nuclear Power Plant Projects in Bangladesh, on cultural cooperation, for the establishment of computer and language labs in 509 schools in Bangladesh, the rehabilitation and improvement of different roads under Rangpur City Corporation (Ministry of External Affairs of India, April 9, 2018).

On September 10, 2018, Indian Prime Minister Narendra Modi, the Prime Minister of Bangladesh, Sheikh Hasina, Chief Minister of West Bengal Ms Mamata Banerjee, and the Chief Minister of Tripura, Shri Biplab Kumar Deb jointly inaugurated three projects in Bangladesh, via video conference. These include: (a) 500 MW additional power supply from India to Bangladesh, through the existing Bheramara (Bangladesh)-Baharampur (India) interconnection, (b) Akhaura–Agartala Rail Link, (c) Rehabilitation of the Kulaura-Shahbazpur section of Bangladesh Railways (Ministry of External Affairs of India, September 10, 2018).

In addition, Narendra Modi, and Sheikh Hasina jointly unveiled e-plaques for the ground-breaking ceremony of two projects [i.e., (a) India-Bangladesh Friendship Pipeline, (b) Dhaka-Tongi-Joydebpur Railway Project], via video conferencing on September 18, 2018. Modi expects that the proposed pipeline and railway projects will be imperative for Bangladesh's development and overall India-Bangladesh relations.

After taking oath as the fourth time Prime Minister of Bangladesh, Sheikh Hasina emphasised her foreign relations with India as demonstrated in the first visit paid to New Delhi by the Bangladesh Foreign Minister A.K. Abdul Momen. To further strengthen the existing multifaceted cooperation between the two countries, Bangladesh Foreign Minister Abdul Momen and Indian External Affairs Minister Sushma Swaraj signed four MoUs on behalf of their respective sides during the fifth meeting of the India-Bangladesh Joint Consultative Commission (JCC). The agreements are MoU on mid-career training of 1,800 Bangladesh civil servants, MoU between AYUSH and the Ministry of Health of Bangladesh on cooperation in the field of medicinal plants, MoU between Anti-Corruption Commission of Bangladesh and Central Bureau of Investigation of India, and between Hiranandani Group and Bangladesh Economic Zones Authority to facilitate investments in the Indian Economic Zone in Mongla (*The Daily Star*, 2019; Ministry of External Affairs of India, 2019a). Notably, Bangladesh and India are enjoying the most significant moments in their bilateral ties between Modi-Hasina regimes. On February 8, 2019, Sushma Swaraj at the 5th India-Bangladesh Joint Consultative Committee Meeting mentioned that as many as 90 bilateral agreements had been signed between Bangladesh and India since Narendra Modi's 2015 visit in Bangladesh (Ministry of External Affairs of India, 2019b). Additionally, in March 2019, through video conferencing, Narendra Modi and Sheikh Hasina inaugurated four development projects in Bangladesh. *The Daily Jugantar* (2019), in its editorial, claimed that such Bangladesh-India cooperation needs to be sustained.

Currently, Bangladesh-India interacts under various bilateral mechanisms like the Joint Consultative Commission, Foreign Secretary and Home Secretary-level talks, Joint Working Group on Security and Border Management, Joint Task Forces on Human Trafficking, Fake Currency Notes etc. To describe the contemporary state of Bangladesh-

India relations, the former High Commissioner of India to Bangladesh, Harsh Vardhan Shringla writes:

> Bangladesh is one of the most important neighbours of India, and India deeply values its relationship. Over the last 10 years, India and Bangladesh have made unprecedented progress in furthering bilateral ties and towards building a multifaceted relationship, which today covers cooperation in a wide range of areas, including security and border management; trade, commerce and investment; connectivity; energy and power; space; developmental projects; culture; and greater people-to-people exchange. Most importantly, several high-level visits have taken place between the two countries, which reflects the value the two countries place on their bilateral relations. The ties can be defined as transformative, and potentially benefit the entire region (Shringla, 2018. p.524).

It is also worthy to look at how the former High Commissioners view the current pattern of Bangladesh-India relations. In this regard, Pinak Ranjan Chakravarty, a former Indian High Commissioner to Bangladesh, writes:

> During the last decade of Ms Hasina's tenure as Prime Minister, high-level Bangladesh-India engagement has intensified. There is an irrevocable and irreversible bipartisan political consensus in India for upgrading relations across a comprehensive interface of ties. India's 'neighbourhood policy' has focused on Bangladesh, which has emerged as a key interlocutor in India's 'Act East Policy' and sub-regional groupings like BIMSTEC (Bay of Bengal Initiative for Multi-Sectoral Technical and Economic Cooperation) and the BBIN (Bangladesh, Bhutan, India, Nepal) Initiative. In Bangladesh too, a growing domestic political consensus, overriding fractious politics, has emerged in favour of close ties with India (Chakravarty, 2019).

Indeed Bangladesh has become an important friend of India in the region and beyond especially for materialising India's Look East Policy. In this regard, the former High Commissioner of India to Bangladesh, Harsh Vardhan Shringla, writes that 'Bangladesh remains India's key partner in the region, and is crucial both for stability in the north-eastern region and as a bridge to South-East Asia. It is also a lynchpin of India's 'Look East' policy'. Bangladesh is also significant for the economic development of the north-eastern region' (Shringla, 2018, p.524). Keeping this in mind, Bangladesh and India enjoy excellent relations at the political and diplomatic level.

The most recent development is that after taking oath as the Prime Minister (for the second time), Narendra Modi continued India's foreign policy priorities on Bangladesh. For instance, the first overseas visit of Subrahmanyam Jaishankar, India's External Affairs Minister, was to Bangladesh in August 2019. According to the press release, 'The visit reflects the highest priority India attaches to its bilateral relationship with Bangladesh, which the two countries describe as transcending a strategic partnership' (Ministry of External Affairs of India, 2019c). In September 2019, on the sidelines of the 74th session of the UN General Assembly, Hasina and Modi held bilateral meetings on different issues. They reiterated zero tolerance for terrorism (*NDTV*, 2019). Narendra Modi assured Sheikh Hasina that Bangladesh should not worry about the NRC issue.

Another development is that at the invitation of India, on October 3, 2019, Bangladesh Prime Minister Sheikh Hasina paid a four-day official visit. The visit resulted in a total of seven MoUs and agreements on Standard Operating Procedure (SOP) on the use of Chattogram and Mongla ports; MoU on withdrawal of 1.82 cusecs of water from Feni river by India for drinking water supply, scheme for Sabroom town, Tripura, India; Agreement concerning the implementation of GoI Line of Credits (LOC) extended to Bangladesh; MoU between the University of Hyderabad and University of Dhaka; Cultural Exchange Programme-Renewal; MoU on Cooperation in Youth Affairs; MoU on providing Coastal Surveillance System.

In August 2020, Harsh Vardhan Shringla, the Foreign Secretary of India, visited Bangladesh in the midst of COVID-19, where he reiterated that Bangladesh receives the 'highest importance' in India's 'Neighbourhood First Policy' (Chaudhury, 2020). During the visit, the secretary met his Bangladeshi counterpart, and the Bangladesh Prime Minister, Sheikh Hasina, and discussed the various issues of mutual interest. Notably, the Indian Foreign Secretary was the first foreign visitor to be received by the Bangladesh Prime Minister after the outbreak of the COVID-19 global pandemic which also underscored the importance that Bangladesh attached to India.

Another contemporary development is the virtual summit between Sheikh Hasina and Narendra Modi, held on December 17, 2020. In the summit, Narendra Modi reiterated Bangladesh's importance for India and thus defined it as a 'significant pillar' for India's 'neighbourhood first policy' (*The Daily Star*, 2020). It is argued that the virtual summit 'showcases the special bond that the two countries share' (Bhattacharjee, 2020). In the summit, Bangladesh and India signed seven bilateral instruments, i.e., Framework of Understanding (FOU) on Cooperation in Hydrocarbon Sector; Protocol on Trans-boundary Elephant Conservation; MoU regarding Indian Grant Assistance for Implementation of High Impact Community Development Projects (HICDPs) through Local Bodies and other Public Sector Institutions; MoU on Supply of Equipment and Improvement of Garbage/Solid Waste Disposal Ground at Lamchori Area for Barishal City Corporation; Terms of Reference of India-Bangladesh CEOs Forum; MoU between Father of the Nation Bangabandhu Sheikh Mujibur Rahman Memorial Museum, Dhaka, Bangladesh and the National Museum, New Delhi, India; and MoU on Cooperation in the field of Agriculture.

Critical Engagement

Bangladesh-India relations at the political and diplomatic level was not always smooth, as mentioned earlier. In fact, though India contributed to the Liberation War of Bangladesh in 1971, a strong anti-India sentiment is manifested in Bangladesh politics even in the initial phase of their ties due to India's hegemonic attitude towards Bangladesh which was termed as 'Indian exploitation' (Muniruzzaman, 1977; Hossain, 1981). Between 1976 and 1995 the relations faced a number of impediments, i.e., anti-India stand in Bangladesh's domestic politics due to Ganga water sharing dispute, Farakka barrage issue, Tin Bigha corridor issue and so forth. In 1996, when the Awami League came to power, the Dhaka-New Delhi ties started to develop. And since 2009, Bangladesh-India is enjoying the best of its relations. It is also pertinent to note that observers in Bangladesh are viewing the outcome of Hasina's 2019 visit to New Delhi as in favour of India. There is no agreement on Teesta water sharing or a formal assurance from the Indian side regarding India's NRC (National Register of Citizens) issue. The NRC issue served the political interest of the Modi government, which badly impacted India's relations with Bangladesh (Ganguly, 2020). Syed Munir Khasru (2018) writes that 'The NRC issue threatens to disturb the equilibrium in India-Bangladesh ties. Plans for the deportation of those not on the NRC list are not only politically imprudent but also risk inciting unrest across the region'. Additionally, Bangladesh's export of gas to India's North East region, withdrawal of 1.82 cusecs of water from the Feni river by India to Sabroom, Tripura or no formal arrangement/stand of India on the repatriation over the Rohingya issue has created negative perceptions in the people's mind of Bangladesh.

Notably, China and India are the major actors giving backups to the Myanmar regime regarding the Rohingya crisis. In the September 26, 2019 vote on a resolution titled 'Situation of human rights of Rohingya Muslims and other minorities in Myanmar' at the United Nations Human Rights Council (UNHRC), India did not support Bangladesh on the Rohingya issue which also raises questions regarding India's perspective on Bangladesh (Bhuiyan, 2019). In fact, Bangladesh has made Rohingya camps in 6,500 acres of land by sacrificing forests, and other resources. And being one of the densely populated countries in the world with limited resources, it becomes a daunting task for Bangladesh to continue its support for the Rohingyas. Prolonging the Rohingya repatriation will be problematic for Bangladesh as stated in the *Christian Science Monitor* (Boston, 3 June 1999); the longer the refugees stay in the refugee camps, the more likely they become a threat to peace (cited in Bariagaber, 1999, p.605). In this context, successful repatriation of the Rohingyas becomes important where India can play a crucial role.

On September 29, 2019, without informing Bangladesh beforehand, India banned onion exports to Bangladesh which created an onion crisis in the market and affected the people of Bangladesh significantly as prices went up. The price of one-kilogram onion in Bangladesh was recorded at 220 BDT (US$ 2.59) after India's ban on onion exports (Hasan, 2019). Onions were being sold at just BDT 45 per kilogram before the export ban was enforced. This impacted millions of poor Bangladeshis badly. And seeing the sufferings of the people, Sheikh Hasina stopped eating onions. According to Sheikh Hasina, 'We stopped eating onion...all foods in my house were cooked on Saturday without onion' (*Dhaka Tribune*, 2019). Though some people might argue the issue is subjective and temporary, it might have more enormous implications in Bangladesh-India relations as people's perceptions and sufferings matter. To understand how onions play a vital role in Bangladesh-India relations, one needs to look at the editorial of the *Indian Express*. It writes:

> That Hasina publicly complained, albeit in a light-hearted manner, about the impact of India's recent move to ban onion exports on her kitchen, underlines the headaches in the neighbourhood that Delhi's economic decisions generate. Hasina was not objecting to the decision itself that has produced immediate onion shortages in Bangladesh. She was pointing to its sudden and unilateral nature. If Delhi had informed Dhaka in advance, Hasina said, her government could have made alternative arrangements for onion import. The problem goes deeper and reveals a lingering autarkic and anti-market orientation in Delhi's economic policy even as India's national strategy calls for regional integration (*The Indian Express* Editorial, 2019).

Therefore, against the ban of onion export, *The Indian Express* suggests that 'India's relations with Bangladesh have never been as good as they are today. They are also the best when viewed in comparison with our other neighbours. But India's economic policymakers can be rather insensitive to the logic of interdependence' (*The Indian Express* Editorial, 2019). In the middle of September 2020, India again banned onion exports to Bangladesh which again impacted the local markets. *The Indian Express* notes that the decision on onion export ban is a 'wrong way out' which should be the last resort when the prices crossed Rs. 40 per kilogram (*The Indian Express* Editorial, 2020). Additionally, India's construction of the 1320 MW coal-based power plant in Rampal, near the Sundarbans area of Khulna, Bangladesh has raised local protests and agitations around the country.

Conclusion

The chapter has surveyed the narratives on Bangladesh-India relations from political and diplomatic dimensions. It argues that though Bangladesh-India relations started warmly, it experienced both ups and downs due to the changing political regimes in Bangladesh and India. An improved political relationship translates into better ties in economic, security, and socio-cultural dimensions. The chapter argues that under the Sheikh Hasina regime in Bangladesh (2009-present), Bangladesh and India have scripted a golden chapter in their bilateral partnership. But calculating its narrowly defined interest, India's policy concerning the

National Register of Citizens, water sharing issues or the Rohingya crisis has impacted the warmth of bilateral ties which merits serious attention.

REFERENCES

Ahmed, K. U. (2008). *Bangladesh and its neighbours*. Dhaka: Asiatic Society of Bangladesh.
Banerjee, S. (2001). Indo-Bangladesh border: Radcliffe's ghost. *Economic and Political Weekly*, 36 (18), pp. 1505-1506.
Bariagaber, A. (1999). States, international organisations and the refugee: Reflections on the complexity of managing the refugee crisis in the Horn of Africa. *The Journal of Modern African Studies*, 37(4), pp. 597-619.
Bhattacharya, V. (1985). India and Bangladesh. *India Quarterly*, 41 (1), pp. 44-52.
Bhuiyan, H.K. (2019, September 30). UNHRC vote on Rohingya: Bangladesh's diplomatic failure exposed yet again. *Dhaka Tribune*. Retrieved from https://www.dhakatribune.com/bangladesh/rohingya-crisis/2019/09/30/unhrc-vote-on-rohingya-bangladesh-s-diplomatic-failure-exposed-yet-again
Bhattacharjee, J. (2020, December 17). Modi-Hasina virtual summit celebrating the bond. ORF Online. Retrieved from https://www.orfonline.org/expert-speak/modi-hasina-virtual-summit-celebrating-bond/
Bindra, S.S. (1984). *India and her neighbours: A study of political, economic and cultural relations and interactions*. New Delhi: Deep & Deep Publications.
Brichieri-Colombi, S. & Bradnock, R.W. (2003). Geopolitics, water and development in South Asia: Cooperative development in the Ganges-Brahmaputra Delta. *The Geographical Journal*, 169 (10), pp. 43-64.
Baxter, C. (1997). *Bangladesh: From a nation to a state*. Cumnor Hill, Oxford: Westview Press.
Chakma, B. (2015). Sheikh Hasina Government's India Policy: A Three-level Game? *Journal of Asian Security and International Affairs* 2(1) pp. 27–51.
Chakravarty, P.R. (2019, January 2). The bilateral transformation. *The Hindu*. Retrieved from https://www.thehindu.com/opinion/lead/the-bilateral-transformation/article25884055.ece
Chaudhury, D.R. (2020, August 19). Highest importance for Bangladesh in India's 'neighbourhood first' policy. *Economic Times*. Retrieved from https://economictimes.indiatimes.com/news/politics-and-nation/highest-importance-for-bangladesh-in-indias-neighbourhood-first policy/articleshow/77638216.cms?utm_source=contentofinterest&utm_medium=text&utm_campaign=cppst
Chowdhury, S. (2018, May 26). Indo-Bangla relations have entered golden phase, says PM Modi. *The Indian Express*. Retrieved from: https://indianexpress.com/article/india/pm-narendra-modi-sheikh-hasina-bangladesh-bhavan-5191560/
Dhaka Tribune (2019, November 16). Food cooked sans onion at PM's house. Retrieved from https://www.dhakatribune.com/bangladesh/politics/2019/11/16/food-cooked-sans-onion-at-pm-s-house
Dutta, J.P. (2005). Challenges and prospects of Bangladesh-India economic cooperation: Trade & investment. In S. Haidar (Ed.), *India-Bangladesh: Strengthening the partnership*, (pp. 31-53). Chandigarh: Centre for Research in Rural and Industrial Development.
Economic Times (2018, October 8). ET Analysis: Indo-Bangla relations enjoy golden

period. Retrievedfrom//economictimes.indiatimes.com/articleshow/ 66118543.cms?utm_source=contentofinterest&utm_medium=text&utm_campaign=cppst

Ganguly, S. (2020, June 23). India is paying the price for neglecting its neighbours. *Foreign Policy.* Retrieved from https://foreignpolicy.com/2020/06/23/india-china-south-asia-relations/

Ghosh, P. S. (1989). *Cooperation and conflict in South Asia.* New Delhi: Manohar Publications.

Hassan, S. (1989). The India factor in the foreign policy of Bangladesh. In M.G. Kabir & S. Hassan (Eds.), *Issues and challenges facing Bangladesh foreign policy* (pp.44-61). Dhaka: Bangladesh Society of International Studies.

Hasan, M. (2019, November 14). Onion price hits Tk220 per kg. *Dhaka Tribune.*

Hossain, I. (1981). Bangladesh-India relations: Issues and problems. *Asian Survey,* 21 (11), pp. 1115-1128.

Hossain, G. (1995). Bangladesh in 1994: Democracy at risk. *Asian Survey,* 35 (2), pp. 171-178.

Hossain, G. (1996). Bangladesh in 1995: Politics of intransigence. *Asian Survey,* 36 (2), pp. 196-203.

Islam, N. (2004). Indo-Bangladesh economic relations: Some thoughts. *Economic and Political Weekly,* 39 (36), pp. 4069-4075.

Jahan, R. (1973). Bangladesh in 1972: Nation-building in a new state. *Asian Survey,* 13 (2), pp. 199-210.

Jahan, R. (2003). Bangladesh in 2002: Imperilled democracy. *Asian Survey,* 43(1), pp. 222-229.

Kashem, M.A. & Islam, M.S. (2016). Narendra Modi's Bangladesh policy and India-Bangladesh relations: Challenges and possible policy responses. *India Quarterly,* 72(3) pp. 250–267.

Khasru, S.M. (2018, December 17). The spectre of deportation. *The Hindu.* Retrieved from https://www.thehindu.com/opinion/op-ed/the-spectre-of-deportation/article25758775.ece

Khan, Z.R. (1993). Bangladesh in 1992: Dilemmas of Democratization. *Asian Survey,* 33 (2), pp. 150-156.

Khan, Z.R. (1994). Bangladesh in 1993: Values, identity, and development. *Asian Survey,* 34 (2), pp. 160-167.

Kochanek, S.A. (1997). Bangladesh in 1996: The 25th year of independence. *Asian Survey,* 37(2), pp. 136-142.

Kochanek, S.A. (1998). Bangladesh in 1997: The honeymoon is over. *Asian Survey,* 38(2), pp. 135-141.

Majumdar, A.J. (2014). Making sense of India-Bangladesh relations. *India Quarterly,* 70, pp. 327–340.

Malone, D.M. (2011). *Does the Elephant Dance?: Contemporary Indian Foreign Policy.* New York: Routledge.

Maniruzzaman, T. (1975). Bangladesh in 1974: Economic crisis and political polarization. *Asian Survey,* 15 (2), pp. 117-128.

Maniruzzaman, T. (1976). Bangladesh in 1975: The fall of the Mujib regime and its aftermath. *Asian Survey,* 16 (2), pp. 119-129.

Maniruzzaman, T. (1977). Bangladesh in 1976: Struggle for survival as an independent state. *Asian Survey,* 17 (2), pp. 191-200.

Ministry of External Affairs, Government of India (2010). *Ministry of External Affairs Annual Report 2009-2010,* New Delhi: Policy Planning and Research Division,

Ministry of External Affairs.
Ministry of External Affairs, Government of India (2014). *Ministry of External Affairs Annual Report 2013-2014*, New Delhi: Policy Planning and Research Division, Ministry of External Affairs.
Ministry of External Affairs of India (2017, October 22). *Press Statement by External Affairs Minister during her visit to Bangladesh. Speeches & Statements*, 22 October. New Delhi: MEA.
Ministry of External Affairs, Government of India (2017), *Ministry of External Affairs Annual Report 2016-2017*, New Delhi: Policy Planning and Research Division, MEA.
Ministry of External Affairs of India (2018, April 9). *Visit of Foreign Secretary to Bangladesh (8-10 April 2018)*. Press Release, 9 April. New Delhi: MEA.
Ministry of External Affairs of India (2018, September 10). *Prime Minister, Prime Minister of Bangladesh and Chief Ministers of West Bengal and Tripura jointly dedicate three projects in Bangladesh*. Press Release, 10 September. New Delhi: MEA.
Ministry of External Affairs of India (2019a, February 8). *Joint Press Release on Joint Consultative Commission between India and Bangladesh*. Bilateral/Multilateral Documents, 8 February. New Delhi: MEA.
Ministry of External Affairs of India (2019b, February 9). *Transcript of opening statement by External Affairs Minister at the 5th India-Bangladesh Joint Consultative Committee Meeting*. Bilateral/Multilateral Documents, 9 February. New Delhi: MEA.
Ministry of External Affairs of India (2019c, August 19). External Affairs Minister's visit to Bangladesh (August 19-21, 2019). Press Release, New Delhi: MEA.
Muniruzzaman, T. (1977). Bangladesh in 1976: Struggle for survival as an independent state. *Asian Survey*, 17 (2), pp. 191-200.
Muni, S.D. (2009). *India's foreign policy: The democracy dimension (With special reference to neighbours)*. New Delhi: Cambridge University Press (under the imprint of Foundation Books).
NDTV (2019, September 28). PM Modi, Sheikh Hasina reiterate zero tolerance for terrorism.
Pant, H.V. (2007). India and Bangladesh: Will the twain ever meet? *Asian Survey*, 47(2), pp. 231-249.
Pant, H.V. (2011). India's relations with Bangladesh. In D. Scott (Ed.), *Handbook of India's international relations*, (pp. 83-94). London and New York: Routledge.
Rashiduzzaman, M. (1978). Bangladesh in 1977: Dilemmas of the military rulers. *Asian Survey*, 18 (2), pp. 126-134.
Rashiduzzaman, M. (2001). Bangladesh in 2000: Searching for better governance? *Asian Survey*, 41 (1), pp. 122-130.
Rashiduzzaman, M. (2002). Bangladesh in 2001: The election and a new political re lity? *Asian Survey*, 42(1), pp. 183-191.
Riaz, A. (2005). Bangladesh in 2004: The politics of vengeance and the erosion of democracy. *Asian Survey*, 45 (1), pp. 112-118.
Riaz, A. (2006). Bangladesh in 2005: Standing at a crossroads. *Asian Survey*, 46 (1), pp. 107-113.
Sharma, M.S. (2011, July 5). The Delhi-Dhaka distance. *The Indian Express*. Retrieved from http://archive.indianexpress.com/news/the-delhidhaka-distance/812740/0
Shankar, K. (2017). *Regional satraps and the battle for India's foreign policy*. New Delhi: Vij Books India Pvt. Ltd. and Indian Council of World Affairs.

Shringla, H.V. (2018). India–Bangladesh relations: An Indian perspective. *Strategic Analysis*, 42(5), pp. 524-528.

Singh, K. (1987). *India and Bangladesh*. Delhi: Anmol Publications.

Singh, R. (2010). *Relation of NDA & UPA with neighbours*. New Delhi: Gyan Publishing House.

Singh, R. (2011). *Contemporary India with controversial neighbours*. New Delhi: Gyan Publishing House.

The *Daily Prothom Alo* (2014, June 27). The power of democracy is to resolve discords peacefully.

The *Daily Samakal* (2013, March 2). Special interview of Pranab Mukherjee with *the Samakal*.

The *Daily Janakantha* Editorial (2018, May 27). (Bangladesh-India relations).

The *Daily Jugantar* Editorial (2019, March 13). (Bangladesh-India relations: Mutual cooperation needs to be sustained).

The *Daily Star* (2016, October 8). Bangladesh-India relations: Progress made and the challenges ahead.

The *Daily Star* (2019, February 8). Bangladesh, India sign 4 MoUs to bolster ties. Retrieved from https://www.thedailystar.net/politics/news/bangladesh-foreign-minister-abdul-momen-meets-sushma-swaraj-india-1699291

The *Daily Star* (2020, December 17). Bangladesh 'significant pillar' of India's Neighbourhood First policy: Modi. Retrieved from https://www.thedailystar.net/world/south-asia/news/bangladesh-significant-pillar-indias-neighborhood-first-policy-modi-2012889

The *Indian Express* Editorial (2019, October 7). Good going but with Dhaka something's missing: Economic policy making in Delhi needs to be more sensitive to the regional dimension. Retrieved from https://indianexpress.com/article/opinion/editorials/sheikh-hasina-modi-meeting-delhi-dhaka-6056781/

The *Indian Express* Editorial (2020, September 16). Wrong way out. Retrieved from https://indianexpress.com/article/opinion/editorials/onion-export-ban-prices-farmers-6597496/

Trivedi, R. (1999). *International relations of Bangladesh and Bangabandhu Sheikh Mujibur Rahman: Documents, messages, and speeches*. [It is a compilation]. Dhaka: Parama.

3

EMERGING TRENDS IN DEVELOPMENT PARTNERSHIP

ABSTRACT

What factors primarily define the development partnership between Bangladesh and India? What are the major challenges that Bangladesh and India face to deepen their development partnership? What might be the policy imperatives to deepen Bangladesh-India development partnership? This chapter investigates these questions. It argues that development partnership has become a new defining characteristic in Bangladesh-India relations. Increasing trade, investment and energy cooperation are hallmarks in this partnership. This chapter contends that millions of people across borders are immensely benefitted from this partnership. This development partnership has also become an example for many in the world. The chapter also concentrates on the challenges and possibilities in the partnership.

Keywords: *Bangladesh-India, Development Partnership, Trade and Investment, Energy Cooperation.*

Introduction

This chapter analyses the Bangladesh-India development partnership which ushers in a new era of cooperation. It argues that Bangladesh-India have expanded their ties from the political dimension to a development partnership. Increasing trade, investment and energy cooperation are hallmarks in this partnership. Until the 1980s, India viewed its neighbours as 'taken for granted', as 'strategic satellites' (Venkataramakrishnan, 2020). Mahfuz Anam, the Editor and Publisher of the *Daily Star* recalls that 'at one time India had counted Pakistan and China as neighbours while the rest of us including Bangladesh are mere geographic entities, to be praised, cajoled, reprimanded, and even punished as the situation would call for' (*The Daily Star*, 2016). Anam contends that Bangladesh has graduated as a neighbour. In this chapter, it is argued that Bangladesh has become one of the important development and strategic partners of India in the region and beyond. In fact, both the countries realised that for their mutual prosperity, there is no alternative to promote cooperation. And especially, for ensuring economic gains of India's landlocked Northeastern region and to implement its Look East, Act East Policy, and security concerns, India realised that Bangladesh is an essential partner as described in the previous chapter. Consequently, Adarsh Swaika, the then Deputy High Commissioner of India to Bangladesh, contends that 'Today India and Bangladesh are partners of progress and development, and our destinies are, in a sense, becoming increasingly intertwined' (*The Daily Star*, 2016). In addition, the former High Commissioner of India to Bangladesh, Harsh Vardhan Shringla, writes: 'Development cooperation has emerged as a key pillar of the bilateral relationship. From modest beginnings in the years after Bangladesh's liberation, India's development cooperation with Bangladesh has grown in size and coverage' (Shringla, 2018, p.527). For instance, Bangladesh-India entered into a Framework Agreement on Cooperation for Development in September 2011. Under this agreement, both parties agreed to narrow the trade imbalance by removing trade and non-tariff barriers. They also agreed to expand their cooperation at the sub-regional level. In fact, a trilateral working group meeting on water, power and connectivity between Bangladesh, Bhutan and India was held in April 2013 (Dubey, 2017). Thus, the Bangladesh-India development partnership goes beyond their bilateral dimensions. Nisha Singh notes that 'India views its development partnership with Bangladesh as a means for strengthening South-South sharing of development experiences and general development cooperation. Over the past few years, this development cooperation between the two countries has grown significantly' (Singh, 2014, p.138).

In the domain of development partnership, this chapter focuses on trade, investment and energy cooperation because these three are the dominant dimensions in the emerging development partnership. It is expected that this development partnership will be imperative to bring a win-win situation. *The Daily Star* in an editorial notes that 'India's short, medium-and long-term interests are in a way tied with economic progress of Bangladesh' (*The Daily Star* Editorial, 2010). Against the above backdrop, this chapter investigates what factors/dimensions primarily define the development partnership between Bangladesh and India? What are the major challenges that Bangladesh-India face deepening their development partnership? What might be the policy imperatives to deepen the Bangladesh-India development partnership?

This chapter is divided into six sections, including Introduction. The second section focuses on the conceptual understanding of development partnership while the third section discusses major dimensions in development partnership focusing on trade and investment perspective and energy cooperation. The fourth section analyses the challenges in the Bangladesh-India development partnership while the fifth section explains the possibilities in the partnership. The final section concentrates on the concluding remarks.

Understanding Development Partnership

Development partnership has become a buzzword in the twenty-first-century development or foreign policy discourse without proper theorisation. Simply, development partnership means arrangements or mechanism of two parties to achieve common development goals. In this chapter, by development partnership, we mean deepening and broadening Bangladesh-India ties by making (new) agreements on developmental aspects based on mutual gain and trust. In fact, no state in this world is self-sufficient and thus cannot live in isolation. Thus, the world witnessed a Bangladesh-India development partnership over the years, considering their mutual compulsions and economic gains. However, in order to understand the Bangladesh-India development partnership, one also needs to understand where Bangladesh is positioned in terms of India's development partnership. In fact, Nepal was one of the top priorities in the case of building India's development cooperation. Chaturvedi (2012, p.560), for instance, writes that 'India has been actively engaged in Nepal and, in terms of India's development cooperation programme, Nepal has always occupied a very eminent place both in terms of quantum and also in terms of innovations in institutional delivery mechanisms'. Chaturvedi (2012, p.569) also notes that in the case of India's development assistance in the South Asian neighbourhood between 1990-91 and 2012-13, Bhutan received the largest amount of aid and concessional loans followed by Afghanistan and Myanmar. Bangladesh-India relations experienced ups and downs over the decades. In fact, the Bangladesh-India development partnership started to grow when the Awami League came in power in 2009. And it was consolidated in Manmohan Singh's visit in Bangladesh in 2011 which resulted in dozens of agreements of mutual interest. One can argue that the continuation of the Awami League government in Bangladesh helped to sustain and consolidate the Bangladesh-India development partnership. On the contrary, the changing attitude of the political regimes in India, i.e., the Manmohan Singh regime and later the Narendra Modi regime also played a crucial role in the development and consolidation of the partnership.

Major Dimensions in Development Partnership

Among the dimensions of the Bangladesh-India development partnership, this chapter focuses on trade and investment, and energy. India's 'Neighbours First' policy also underscores the importance India currently attaches to its neighbours. The Bangladesh-India development partnership is a case in point.

Trade

Trade is seen as a catalyst of peace and stability in bilateral or multilateral relations since trade creates interdependence between states which makes war less likely. Also, increased trade results in increased communications and reduced mutual distrust. In April 1972 (p.763), Sunanda Sen saw the prospects and benefits of India-Bangladesh bilateral trade and wrote that 'The special circumstances in which Bangladesh became independent bring to the forefront the issue of its trade prospects with India'. And consequently, from the beginning of their diplomatic relations, trade constitutes a crucial component in Bangladesh-India ties. Thus, this section focuses on the trade and investment perspective in the formation of the Bangladesh-India development partnership. It is argued that 'The phenomenon of economic cooperation between Bangladesh and India, particularly with respect to trade and investment, is of recent origin'

(Dutta, 2005, p.31). Despite the 'recent origin', former India's High Commissioner to Bangladesh M. Dubey (2017, p.122) writes that 'The economic relations between India and Bangladesh constitute a very significant aspect of the overall relations between the two countries'. Dubey also notes that Bangladesh has been India's largest export destination in South Asia for several decades.

Institutional/Instrumental Development

During Bangladesh Foreign Minister Abdus Samad Azad's January 1972 New Delhi visit, detailed discussions on economic cooperation were held. In the discussion, both Bangladesh and India agreed on the importance of restoring trade and economic cooperation between them. Consequently, on 28 March 1972, Bangladesh and India signed a Trade Agreement bearing 11 articles. The Agreement came into force on 28 March 1972 for a period of one year for the first time. According to the Agreement, both sides expressed an interest to strengthen 'economic relations between the two countries on the basis of equality and mutual benefit'. In the Agreement, people were identified as the 'beneficiaries' of close economic cooperation. State-to-State basis trade was identified as the organising trade between Bangladesh and India as far as possible. According to Article 1 of the Agreement 'The two Governments recognising the need and requirements of each other in the context of their developing economies undertake to explore all possibilities for expansion and promotion of trade between the two countries on the basis of mutual advantage'. Notably, border trade was allowed within a sixteen-kilometre belt of the border between West Bengal, Assam, Meghalaya, Tripura and Mizoram on the one hand and Bangladesh on the other. According to Article V of the Agreement, in order to promote Bangladesh-India trade and commerce, the mutual arrangements on the use of waterways, railways, and roadways will be made. For Nachiketa (1972, p.746), 'With the signing of the trade treaty between India and Bangladesh, much of the uncertainty surrounding the nature of trade relations between the two countries has been removed'.

It was agreed that both Bangladesh and India could export goods to each other valued to Rs. 2,500 lakh. But over time, we see that Bangladesh's exports to India have been marginalised substantially while India's exports to Bangladesh have been increased significantly. Notably, the 1972 agreement established the foundation of Bangladesh-India trade relations. On 5 July 1973, Bangladesh-India signed another trade agreement which came into force on 28 September 1973 for a period of three years. Again on 4 October 1980, Bangladesh-India signed a Trade Agreement which came into force on the date of signing for a period of three years with the possibility of extension for a further period of three years. After 35 years, on 6 June 2015, Bangladesh and India signed a Trade Agreement for a period of five years with effect from the first day of April 2015. The Agreement was supposed to automatically be extended for successive terms of five years unless either Government terminated the Agreement by giving written notice of its intention to terminate to the other Government at least six months before the end of such a term. Thus, we see that there is instrumental/institutional development in the Bangladesh-India trade relations which paved the way for the increased volume of trade between them. Additionally, on September 6, 2011, to expedite developmental cooperation, Bangladesh and India signed a Framework Agreement on Cooperation for Development. According to Article I of the Agreement:

> To promote trade, investment and economic cooperation, which is balanced, sustainable and builds prosperity in both countries: Both Parties shall take steps to narrow trade imbalances, remove progressively tariff and non-tariff barriers and facilitate trade, by road, rail, inland waterways, air and shipping. Both parties will encourage the development of appropriate infrastructure, use of seaports, multimodal transportation and standardisation of means of transport for bilateral as well as sub-regional use.

During the 14th South Asian Association for Regional Cooperation (SAARC) Summit in New Delhi, India announced duty-free access to exports from Least Developed Countries (LDCs) in the SAARC region including Bangladesh from January 1, 2008, and reduced the sensitive lists. In addition, India and Bangladesh signed an MoU in September 2007 on duty-free access of eight million pieces of readymade garments from Bangladesh to India which came into effect in April 2008. During Sheikh Hasina's 2010 New Delhi visit, India widened duty-free access and thus dropped 47 more items from its negative list giving Bangladeshi goods duty-free access to the Indian market. Earlier 56 Bangladeshi products were given duty-free access to the Indian market (*The Daily Star*, 2010).

The India-Bangladesh Chamber of Commerce and Industries (IBCCI) was formed in 2007 to promote bilateral trade, to reduce the trade imbalance, to resolve bilateral business-related issues, to increase Bangladesh's export to India, and to encourage India's investors to invest in Bangladesh. It can also be mentioned that a 30 member business delegation from Merchant's Chamber of Commerce and Industry (MCCI) visited Bangladesh in 2010 to explore business opportunities and consequently an MoU was signed between MCCI and India-Bangladesh Chamber of Commerce and Industries (IBCCI) on trade and investment. In addition, India provided duty-free access to Bangladeshi products except for drugs and tobacco-related products in November 2011. But Bangladesh could not utilise this facility due to several limitations which are explained later.

The institutional framework in facilitating trade and commerce was strengthened in 2013 through the signing of another MoU on cooperation in fashion technology, skills exchange, productivity enhancement, and techno-commercial collaboration in the development of textiles. Thus, a strong institutional framework has been developed over the decades in promoting bilateral trade between Bangladesh and India.

Changing Volume of Trade

In 1980, Bangladesh's exports were worth US$ 12.35 million, while imports amounted to US$ 105.52 million (see Table 1). According to the Indian Department of Commerce, as per 2016-17 data, Bangladesh is the largest trading partner of India in South Asia. Among 83 per cent of total Indian exports in South Asia, Bangladesh alone accounts for 35 per cent. The total bilateral trade was valued at US$ 7.4 billion during 2016-17, while Bangladesh's exports to India are valued at only US$ 703 million. Overall, Indian exports to Bangladesh increased by 30.8 per cent from 2012-13 to 2016-17, while imports increased by 10 per cent in the same period (Department of Commerce, Government of India 2017). According to the IMF data, between 2012 and 2017, Bangladeshi exports to India were worth US$ 3,172.5 million while imports amounted to US$ 34,511.8 million (International Monetary Fund, 2018, p.87). In the last five years (from the financial year 2012-13 to 2016-17), total trade between India and Bangladesh has grown at 11.45 per cent (Ministry of External Affairs, 2018, p.6). Thus over the years, Bangladesh's trade imbalance with India has widened substantially (see Table 1). This huge trade deficit needs to be addressed for a sustainable Bangladesh-India partnership.

Jayanta Kumar Ray wrote in 2011 that 'Bangladesh, like Pakistan, believes in cutting its nose to spite India's face. So, it may not agree to offer land-water transhipment rights to India to supply goods to its northeast region for appropriate fees, and thereby substantially reduce the trade gap with India' (Ray, 2011, p.405). Kumar believed that if transit is given to India, the Indo-Bangla trade deficit would be reduced. Bangladesh has already given that transit facility to India and hence the ball is in India's court. Now, India needs to address Bangladesh's trade deficit with the country by abolishing all types of tariff and non-tariff barriers.

The introduction of border *haats* is a new dimension in Bangladesh-India economic relations. Bangladesh approved two border *haats* at Srinagar and Kamalasagar. Against the Indian proposal of 22 border *haats* along the Meghalaya border in May 2013, Bangladesh approved four border *haats*. Among them, the border *haat* in Srinagar (in Feni district) was inaugurated in January 2015. If more border *haats* can be operationalised successfully, this can contribute to Bangladesh-India trade volume in a significant way. In fact, as mentioned earlier, though border trade was encouraged in the 1972 Agreement, it could not be developed due to lack of political will from both sides.

Table 1: Evolution of Trade between Bangladesh and India (in US $)

Year	Bangladesh's Exports to India	Bangladesh's Imports from India
1980	12.35 million	105.52 million
1981	13.55 million	49.01 million
1982	18.61 million	60.18 million
1983	5.75 million	41.97 million
1984	26.74 million	89.97 million
1985	28.90 million	104.19 million
1986	7.90 million	112.59 million
1987	14.11 million	145.49 million
1988	12.28 million	169.99 million
1989	13.95 million	176.23 million
1990	15.26 million	297.11 million
1991	5.73 million	324.56 million
1992	9.78 million	353.18 million
1993	12.93 million	429.62 million
1994	34.27 million	521.00 million

Year	Bangladesh's Exports to India	Bangladesh's Imports from India
1995	78.82 million	959.62 million
1996	57.96 million	832.45 million
1997	53.65 million	807.13 million
1998	59.50 million	943.33 million
1999	74.25 million	726.13 million
2000	79.85 million	860.33 million
2001	66.88 million	1,086.81 million
2002	61.32 million	1,132.54 million
2003	73.73 million	1,599.55 million
2004	60.57 million	1,624.82 million
2005	130.77 million	1,773.85 million
2006	168.11 million	2,061.71 million
2007	232.93 million	2,646.58 million
2008	318.82 million	3,498.15 million
2009	268.23 million	2,748.59 million
2010	320.90 million	3,859.82 million
2011	523.02 million	4,870.25 million
2012	520.0 million	4,704.2 million
2013	473.0 million	5,246.1 million
2014	432.0 million	6,174.4 million
2015	546.8 million	5,575.2 million
2016	642.8 million	5,530.2 million
2017	557.9 million	7,281.7 million
2017-18	685.65 million	8,614.35 million
2018-19	1.04 (billion)	9.21 (billion)

Source: 1980-2005 (Das, 2008, p.11); 2006-2011 (Dubey, 2017, p.126), 2012-2017 (IMF, 2018, p. 87), 2017-18, 2018-19 (MEA Annual Reports, 2018-19, p.38; 2020, p.42).

Table 1 demonstrates the increasing volume of Bangladesh-India bilateral trade. One can argue that if informal trade is included, the volume would be much higher. It is argued that informal trade between Bangladesh and India is 'nearly equal the official trade statistics' (Behera, 2002, p.453). Nurul Islam (2004, p.4069) contends that 'there is a very large illegal trade; illegal imports are estimated to be almost as large as legal imports and illegal exports as small. Legal and illegal imports most probably tantamount to more than 20 per cent of total imports of Bangladesh'. The number of Bangladeshi tourists and medical patients visiting India is growing every year, which can also be taken into account in the context of Bangladesh-India bilateral trade.

Bangladesh's Imports of Services: Health and Education Sector in Focus
Dutta (2005, p.36) notes that 'The bilateral trade deficit of Bangladesh with India...will register a further rise if the imports of services by the

citizens of Bangladesh from India are taken into consideration'. Rahman in 1998 mentioned that such import services exceed US$ 100 million annually (cited in Dutta, 2005, p.36). It was estimated that the annual number of service seekers was 103,000 (health service 50,000, education 53,000) in 1998/99. On an average, each health service seeker spent US$ 600 while education service seekers spent an average of US$ 1,400. (Dutta, 2005, p.36). Notably, the number of service seekers has increased substantially in contemporary times. India has become the most favourite destination for Bangladeshi patients considering the close neighbour, comparably reasonable to other Asian and European countries. Padam Vanish, director of the Indian consultancy firm VAP Global, mentions that 'On an average 1,000 Bangladeshis go to India daily to take treatment' (*The Daily Star*, 2018b). Considering the growing demands, VAP Global has opened a local office in Dhaka to provide information about Indian doctors and hospitals. According to Vanish, 'we opened an office in Dhaka three months ago to provide Bangladeshis with information. On an average, 100 people visit our Dhaka office every day to know about hospitals and doctors in India' (*The Daily Star*, 2018b). Notably, VAP Global has already established contacts with 80 Indian hospitals. In addition, Apollo Hospitals of India has also opened its local office in Dhaka for Bangladeshi medical tourists to provide information who want to visit its medical institute in Chennai for medical treatment (*The Daily Star*, 2018b). According to Noerita Mahmood Farin, customer relationship officer of Health Connect at Apollo Hospitals India, around 150 Bangladeshi patients visit their office every day for information concerning treatment and appointment of doctors in India (*The Daily Star*, 2018b). There is a growing demand for Indian treatment for Bangladeshi patients. In 2017, for instance, Bangladeshis constituted about 55 per cent of the total medical tourists coming to India. According to the Indian Ministry of Tourism, the inflow of medical tourists coming from Bangladesh increased to as much as 83 per cent between 2015 and 2017. In 2015, the number was 120,388 while it increased to 221,751 in 2017, which is almost double (Kumar, 2018). There is a strong political economy involved in this medical tourism. In addition, the huge number of Bangladeshis travelling every day to India, are staying for a few days or few months in case of medical treatment, and are spending millions of dollars for their accommodation, food, treatment and obviously for shopping. Additionally, though there are no exact statistics available, it is assumed that thousands of Bangladeshis are taking education services from Indian institutions. Thus, this import of services in health services and education accelerates the trade deficit/imbalance in favour of India, which needs to be taken into account in discussing Bangladesh-India trade relations.

Investment

Though trade has been a critical feature in Bangladesh-India relations since the establishment of the ties, bilateral investment has been a recent development. Despite being close neighbours, Bangladesh and India could not utilise their investment potential for mutual benefit for a long time. The Bangladesh-India development partnership can be strengthened through increasing the flow of bilateral investments. They have liberalised their investment policies which attract billions of dollars in foreign direct investment (FDI) from other countries. Compared to other countries, India's investment in Bangladesh and vice versa remains at a minimal level.

In February 2009, Bangladesh and India signed an agreement for the promotion and protection of investments for ten years, and thereafter it shall be deemed to have been automatically extended unless there is any opposition. In fact, Bangladesh and India are the fastest-growing economies in the world today. The business community in each country can take advantage of such impressive economic growth for their investments.

In June 2013, the Board of Investment, Bangladesh, in partnership with the Confederation of Indian Industries and the India-Bangladesh Chamber of Commerce and Industry organised investor roadshows in Mumbai, Chennai and Kolkata which resulted in signing an MoU between Indian and Bangladeshi companies amounting to almost US$ 100 million for investment in Bangladesh.

Bangladesh has identified 13 possible investment areas including agro-processing, automobiles, ceramics, chemicals, gems and jewellery, light engineering, ICT, hospital, medical equipment, pharmaceuticals, and textiles where the country is seeking India's investment on a joint venture basis (Bhattacharya, 2018). Bangladesh's former High Commissioner to India, Syed Muazzem Ali, contends that 'The most practical cause of action would be to set-up a series of buy-back projects where Indian investors will set-up industries in Bangladesh and re-export to India and some other neighbouring countries' (cited in Bhattacharya, 2018). Indian companies, i.e., Hero Honda, Tata Group, CEAT Tyres have already set-up projects in Bangladesh. In this regard, the High Commissioner notes that 'these are small projects. What we need is a much bigger investment. If we could engage in the bigger projects, it will also ensure the stability of our relationship'. Notably, the volume of Indian investment in Bangladesh is US$ 3.11 billion, including Reliance's US$ 642-million in the 745 MW gas-fired project and Adani's US$ 400 million in the Mirsarai Economic Zone (Khasru, 2020). The volume is minimal compared to other countries. In addition, India and Bangladesh had signed an MoU for the implementation of small development projects in Bangladesh. Notably, BDT 58.24 crore was sanctioned in the 2014-2015 fiscal year for the implementation of small development projects in Bangladesh. India also extended its second Line of Credit (LoC) of US$ 2 billion in 2015 for 14 developmental projects in Bangladesh. Notably, Tk 6.78 billion will be spent to rebuild the 53 km-long Kulaura-Shahbazpur rail connection, of which Tk 5.55 billion will be paid by an Indian LoC, while the Bangladesh government pays the remaining 1.23 billion. The project will build railway bridges, road bridges and station buildings, platforms, rail lines and other rail infrastructure (*bdnews24.com*, 2018). It is also worthy to note that India supplied 400 deep tubewells in Naogaon district which was completed in May 2014. During her second visit to Dhaka in October 2017, former Indian External Affairs Minister, Sushma Swaraj noted that

> India has been a long-standing and reliable development partner of Bangladesh. Totally, three lines of credit amounting to US$ 8 billion have been extended by India to Bangladesh so far. This is by far the largest development assistance that India has extended to any country worldwide (Ministry of External Affairs of India, 22 October 2017).

Special Investment Zones
In February 2019, the Executive Committee of the National Economic Council (ECNEC) of Bangladesh had approved a project involving Tk 845 crore to acquire 1,000 acres of land in Chattogram's Mirsarai for Indian investors. Notably, the project will be financed through a third line of credit of $4.5 billion from India (*The Daily Star*, 2019). Bangladesh is also

considering two more economic zones for India's investors in Mongla and Bheramara. When implemented, these economic zones will facilitate Bangladesh-India bilateral investment volume. In a joint venture, India's Adani Group with Singapore-based Wilmar expressed an interest to invest US$ 350 million in agro-based foods and allied products (*The Daily Star*, 2018a).

Energy Cooperation

If one looks at the history of Bangladesh-India cooperation on power, on 4 January 1973, they signed an MoU regarding Joint Power Coordination Board that aimed primarily 'to maintain liaison between the participating countries in order to ensure the most effective joint efforts in maximising the benefits from the power systems and energy resources to their mutual benefit'. But it took almost four decades for electricity exchange between Bangladesh and India.

The energy demand of Bangladesh and India is increasing day by day due to urbanisation and industrialisation. Both countries are emerging economies in the region and beyond, for which enough power supply will be mandatory. In this context, energy cooperation between them and along with others in the region will be imperative. Bangladesh and India under Sheikh Hasina-Manmohan Singh, Sheikh Hasina-Narendra Modi regime has created an instance in energy cooperation for many.

Regarding energy cooperation, it is worthy to note that the second meeting of the Joint Working Groups on Cooperation in Power Sector was held in Dhaka and Delhi in May and June 2010, respectively. The notable development was the signing of a 35-year power transmission agreement between Power Grid Corporation of India Ltd (PGCIL) and Bangladesh Power Development Board (BPDB). In addition, in August of the same year, an MoU was signed between National Thermal Power Corporation (NTPC) and Bangladesh Power Development Board (BPDB) for setting up two coal-fired power plants of 1,320 megawatts each in Chattogram and Khulna under a joint venture. In addition, during the visit of India's power secretary, Uma Shankar, to Bangladesh in April 2013, three agreements, i.e., Power Purchase Agreement, Implementation Agreement, and Supplementary Joint Venture Agreement were signed for the joint venture 1320 MW power plant in Rampal, Khulna. In April 2017, the Bangladesh-India Friendship Power Company began the construction of the Rampal power plant, which is close to Sundarbans. The project acquired an area of over 1,834 acres of land. It is argued that the project will lead to large scale ecological disasters and face local resistance (Islam & Al-Amin, 2019).

In February 2014, Bangladesh's Petrobangla and India's ONG Videsh Ltd (OVL) signed two production-sharing contracts for the exploration and production of oil and gas in two shallow-water blocks in the Bay of Bengal. This is the first time in history that Bangladesh has awarded an Indian company to explore oil and gas in the Bay of Bengal. In August 2014, Larsen and Toubro Limited (L&T) signed a contract with Bangladesh Power Development Board to construct a 225 MW combined cycle (dual-fuel) power plant at Sikalbaha in Patiya of Chattogram at the estimated cost of US$ 202.22 million. Notably, L&T was working on a 360 MW project at Bheramara, Rajshahi with Marubeni Corporation.

In 2017, Adani Power (Jharkhand) India inked a long-term pact with Bangladesh Power Development Board to supply electricity from its upcoming 1,600 MW coal-based power plant at Godda in Jharkhand for 25 years (*The Hindu*, 2017). On September 10, 2018, through video conferencing, Sheikh Hasina and Narendra Modi jointly inaugurated three major Bangladesh-India joint venture projects including supply of 500 MW of electricity from India to Bangladesh. The power transfer will be from West Bengal's Baharampur grid to Kushtia's Bheramara grid. According to the agreement, 300 MW of power will come from India's public sector National Thermal Power Plant and 200 MW from the private sector Power Trading Corporation. Currently, India exports 660 MW of power to Bangladesh, 500 MW of which are transferred through the Baharampur-Bheramara connection and 160 MW from Tripura to the Comilla power grid.

The former High Commissioner of India to Bangladesh, Harsh Vardhan Shringla, writes that 'India–Bangladesh cooperation in the power and energy sector has advanced substantially in the last few years. India is committed to supporting Bangladesh in its vision of "Power to All" by 2021. At present, 660 MW of power is already flowing from India to Bangladesh, and to this an additional 500 MW is expected to be added shortly' (Shringla, 2018, p.526). Echoing this, the former Bangladesh High Commissioner to India, Syed Muazzem Ali identifies cooperation in the energy sector as the hallmark in Bangladesh-India relations (*ANI*, March 19, 2019). The envoy also notes that a trilateral investment of MW 1125 MW hydro-power project in Bhutan by Bangladesh-India and Bhutan is under discussion. The former High Commissioner of India to Bangladesh, Harsh Vardhan Shringla, points out that 'India will provide transit for transmitting electricity to Bangladesh' (Shringla, 2018, p.527). Another trilateral hydro-power project in Nepal by Bangladesh-India-Nepal is also under discussion (*ANI*, 2019). In fact, these are incredible developments in Bangladesh-India relations. It is also pertinent to note that the pricing of the energy needs to be reasonable, focusing on the people's perspective.

Challenges

Table 1 shows that there is a considerable trade imbalance that favours India. Notably, during the signing of the first trade agreement in 1972, it was agreed that both Bangladesh and India could export goods to each other valued to Rs. 2,500 lakh. Coming in 2017, the volume of Bangladesh's exports to India were worth US$ 557.9 million while imports were worth US$ 7,281.7 million. In the fiscal year 2018-19, the volume of Bangladesh's exports to India increased to US$ 1.04 billion while the volume of imports also increased to US$ 9.21 billion. In this case, Das (2008, p.40) argues that 'The asymmetry in Indo-Bangladesh bilateral trade in favour of India is mainly due to the very narrow export basket of Bangladesh' that needs to be problematised. In fact, imposing tariff and non-tariff barriers from the Indian side remain a major challenge in Bangladesh-India economic relations (Bhattacharya, 2004). Hossain and Rahman (2008, p.58) note that:

> Bangladesh's current exports face tariff rates between 15 % and 35 % with the exception of mustard oil and soybean oil which face 85 % and 45 % tariff rates respectively. Tariff rates on the agro-based products are on the higher side. Besides, many products are subjected to countervailing duties (CVD) and special additional duties (SAD). High tariff and non-tariff barriers reduce market access for Bangladeshi products.

In addition, though Bangladesh enjoys duty-free access to the Indian market except for a few products, non-tariff barriers impede Bangladesh's exports to India. It is argued that 'Non-tariff barriers (NTB) are also a major deterrent to Bangladesh's exports to India, as India's NTB coverage ratio is much higher than Bangladesh' (Bhattacharya, 2004, p.5152). Rajeet

Mitter, the former Indian High Commissioner to Bangladesh, acknowledges that 'Non-tariff barriers are a hindrance to bilateral trade. It could be good for both countries to have an expert level task force to identify the barriers and solutions' (*The Daily Star*, 2016). Notably, seven to nine documents are required to trade between Bangladesh and India (The Asia Foundation, 2018). If these barriers are well taken care of, the World Bank figures argue that there is a potential for a 300 per cent increase in Bangladeshi exports to India (The World Bank, 2016).

There is still a standardisation problem for Bangladeshi products to enter the Indian market, which links with the non-tariff barriers. Arif Dowla, Managing Director, ACI Limited, Bangladesh, mentions a lack of laboratories on the land ports to check the quality of products. Thus, samples are sent to Khulna or to other places which take 7-15 days. Trucks loaded with products need to wait till the test results arrive, which increases the cost of doing business by 2 per cent (*The Daily Star*, 2016).

In addition, anti-dumping duty (ADD) imposed on Bangladesh jute goods by India is hurting Bangladesh's export volume to India. *The Financial Express*, in its editorial, noted that:

> the imposition of ADD on jute goods is hurting Bangladesh's interest most—its export earnings from the same dropped by more than 20 per cent in 2018-19. The Bangladesh government, since the levying of ADD on jute goods, has requested its Indian counterpart to reconsider the issue, but to no avail. Most Bangladeshi jute goods exporters who had approached the relevant Indian authorities for a review of the ADD imposition got no relief (*The Financial Express* Editorial, 2020).

The Financial Express, in its editorial, further claims that 'the renewed move to put up fresh tariff and non-tariff barriers to the access of Bangladesh goods to the Indian market has triggered frustration among businesses here. Many might find the approach on the part of India a bit harsh and not in line with the much-touted claim that the good neighbourly relations between the two countries are now at its peak'. In the editorial, it is also noted that 'the relevant policymakers of that country [India] cannot be oblivious of the interests of a close neighbour [Bangladesh] that has been a victim of significant and ever-widening trade deficit for decades'. Consequently, it is suggested that 'Bangladesh policymakers should make forceful efforts to dissuade India from levying punitive duties on its exports. In the event of failure to do so, they should take the issues to the WTO and seek justice' (*The Financial Express* Editorial, 2020).

In addition, the Bangladesh business community fears that Indian Customs Rules-2020 is likely to make a tariff preference in its market most challenging for anyone, including Bangladesh, which might affect the Bangladeshi export volume to the Indian market. The importers should enter details of certificate of origin which include the reference number, date of issuance, originating criteria, indicate if accumulation/cumulation is applied if the certificate is issued by a third country and if goods have been transported directly from the country of origin. The claim for a preferential rate of duty can be denied without verification if the certificate of origin is incomplete and not in accordance with the format as prescribed by the rules of origin (Islam, 2020). Khondaker Golam Moazzem, research director of Centre for Policy Dialogue, notes that 'Bangladeshi exporters may face various types of constraints and challenges in compliance with the documentation and following proper submission process' (Islam, 2020).

With regard to the investment aspect, it is argued that the poor state of political relations mainly impeded bilateral investments (Dubey, 2013). Dubey also noted that in 2005, the Indian Tata Group proposed nearly US$ 3 billion investment for setting up a steel plant, fertiliser factories and power plants in Bangladesh, mainly based on the local supply of gas. After three years, the proposal was rejected citing the lack of natural gas while Dubey asserted that it is due to the bad political ties between Bangladesh and India. Thus, it is argued that 'The real breakthrough in Indian investment in Bangladesh will come only if there is a marked improvement in the political relations between the two countries' (Dubey, 2013). Against the findings of Dubey (2013), this chapter argues that despite having good political relations since 2009, the volume of bilateral investment remained minimal. In this case, the Indian policy towards Bangladesh is not investment-friendly. In this context, it is argued that 'Despite India-Bangladesh relations being referred to as a "role model", the irony is that in India's Consolidated FDI policy 2017, Bangladesh is put in the same category as Pakistan' (Khasru, 2020). The FDI policy's para 3.1.1 says, 'A non-resident entity can invest in India.... However, a citizen of Bangladesh/Pakistan or an entity incorporated in Bangladesh/

Pakistan can invest only under the Government route' which discourages Bangladeshi investments in India and therefore needs to be taken into account seriously.

Policy Imperatives

First, it becomes essential to diversify the Bangladeshi export basket to India. In this regard, Bangladesh's major export items included raw jute, jute items, fertiliser, and frozen products which need to be diversified. In a study by the Centre for Policy Dialogue, it was found that Bangladesh enjoys a comparative advantage in some items like bicycles, optical elements, leather items, handbags, footwear, outer soles and sleeping bags (*The Daily Star*, 2014a). Bangladesh policy and the business community need to take strong policy initiatives to place these products in the Indian colossal market. *The Daily Star* (2014b) in its editorial notes that 'Although over the decade 2003-2013, export volume has increased fivefold to more than US$ 500 million per annum, it is a paltry figure considering that the rest of the world exports worth US$ 350 billion to India every year'.

Second, as mentioned earlier, tariff, para-tariff and non-tariff barriers impede Bangladesh-India trade volume. It is also argued that 'tariffs and non-tariff barriers, including cumbersome customs procedures for legal imports, make illegal trade attractive' (Islam, 2004, pp.4069-70). Hence, India needs to take decisive, practical steps to increase Bangladesh's export volume to the former by reducing tariff, para tariff and non-tariff barriers.

Third, opening more border *haats* would be imperative for the promotion of Bangladesh-India trade volume. In fact, border *haats* can play an effective role in empowering local people economically as local and indigenous products ranging from vegetables and fruits to aluminium and plastic products are mainly transacted. Effective border governance becomes imperative in proper border *haats* management. Joyeeta Bhattacharjee, senior fellow, Observer Research Foundation, New Delhi contends that 'Effective border management would require adopting a people-centric approach like establishing more number of border *haats*' (*The Financial Express*, 2020). It is also expected that opening more border *haats* will diminish illegal trade volume substantially as local people and businessmen will be able to do trade legally. More border *haats* will also impact on socio-cultural exchanges between Bangladesh and India.

Finally, attracting more of India's investment through effective nation branding becomes necessary for Bangladesh. After peaceful maritime dispute resolution with Myanmar and India in 2012 and 2014, respectively, Bangladesh got the scope to explore and exploit its blue economy. Bangladesh can explore its marine resources for national development. Blue economy is still untapped in Bangladesh with huge potential. This area can be one area where more of India's investment can be attracted. In this case, effective nation branding becomes important.

Conclusion

The chapter has analysed the emerging development partnership between Bangladesh and India. From the traditional focus of trade and aid, investment and energy cooperation have become the defining features in the development partnership. The introduction of border *haats* has added a new dimension to Bangladesh-India economic cooperation. In fact, Bangladesh-India development partnership has become an example to many in the world. The chapter additionally contends that in this age of shared prosperity and development, development partnership becomes important to harness the untapped potentials of these two countries. Therefore, the chapter concludes by saying that the Bangladesh-India development partnership based on mutual interest will bring emancipatory potentials from poverty and hunger to tens of thousands of people in these countries. Thus, untapped potential in this partnership needs to be explored and harnessed for the benefit of the people of these two countries and beyond. In this context, a strong political will on the Indian side is necessary to reduce the trade gap and widen development partnership.

REFERENCES

ANI (2019, March 19). Power sector is hallmark of Indo-Bangla cooperation, says Bangladesh envoy.

bdnews24.com (2018, September 10). India supplies 500MW additional power to Bangladesh. Retrieved from https://m.bdnews24.com/en/detail/economy/1538326

Behera, N.C. (2002). Regionalism from below: The domain of civil society. In S. Afroze (Ed.), *Regional cooperation in South Asia: New dimensions and perspectives*, (pp. 448-461). Dhaka: Bangladesh Institute of International and Strategic Studies.

Bhattacharya, S.K. (2004). Does Bangladesh benefit from preferential trade with India? A gravity analysis. *Economic and Political Weekly*, 39 (48), pp. 5152-5162.

Bhattacharya, P. (2018, July 25). Bangladesh seeks big Indian investment in 13 sectors. *The Daily Star*.

Chaturvedi, S. (2012). India's development partnership: Key policy shifts and institutional evolution. *Cambridge Review of International Affairs*, 25 (4), pp. 557-577.

Das, G. (2008). Indo-Bangladesh economic relations: Issues in trade, transit and security. In G. Das and C.J. Thomas (Eds.), *Indo-Bangladesh border trade: Benefiting from neighbourhood*, (pp. 3-44). New Delhi: Akansha Publishing House.

Department of Commerce, Government of India (2017). *India's trade with South Asia in 2016-17: An analysis*. New Delhi: Department of Commerce, FT-South Asia Foundation.

Dubey, M. (2013, March 25). Indo-Bangladesh economic relations. *Mainstream Weekly*, vol. 51, no. 14. Retrieved from http://www.mainstreamweekly.net/article4074.html

Dubey, M. (2017). *India's foreign policy: Coping with the changing world*. Telangana: Orient Blackswan Private Limited.

Dutta, J.P. (2005). Challenges and prospects of Bangladesh-India economic cooperation: Trade & investment. In S. Haidar (Ed.), *India-Bangladesh: Strengthening the partnership* (pp. 31-53). Chandigarh: Centre for Research in Rural and Industrial Development.

Hossain, M.I. and Rahman, M.H. (2008). Bangladesh-NEI Trade: Can there be a better future? In G. Das and C.J. Thomas (Eds.), *Indo-Bangladesh border trade: Benefiting from neighbourhood*. (pp. 45-65). New Delhi: Akansha Publishing House.

International Monetary Fund (2018). *Direction of Trade Statistics Yearbook*, Washington DC: IMF.

Islam, N. (2004). Indo-Bangladesh economic relations: Some thoughts. *Economic and Political Weekly*, 39 (36), pp. 4069-4075.

Islam, M.N. & Al-Amin, M. (2019). The Rampal power plant, ecological disasters and environmental resistance in Bangladesh. *International Journal of Environmental Studies*, DOI: 10.1080/00207233.2019.1662183

Islam, S. (2020, October 15). India's new customs rules may toughen tariff preferences, fear Bangladesh stakeholders. *The Financial Express*. Retrieved from https://www.thefinancialexpress.com.bd/trade/indias-new-customs-rules-may-toughen-tariff-preferences-fear-bangladesh-stakeholders-1602732339

Khasru, S.M. (2020, December 16). 49 years on, India, Bangladesh should deal with unresolved issues. *Hindustan Times*. Retrieved from https://www.hindustantimes.com/opinion/49-years-on-india-bangladesh-should-deal-with-unresolved-issues/story-U89UhWKCvatR08Og1YjvPP.html

Kumar, N. (2018, August 4). Over 50% medical tourists to India are from Bangladesh. *Sunday Guardian Live*. Retrieved from https://www.sundayguardianlive.com/news/50-medical-tourists-india-bangladesh

Ministry of External Affairs of India (2017, October 22). *Press Statement by External Affairs Minister during her visit to Bangladesh*. Retrieved from https://www.mea.gov.in/Speeches-Statements.htm?dtl/29039/

Ministry of External Affairs, Government of India (2018). *Ministry of External Affairs Annual Report 2017-18*, New Delhi: Policy Planning and Research Division, Ministry of External Affairs.

Nachiketa (1972). India-Bangladesh trade treaty. *Economic and Political Weekly*, 7 (15), p, 746.

Ray, J.K. (2011). *India's foreign relations, 1947-2007*. New Delhi: Routledge.
Sen, S. (1972). Indo-Bangladesh trade: Problems and prospects. *Economic and Political Weekly*, 7 (15), pp. 763-768.
Shringla, H.V. (2018). India–Bangladesh relations: An Indian perspective. *Strategic Analysis*, 42 (5), 524-528, DOI: 10.1080/09700161.2018.1523080
Singh, N. (2014). India and development partnership: Special reference with Bangladesh in 21st century. *Procedia - Social and Behavioral Sciences*, 157: pp. 137-142.
The Asia Foundation (2018). Intra-regional trade in South Asia.
The Daily Star Editorial (2010, January 10). Expectations from Indo-Bangla summit: Taking the relationship on to a new plane.
The Daily Star (2010, January 12). Duty-free access to India widens: 47 more Bangladeshi products dropped from negative list.
The Daily Star (2014a, April 23). Product diversity holds key to wider access to Indian markets: CPD.
The Daily Star Editorial (2014b, April 25). Boosting exports to India, Major bottlenecks need addressing.
The Daily Star. (2016, October 8). Bangladesh-India relations: Progress made and the challenges ahead.
The Daily Star (2018a, April 19). Wilmar-Adani to invest $350m in Mirsarai economic zone.
The Daily Star (2018b, May 4). Bangladesh a key source market for medical tourism. Retrieved from https://www.thedailystar.net/business/tourism/bangladesh-key-source-market-medical-tourism-1571314
The Daily Star (2019, February 28). Economic zone for Indians gets nod.
The Hindu (2017, November 8). Adani Power inks power purchase agreement with Bangladesh Power Development Board. Retrieved from https://www.the hindubusinessline.com/companies/adani-power-inks-power-purchase-agreement-with-bangladesh-power-development-board/article9949195.ece
The Financial Express Editorial (2020, May 16). Fresh tariff barrier to Bangladesh exports to India. Retrieved from https://www.thefinancialexpress.com.bd/editorial/fresh-tariff-barrier-to-bangladesh-exports-to-india-1589641379
The Financial Express (2020, October 31). 'Bangladesh-India border haats are places for socio-cultural exchanges'. Retrieved from https://www.thefinancialexpress.com.bd/trade/bangladesh-india-border-haats-are-places-for-socio-cultural-exchanges-1604146751
The World Bank (2016, May 24). The potential of intra-regional trade for South Asia. Retrieved from http://www.worldbank.org/en/news/infographic/2016/05/24/the-potential-of-intra-regional-trade-for-south-asia
Venkataramakrishnan, R. (2020, August 22). 'India cannot afford to think of permanent friends anymore in its neighbourhood': Constantino Xavier. *Scroll.in*. Retrieved from https://scroll.in/article/971091/india-cannot-afford-to-think-of-permanent-friends-anymore-in-its-neighbourhood-constantino-xavier

4

UNDERSTANDING SECURITY COOPERATION

ABSTRACT

Why is Bangladesh-India security cooperation important? What are the major areas of security cooperation between Bangladesh and India? This chapter investigates these questions. It argues that from the traditional trade and aid dimensions, Bangladesh-India relations have turned into a security and strategic partnership. Increased military cooperation, cooperation over fighting terrorism and increased maritime cooperation defines the current security and strategic partnership. It is also argued that strong Bangladesh-India security cooperation is in the interest of not only these countries but also for the region.

Keywords: *Security Cooperation, Terrorism, Military Cooperation, Defence, Maritime Cooperation.*

Introduction

This chapter analyses how the Bangladesh-India security relationship has developed in contemporary times. It discusses the major areas of security cooperation. Indeed, since the emergence of the states, security remains its core concern, whether internal or external. In the early nineteenth century, states formed security groups to avoid war. In the post-Cold War period, the nature of security threats changed substantially from traditional to non-traditional security challenges. Inter-state war is no longer a common phenomenon in the twenty-first century. Cross-border terrorism, marine piracy, cyber insecurity and other non-traditional security threats have become common features in the twenty-first century. In fact, no single state can address twenty-first-century security challenges alone. This requires security cooperation at the bilateral, regional and global levels. Thus, security cooperation becomes one of the major dimensions of any bilateral relation.

Bangladesh and India face several common security challenges, including cross-border terrorism which requires cooperation. The former High Commissioner of India to Bangladesh, Harsh Vardhan Shringla, writes that 'The transnational nature of crime syndicates, terror and other criminal networks requires effective cooperation of both countries' (Shringla, 2018, p.524). Against this backdrop, this chapter investigates two questions: why is Bangladesh-India security cooperation important? What are the major areas of this cooperation? If one looks at it historically, the security and strategic dimension in Bangladesh-India relations dates back to the emergence of Bangladesh. One can argue that Bangladesh-India defence cooperation started in 1971 when the Indian armies fought alongside Bangladeshi soldiers. Similarly, one cannot deny that the emergence of Bangladesh also served the security and strategic interests of India. For instance, S.S Bindra (1984, p.141) notes that 'Bangladesh's birth has lessened the worries of the Government of India about Mizos and Nagas who were previously getting training facilities as well as the arms from Pakistan via East Pakistan'. Bindra (1984, p.141) further contends that 'The emergence has given a severe blow to their hostile activities and has shielded the safety of India on Siliguri bottleneck against a possible attack by China because of the friendly interaction of India and Bangladesh since 1971'. Thus, the geostrategic dimension worked as a building block in Bangladesh-India security relations. To discuss Bangladesh-India security cooperation, one can also cite the 1972 Treaty of Peace and Friendship for 25 years. However, it was ineffective due to the continued mistrust between the Dhaka and New Delhi regimes.

To understand Bangladesh-India security cooperation, one also needs to understand the geostrategic importance of Bangladesh to India. Y.M. Bammi, for instance, notes that 'Bangladesh's strategic importance to India lies in the fact that she dominates the Siliguri Corridor (a narrow space of approximately 20 km between Nepal and Bangladesh near Siliguri), in West Bengal' (Bammi 2010, p.52). In an editorial of *The Hindu*, it is argued that 'Mr. Modi's team made Ms. Banerjee understand the geostrategic significance of Bangladesh ...which made two quick visits to Dhaka, after having refused to accompany the then Prime Minister on his visit in 2011' (*The Hindu*, 2015). In addition, according to the analysis of the *Times of India*, India's access to use Bangladesh's Chattogram and Mongla ports 'has huge strategic implications' for India (*Times of India*, 2015). Prior to Manmohan Singh's 2011 Dhaka visit, the IDSA Task Force authored a report where it is argued that 'Bangladesh is critical to India's security concerns and can make a positive contribution to the social and economic prosperity, particularly that of the Northeastern states. India's "Look East policy" cannot be successful without a durable relationship with Bangladesh' (IDSA Task Force, 2011, p.13).

After decades of trust deficit, in 2009, when the Awami League came to power, security and strategic cooperation received a momentum in Bangladesh-India relations. In this regard, the *Hindustan Times* (2020), in its editorial notes that 'Ms Hasina's government has provided a model of security cooperation'. In November 2016, Indian Defence Minister Manohar Parrikar visited Bangladesh, the first-ever visit by an Indian Defence Minister. The visit underscores the evolving security ties between Bangladesh and India. During his trip, Parrikar met with a range of senior officials, including Prime Minister Sheikh Hasina, the President, the Security Adviser to the Prime Minister, and Chiefs of the Army, Navy, Air Force and Coast Guard (Parameswaran, 2016). Thus, this chapter argues that from the traditional trade and aid dimensions, Bangladesh-India relations have turned into a security and strategic partnership. Increased military cooperation, cooperation over terrorism and increased maritime cooperation define the current security and strategic partnership between Bangladesh and India. It is also argued that strong Dhaka-New Delhi security cooperation is in the interest of not only these countries but also others of the region.

This chapter is divided into four sections. The first discusses the rationale and background of Bangladesh-India security cooperation. The second section provides a conceptual understanding of security cooperation. It subsequently focuses on the major areas of security cooperation, concentrating on military cooperation, cooperation on terrorism, maritime cooperation, cooperation on cybersecurity and cooperation within Indian Ocean Regional institutions. Finally, this chapter presents the concluding remarks.

Conceptualising Security Cooperation

Though security has become a household word, it is very much contested and subjective. Simply, security means the absence of insecurity, or it is associated with a perceived threat. Scholars define security from their own perspective/school of thought. For instance, a realist scholar like Stephen M. Walt (1991) links security with military security, while a critical scholar like Ken Booth (2007, 1991) sees security as 'survival-plus' or linked with 'emancipation'. While there is no consensus on the meaning of security, 'most scholars within International Relations work with a definition that involves the alleviation of threats to cherished values' (Williams 2008, p.1). Consequently, in the traditional security studies, states are seen as the central unit of analysis and threats are perceived as external aggression. In critical security studies, the individual is seen as the referent object of security and security is broadly seen as human well-being. Critical security studies broaden and deepen the security agendas ranging from health challenges to poverty to piracy (Krause and Williams, 1996, 1997).

Security cooperation means deepening or promoting cooperation between or among states in the security areas, i.e., terrorism, maritime issues and food insecurity. It is argued that 'The conceptual shift that has occurred after the end of the Cold War is that security can be dealt with through cooperation rather than confrontation' (Gupta, 2011). Woodrow Wilson viewed that security cooperation at the international level is necessary to avert war (cited in Jervis, 1985). This resulted in the creation of the League of Nations. It is also argued that states benefit from cooperation on common problems (Jervis, 1985). According to L. Cordner 'States are most likely to embrace cooperative security measures when there is a compelling, shared belief that the defence of their own interests can be usefully enhanced through that course' (Cordner, 2011, p.69). In the case of Bangladesh-India relations, one can argue that there are many common security challenges including terrorism, maritime challenges, cyber insecurity, and other non-traditional security threats which can be addressed through enhancing security cooperation. Thus, Bangladesh-India security cooperation means promoting cooperation in the common security challenges to ensure the security and well-being of the state and its people. In the domain of security cooperation, this chapter discusses military cooperation, maritime cooperation, cooperation on preventing terrorism, cybersecurity and security cooperation at the Indian Ocean regional institutions. Mahfuz Anam, the editor and publisher of *The Daily Star*, contends that 'The primary concern of India regarding Bangladesh is security in the east. The other major concern is terrorism...terrorism is also a major concern for Bangladesh' (*The Daily Star*, 2016a). Notably, Bangladesh has already addressed India's security issues significantly in its Northeast region. Thus, Bangladesh-India security cooperation has been identified as 'unparalleled' by the Indian Ministry of External Affairs (Ministry of External Affairs, 2016). It is also worthy to note that all umbrella agreements with regard to security cooperation have been signed and ratified by both India and Bangladesh, which also implies the importance they attach to the dimension of security cooperation.

Major Areas of Security Cooperation

After the Awami League came to power in 2009 through the 2008 election, the world witnessed a series of agreements and Memorandum of Understanding (MoU) on security/defence cooperation between Bangladesh and India. Consequently, from the trade and economic perspectives in Bangladesh-India relations, security and strategic perspectives have gained momentum in the areas of military affairs, maritime domain, terrorism, cybersecurity, etc. It becomes important to understand how security cooperation is perceived both in Bangladesh and India. In this regard, the former Foreign Secretary of Bangladesh, Farooq Sobhan, in an interview with *Prothom Alo English* notes that 'after coming to power in 2009, the Awami League-led government gave special importance to strengthening security cooperation between the two countries. Today this cooperation is very strong, effective and successful' (Khan, 2017). On the contrary, Joyeeta Bhattacharjee from Observer Research Foundation, India, contends that 'bilateral relations between India and Bangladesh improved significantly after Sheikh Hasina-led Awami League formed government in 2009 in Bangladesh. The core of this relationship was the security cooperation between the two countries.

Security cooperation resulted in Bangladesh's action against the anti-India forces; they were active in its soil, mainly the insurgent groups of India's North-eastern region' (Bhattacharjee, 2012, p.114). Bhattacharjee further contends that 'Bangladesh became important to NE [Northeast] insurgency. Bangladesh's importance could be analysed from India's repeated requests to that country to react against the insurgent groups' (Bhattacharjee, 2012, p.116).

During Sheikh Hasina's 2010 New Delhi visit, she ensured that 'Bangladesh will not allow its territory to be used for terrorist activities against any country in the neighbourhood or around the world. I can give you this assurance that Bangladesh is committed to eliminating all forms of terrorism from within its territory' (*The Daily Star*, 2010). India was facing insurgencies in its Northeastern states for more than 60 years. In April 2010, both the Bangladesh and Indian governments took firm action against militants from India's Northeast. Notably, Bangladesh security forces launched massive operations against the militants, resulting in the surrender of around 110 militants of the National Liberation Front of Tripura and the All Tripura Tiger Force to Indian security forces in late June 2010 (D'Costa, 2011). Additionally, the Sheikh Hasina regime addressed India's major security concerns by arresting and handing over top United Liberation Front of Asom (ULFA) insurgent group leaders which is well recognised by the policy and academic community of India. During his visit as the Indian President to Bangladesh, Pranab Mukherjee appreciated the contributions of Bangladesh to address the cross-border security concerns of India (*The Daily Samakal*, 2013). Similarly, Bangladesh also faces cross-border terrorism, piracy and other common security challenges. Among these, the major areas of security cooperation are discussed here.

Narratives on Military Cooperation
Bangladesh-India military cooperation can be explained through the exchange of visits, joint military exercises, training programmes and India's line of credit. Amit Sarin writes that 'India's military engagement with the armed forces of Bangladesh had been virtually non-existent until the late 2000s. India has recognised the importance of engaging the Army as an institution and has actively sought to intensify its ties since 2008' (Sarin, 2016, p.20). In July 2008, Indian Chief of Army Staff, General

Deepak Kapoor, visited Bangladesh and discussed various steps to accelerate defence cooperation. After Sheikh Hasina came to power, military cooperation started to develop. And after that, there have been regular exchanges of visits and meetings between the defence personnel of Bangladesh and India. The Chief of Army Staff of India visited Bangladesh in March 2017 while the Bangladesh Army Chief visited India to review the Passing-out Parade at the Indian Military Academy, Dehradun, in December 2017.

Defence cooperation was strengthened by the fourth Army-to-Army-Staff talks held in Dhaka in August 2013. In addition, the first Navy-to-Navy-Staff talks were also held in New Delhi in April 2013. Army and Navy staff talks continued in 2014 as well. In 2014, India offered 123 courses to Bangladesh defence personnel and availed 14 courses offered by Bangladesh. In addition, *Sampriti 2017*, which was held in Mizoram, was the seventh round of joint military exercises between Bangladesh and the Indian army. According to officials, this was imperative to boost not only army-to-army cooperation and understanding but also comprehensive bilateral relations (*Firstpost*, 2017). In addition, in February 2020, Bangladesh and the Indian Army conducted a two-week prolonged military exercise known as *Sampriti-IX* at Umroi in the northeastern Indian state of Meghalaya. Reportedly, more than 160 Bangladesh Army personnel, including 31 officers participated. One of the key aims of the exercise was building 'military trust' between the Bangladesh Army and the Indian Army (Panda, 2020).

India expressed interest for a comprehensive, 25-year agreement on defence cooperation. In December 2016, India's Defence Minister, Manohar Parrikar, visited Dhaka and sought greater defence cooperation with Bangladesh. India's proposed defence agreement would cover 'greater military-to-military cooperation, sale and supply of military hardware from India to Bangladesh and coordinated operations against mutually perceived threats' (Bhaumik, 2017). India offered US$ 500 million line of credit to Bangladesh for the purchase of military hardware from India.* During Sheikh Hasina's 2019 New Delhi visit, India urged Bangladesh to expedite the implementation of the line of credit that was offered in the field of defence cooperation.

---
*Bangladesh buys its military hardware mostly from China.

Cooperation on Combating Terrorism

There is no single state in the world that is immune/exempt from terrorism. Among traditional security threats, terrorism dominates the security discourse of Bangladesh and India. If one looks at Bangladesh, the grenade attack on Sheikh Hasina, the then opposition leader of the Bangladesh Parliament, at Bangabandhu Avenue on 21 August 2004, was one of the most dreadful terrorist incidents in the world which killed 24 Awami League activists and leaders including one of the senior members of the Awami League—Ivy Rahman (Talukdar, 2016). Bangladesh also experienced countrywide bomb blasts by extremist Islamist groups in August 2005. Additionally, Bangladesh gained attention from the world community because of the Holey Artisan Cafe terror attack, Dhaka, on July 1, 2016. This incident resulted in 22 deaths, including that of two police officers and around 42 people injured (*The Daily Star*, 2016b). In *The State of Terrorism in Bangladesh 2010-2011*, Farooq Sobhan (2011, p.3) contends that 'Bangladesh had witnessed sporadic acts of terrorism in the first half of the last decade'. Thus, terrorism becomes one of the significant security threats in Bangladesh.

Terrorism has also become a grave concern for India (Puroshotham and Prasad, 2009; Sakthival, 2010; Zafar and Wasi, 2010). P.W. Puroshotham and M. Veera Prasad (2009, p.553) write that 'India since its independence has been facing the problem of insurgency and terrorism in different parts of the country and frontier-terrorism has been the unending vexed issue'. Indeed, the 2001 attack on the Indian Parliament and the 2008 Mumbai terror attack shows the severity of terrorism in the country and stresses the importance of regional and global cooperation.

Terrorists are today regionally and globally interconnected. Globalisation has made the process easier for terrorists to maintain regional and global networks. Consequently, cross-border terrorism has become a common feature in the twenty-first century. It is seen in the fact that Bangladeshi terrorists take refuge in India while the terrorists of India's Northeast region take refuge in Bangladesh (Bammi, 2010; Ministry of External Affairs, 2006; 2007). For instance, in December 2009, some Indian insurgents were arrested in Bangladesh and were handed over to India. Similarly, in April 2014, there were seven murders in Narayanganj, a city near Dhaka. Noor Hossain and his associates were the prime suspects. Later, they absconded and took shelter in Kolkata. In June 2014, he, along with his associates, was arrested in Kolkata (*The Daily Kaler Kantha*, 2014). It was also reported that 52 Bangladeshi terrorists were arrested in India (Alam, 2014). In such a scenario, one of the major developments in Bangladesh-India security cooperation was the arrest of the ULFA chief Aravinda Rajkhowa (who was leading the ULFA for three decades) and his associates by Bangladesh authorities and handing them over to India as mentioned earlier. Rajkhowa was the most wanted insurgent for India's security agency. In addition, the *Indian Express* notes that 'The Bangladesh PM's unreserved cooperation on terrorism and a readiness to think out of the box have been key to constructing a genuine partnership between Delhi and Dhaka' (*The Indian Express* Editorial, 2015). Mahfuz Anam, the editor and publisher of the *Daily Star*, writes

> India truly needs to be grateful to Sheikh Hasina for her determined and successful effort at dismantling all the camps of the insurgents from the north-east that the Khaleda Zia government had allowed in a mistaken policy to keep "pressure" on India. Over time, these insurgents had become a genuine worry as their destructive power rose with sanctuary on Bangladesh's side of the border (Anam, 2017).

Therefore, to address cross-border terrorism, Bangladesh and India have signed several agreements and MoUs. For instance, during the visit of Sheikh Hasina to India in January 2010, India and Bangladesh signed three agreements related to terrorism. These agreements are: A) Agreement on Mutual Legal Assistance in Criminal Matters; B) Agreement on Combating Terrorism, organised Crime and Illicit Drug Trafficking; and C) Agreement on Transfer of Sentenced Persons. In 2013, Bangladesh and India also signed an Extradition Treaty to suppress crimes. In addition, an MoU on prevention of human trafficking, MoU on prevention of smuggling and circulation of fake currency notes were signed in 2015. These agreements and Memorandum of Understanding are imperative in forging Bangladesh-India cooperation on terrorism. It is also worthy to note that in a joint media event, Sheikh Hasina and Narendra Modi expressed their firm commitment to extend anti-terror cooperation. According to Narendra Modi, 'While our partnership brings prosperity to our people, it also works to protect them from forces of radicalisation and extremism. Their spread poses a grave threat, not just to India and Bangladesh but to the entire region' (*The Economic Times*, 2018). Thus, a firm commitment is manifested by Sheikh Hasina and Narendra Modi to deal with cross-border terrorism and ensure peace and stability for the people of Bangladesh and India. It is also pertinent to note that in September 2019, on the sidelines of the 74th session of the United Nations General Assembly, Sheikh Hasina and Narendra Modi held bilateral meetings on different issues. They reiterated zero tolerance on terrorism (*NDTV*, 2019). Thus, one can argue that addressing cross-border terrorism is one of the priority areas in Bangladesh-India relations.

Maritime Cooperation

Oceans have traditionally been the source of resources, an important source of food security, energy security, and an essential medium of international trade. Thus, controlling the seas were significant concerns for the great powers once upon a time. But today, coming to the twenty-first century, it is argued that oceans have become a source of cooperation among the nation-states to harness their potential. In this regard, Kyunghan Lim contends that 'the seas of the 21st century are no longer a stage for nations to compete or rival over. The significance of today's maritime environment goes beyond a territorial space of each nation's operations' (Lim, 2015, p.135). It seems that states today confront less and cooperate more in the maritime domain. It raises the question: When do states cooperate in the maritime domain? In this context, Lee Cordner contends that 'If progress is to be made toward effective maritime security cooperation among nation-states, there needs to be a strong sense that commonly held interests are threatened, at risk, or vulnerable and that cooperative action among states will help to protect them' (Cordner, 2011, p.69). In the case of Bangladesh and India, both face common maritime challenges, i.e., piracy which hampers their common interests, as both depend on secured seas for their trade or harnessing marine resources. For instance, between 2001 and 2010, approximately 85 per cent of piracy worldwide was accounted for by 15 states. Among these, Bangladesh was ranked the fourth-highest piracy incident country (7.5 per cent) while India was ranked fifth (3.8 per cent) (Twyman-Ghoshal and Pierce, 2014, p.656). It is argued that 'Though transnational maritime crime rarely presents a direct threat to states, piracy and robbery at sea are such severe problems that they are now perceived to do just that' (Bradford, 2005, p.66). Thus, it is essential to promote cooperation at the bilateral, regional and global level in the maritime domain.

Another important aspect is that more than 90 per cent of the international trade of Bangladesh and India happens through the sea. Additionally, Bangladesh and India depend on the seas for their energy supplies from the Middle East and other parts of the world as well as for exporting their (manufactured) products to other parts of the world which creates sea dependence. This requires a safe sea where uninterrupted seaborne trade is possible. In addition, to explore and harness the marine resources sustainably, Bangladesh and India need to promote cooperation in the Bay of Bengal region (Hossain and Islam, 2019).

Therefore, Bangladesh and India signed an MoU on cooperation between the Coast Guards of their countries in 2015. In December 2016, the Indian Coast Guard (ICG) hosted a four-member delegation led by the Director General of the Bangladesh Coast Guard, Rear Admiral Aurangzeb Chowdhury, to discuss cooperation in the maritime realm. Bangladesh and India have instituted a Coordinated Patrol (CORPAT) as an annual feature between the two navies. CORPAT was inaugurated on 27 June 2018 which is expected to consolidate Bangladesh-India naval cooperation. According to the Indian Navy, 'CORPAT is a major step towards enhanced operational interaction between both Navies. Naval cooperation between India and Bangladesh has been traditionally strong, encompassing a wide span which includes operational interactions through port calls, passage exercises along with capacity building, capability enhancement and training initiatives' (*The Hindu*, 2018). In August 2018, a delegation of the Bangladesh Coast Guard visited Goa as part of an engagement programme and met the Coast Guard Goa's district commander, DIG Himanshu Nautiyal. They discussed issues of maritime law enforcement and enhanced cooperation (*The Times of India*, 2018).

During Sheikh Hasina's 2019 New Delhi visit, Bangladesh and India signed an MoU for setting up a coastal surveillance system radar in Bangladesh. Dipanjan Roy Chaudhury writes in the *Economic Times* that 'The coastal surveillance system will pave the way for Indo-Bangladesh White Shipping Agreement in future. This will be useful amid growing terror threats via seas' (Chaudhury, 2019). After signing the MoU, a question arose in Bangladesh regarding the control of the radar. Though there is no data available yet, we can expect that the controlling power of the radar will be in the hands of Bangladesh.

It is also worthy to note that the Bangladesh Navy and Indian Navies conducted the second edition of 'Exercise Bongosagar' in the Bay of Bengal in October 2020 which was aimed at 'developing interoperability and joint operation skills' (*The Times of India*, 2020). Notably, the Exercise was followed by the third edition of CORPAT in the northern Bay of Bengal on October 4 and 5, 2020.

Cooperation in the Area of Cyber Security
The states and its people in the world today have become dependent on the cyber world/internet for their business, commerce, banking, communications, and other daily activities. Due to increasing cyber insecurities, those critical infrastructures are vulnerable today. For instance, in February 2016, the Bangladesh Bank heist proved how vulnerable the states and people are today. Notably, US$ 101 million was stolen from the Bangladesh Bank's account with the New York Federal Reserve Bank by hackers (*The Daily Star*, 2016c). In fact, it was a massive loss for a country like Bangladesh. In the case of India, according to the 'Internet Security Threat Report', India was the third-most vulnerable country to cyber threats. Notably, 5.09 per cent of global threats were detected in India in 2017 (Bhargava, 2018). It is worthy to note that Bangladesh and India are growing economic powers in Asia. Thus, they will also be targeted by cyber attackers. Considering such growing challenges, Bangladesh and India signed an MoU on cyber security in 2017 to promote cooperation in the area of cyber security. According to the MoU, Dhaka and New Delhi will focus on establishing a framework for dialogue, exchanging of information and mutual response related to cyber-attacks, cooperation on technology, and capacity building.

Cooperation within Indian Ocean Regional Institutions
Bangladesh and India cooperate in the Indian Ocean regional institutions like Indian Ocean Rim Association (IORA) and Indian Ocean Naval Symposium (IONS). India was the former chair of IORA and Bangladesh is going to be the chair in 2021. Notably, Bangladesh hosted the Third IORA Ministerial Blue Economy Conference in September 2019. Bangladesh-India work closely in maritime-related matters of the IORA and IONS. Thus, Dhaka-New Delhi security cooperation spanned beyond its bilateral frameworks. In order to establish rule-based maritime order

in the Bay of Bengal and the Indian Ocean Region, Bangladesh-India security cooperation will be imperative.

Conclusion

This chapter has analysed the necessity, nature and scope of Bangladesh-India security cooperation. Though Bangladesh-India ties began with security cooperation, due to the existing political differences between Dhaka and New Delhi and for the sake of narrowly defined regime interests, the security partnership could not develop. Bangladesh-India security cooperation has reached a new height after Sheikh Hasina came to power in 2009. This chapter argues that Bangladesh-India security cooperation is imperative considering the increasing number of security challenges, i.e., piracy, cyber insecurity or cross-border terrorism. Thus, it concludes by arguing that Dhaka-New Delhi security cooperation needs to be sustained based on mutual benefit. Such security cooperation might also be imperative for the betterment of the South Asian region and beyond as everyone is connected in this networked world. It is also worthy to note that Bangladesh-India security and strategic cooperation needs to be based on a win-win situation for the greater interest of all.

REFERENCES

Alam, S. (2014, March 17). 52 terrorists arrested in India will be handed over to Bangladesh [In Bangla]. *The Daily Kaler Kantha*.

Anam, M. (2017, March 25). The new power play in South Asia. *The Straight Times*. Retrieved from https://www.straitstimes.com/asia/south-asia/the-new-power-play-in-south-asia

Bammi, Y.M. (2010). *India-Bangladesh relations: The way ahead*. New Delhi: United Service Institution of India and Vij Books India Pvt. Ltd.

Bhattacharjee, J. (2012). India-Bangladesh security cooperation impacting NE India's Insurgency. In K. Lange, K. Knapp, & J.P. Panda (Eds.), *Revisiting contemporary South Asia: Politics, economics and security* (pp.114-126). New Delhi: Pentagon Press.

Bhaumik, S. (2017, March 1). Keener on arms from China, Bangladesh dithers on defence pact with India. *South China Morning Post*. Retrieved from https://www.scmp.com/week-asia/geopolitics/article/2075152/keener-arms-china-bangladesh-dithers-defence-pact-india

Bhargava, Y. (2018, April 5). India third most vulnerable country to cyber threats. *The Hindu*. Retrieved from https://www.thehindu.com/news/national/india-third-most-vulnerable-country-to-cyber-threats/article23437238.ece

Bindra, S.S. (1984). *India and her neighbours: A study of political, economic and cultural relations and interactions*. New Delhi: Deep & Deep Publications.

Booth, K. (1991). Security and emancipation. *Review of International Studies*, 17 (4), 313-326.

Booth, K. (2007). *Theory of world security*. New York: Cambridge University Press.

Bradford, J.F. (2005). The growing prospects for maritime security cooperation in Southeast Asia. *Naval War College Review*, 58 (3), pp. 63-86.

Chaudhury, D.R. (2019, October 7). India, Bangladesh sign MoU for setting up a coastal surveillance system radar in Bangladesh. *Economic Times*. Retrieved from // economictimes.indiatimes.com/articleshow/71457316.cms

Cordner, L. (2011). Progressing maritime security cooperation in the Indian Ocean. *Naval War College Review*, 64 (4), pp. 68-88.

D'Costa, B. (2011). Bangladesh in 2010: Digital makeover but continued human and economic insecurity. *Asian Survey*, 51(1), 138-147.

Firstpost (2017, November 17). India-Bangladesh joint military exercise 'Sampriti 2017' concludes in Mizoram; officials say bilateral ties strengthened. Retrieved from https://www.firstpost.com/india/india-bangladesh-joint-military-exercise-sampriti-2017-concludes-in-mizoram-officials-say-bilateral-ties-strengthened-4214003.html

Gupta, A. (2011, November 19). Will cooperative security work in South Asia? *The Daily Star*. Retrieved from https://www.thedailystar.net/news-detail-210669

Hindustan Times Editorial (2020, December 18). The Delhi-Dhaka bond: Sustain the partnership, reconcile domestic narratives, and manage China. Retrieved from https://www.hindustantimes.com/editorials/the-delhi-dhaka-bond-ht-editorial/story-pVlB1Yhp0J9DAHA2xyzWXJ.html

Hossain, D. and Islam, M.S. (2019). Unfolding Bangladesh-India maritime connectivity in the Bay of Bengal region: A Bangladesh perspective. *Journal of the Indian Ocean Region*, 15(3), pp, 346-355, DOI: 10.1080/19480881.2019.1646570

IDSA Task Force (2011). *India-Bangladesh relations: Towards convergence*. IDSA: New Delhi.

Jervis, R. (1985). From balance to concert: A study of international security cooperation. *World Politics*, 38 (1), pp. 58-79.

Khan, M.R. (2017, April 3). Exclusive Interview with Farooq Sobhan: 'India needs to be sensitive about Bangladesh's public opinion'. *Prothom Alo English*. Retrieved from https://en.prothomalo.com/opinion/%E2%80%98India-needs-to-be-sensitive-about-Bangladesh%E2%80%99s

Krause, K. and Williams, M.C. (1996). Broadening the agenda of security studies: Politics and methods. *Mershon International Studies Review*, 40 (2), pp. 229-54.

Krause, K. Williams & Michael C. (Eds.) (1997). *Critical security studies: Concepts and cases*, Minneapolis, MN: University of Minnesota Press.

Lim, K. (2015). Non-traditional maritime security threats in Northeast Asia: Implications for regional cooperation. *Journal of International and Area Studies*, 22(2), pp. 135-146.

Ministry of External Affairs, Government of India (2006). *Ministry of External Affairs Annual Report 2005-2006*, New Delhi: Policy Planning and Research Division, Ministry of External Affairs.

Ministry of External Affairs, Government of India (2007). *Ministry of External Affairs Annual Report 2006-2007*, New Delhi: Policy Planning and Research Division, Ministry of External Affairs.

Ministry of External Affairs, Government of India (2016). *Ministry of External Affairs Annual Report 2015-2016*. New Delhi: Policy Planning and Research Division, Ministry of External Affairs.

NDTV (2019, September 28). PM Modi, Sheikh Hasina reiterate zero tolerance for terrorism. Retrieved from https://www.ndtv.com/india-news/pm-modi-bangladesh-pm-sheikh-hasina-reiterate-zero-tolerance-for-terrorism-2108515

Panda, A. (2020, February 4). Armies of India, Bangladesh Begin Military Exercise in Indian Northeast. *The Diplomat.* Retrieved from https://thediplomat.com/2020/02/armies-of-india-bangladesh-begin-military-exercise-in-indian-northeast/

Parameswaran, P. (2016, December 10). India, Bangladesh talk Coast Guard cooperation. *The Diplomat.* Retrieved from https://thediplomat.com/2016/12/india-bangladesh-talk-coast-guard-cooperation/

Puroshotham, P.W. & Prasad, M.V. (2009). Addressing frontier-terrorism: India needs global counter terrorism strategy. *The Indian Journal of Political Science,* 70 (2), 553-568

Sakthival, P. (2010). Terrorism in India: The unholy neighbours. *The Indian Journal of Political Science,* 71 (1), pp. 153-162.

Sarin, A. (2016). Military diplomacy: A tool for foreign policy. In S. Kumar, D. Dwivedi & M.S. Hussain (Eds.) *India's defence diplomacy in 21st century: Problems & prospects* (pp. 9-22). New Delhi: G. B. Books.

Shringla, H.V. (2018). India–Bangladesh relations: An Indian perspective, *Strategic Analysis,* 42 (5), 524-528, DOI: 10.1080/09700161.2018.1523080

Sobhan, F. (2011). *The state of terrorism in Bangladesh 2010-2011.* Dhaka: BEI.

Talukdar, M.R.I. (2016, August 23). Grenade attack on 21 August 2004. *The Independent.* Retrieved from http://www.theindependentbd.com/arcprint/details/57049/2016-08-23

The Daily Samakal (2013, March 2). Special interview of Pranab Mukherjee with the Samakal.

The Daily Kaler Kantha (2014, June 16). 8 days remand in India's court, many names come out in investigation [in Bangla].

The Daily Star (2010, January 12). Hasina wants deal on Teesta water: Bangladesh must get guaranteed water flow of all common rivers, she tells banquet.

The Daily Star (2016a, October 8). Bangladesh-India relations: Progress made and the challenges ahead.

The Daily Star (2016b, July 2). Terror strikes Dhaka.

The Daily Star (2016c, March 15). 101m heist: Atiur quits as governor of Bangladesh Bank.

The Economic Times (2018, July 12). India, Bangladesh to step up anti-terror cooperation. Retrieved from https://economictimes.indiatimes.com/news/defence/india-bangladesh-to-step-up-anti-terror-cooperation/articleshow/58081100.cms?utm_source=contentofinterest&utm_medium=text&utm_campaign=cppst

The Hindu Editorial (2015, June 8). Modi's day in Dhaka. Retrieved from http://www.thehindu.com/opinion/editorial/modis-day-in-dhaka/article7291974.ece

The Hindu (2018, June 24). India, Bangladesh Navies to join hands. Retrieved from https://www.thehindu.com/news/national/india-bangladesh-navies-to-join-hands/article24247739.ece

The Indian Express Editorial (2015, June 8). Taking the leap: Prime Minister Modi's Bangladesh visit affirms a more purposeful and problem-solving neighbourhood policy. Retrieved from https://indianexpress.com/article/opinion/editorials/taking-the-leap/

The Times of India (2015, June 7). Now, India gets to tug at China's 'string of pearls'. *Times of India,* Retrieved from http://timesofindia.indiatimes.com/india/Now-India-gets-to-tug-at-Chinas-string-of-pearls/articleshow/47570510.cms

The Times of India (2018, August 30). Bangladesh coast guard visits Goa. Retrieved from https://timesofindia.indiatimes.com/city/goa/bangladesh-coast-guard-visits-goa/articleshow/65599699.cms

The Times of India (2020, October 4). India-Bangladesh naval exercise commences. Retrieved from https://timesofindia.indiatimes.com/city/visakhapatnam/india-bdesh-naval-exercise-commences/articleshow/78468072.cms

Twyman-Ghoshal, A. A. and Pierce, G. (2014). The Changing Nature of Contemporary Maritime Piracy. *The British Journal of Criminology: An International Review of Crime and Society*, 54, 652–672.

Walt, S.M. (1991). The renaissance of Security Studies. *International Studies Quarterly*, 35 (2), 211-239.

Williams, P.D. (2008). Security Studies: An Introduction. In P.D. Williams (Ed.), *Security Studies: An Introduction* (pp.1-12). Oxon: Routledge.

Zafar, S. and Wasi, A.B. (2010). Terrorism in India: Method in madness? *Policy Perspectives*, 7 (2), pp. 51-74.

5

BORDER ISSUE:
CHALLENGES AND RESPONSES

ABSTRACT

Bangladesh and India share 4,096 km of land borders. This border demarcation and its governance has always been a matter of discussion and debate in Bangladesh-India relations. Though the Land Boundary Agreement has been ratified, tensions still remain in the Bangladesh-India border area including cross-border terrorism, smuggling, and border killings. This chapter argues that this long border can be turned into possibilities for the people of these countries. Against this backdrop, this chapter tries to understand: What is a border? How can one understand the Bangladesh-India border both historically and theoretically? What kind of challenges are there in the Bangladesh-India border management on the ground? How can the Bangladesh-India border be turned into greater possibilities instead of conflicts or tensions?

Keywords: *Bangladesh-India border, LBA, border cooperation, mental border, border killings, smuggling, trafficking.*

Introduction

Through the Peace of Westphalia in 1648, the modern nation-state was born where borders were demarcated. From that point of time, borders are protected by the state and its machinery, i.e., security forces. These borders provide identity to particular groups or communities of people. In fact, borders are not only physically but also mentally constructed throughout the decades. These borders can be from land, maritime, and air dimensions. India shares a 4,096-km border with Bangladesh along with the States of West Bengal (the longest at 2,216 km), followed by Tripura (856 km), Meghalaya (443 km), Mizoram (318 km) and Assam (263 km) (Singh, 2017). In fact, Bangladesh inherited border disputes with India as a legacy of the partition of the subcontinent in 1947. After the partition, the border was not fully demarcated between India and Pakistan and that persisted throughout decades. Consequently, after Bangladesh was liberated from Pakistan in 1971, the border with India remained undemarcated which resulted very often in conflicts though, in 1972, Bangladesh and India emphasised on maintaining 'fraternal and good-neighbourly relations and transforming their border into a border of eternal peace and friendship'. To resolve the dispute, on May 16, 1974, Bangladesh and India signed the Land Boundary Agreement (LBA). Later, on September 6, 2011, Bangladesh and India signed a Protocol to implement the 1974 Land Boundary Agreement which has been ratified in 2015 by the Indian Parliament. Now, the conventional wisdom is that the LBA ratification has addressed the border problem, and it is peaceful now. Against this backdrop, this chapter argues that though the Bangladesh-India border has been demarcated, border management still remains a major challenge. Border challenges, i.e., border killings have always been a matter of discussion and debate in Bangladesh-India relations. This chapter argues that the Bangladesh-India lengthy border can be turned into possibilities for the benefit of the people of both these countries. In such a scenario, this chapter tries to understand: What is a border? How can one understand the Bangladesh-India border both historically and theoretically? What kinds of challenges are there in Bangladesh-India border management on the ground? Why should Bangladesh and India cooperate on border management? How can the Bangladesh-India border be turned into greater possibilities instead of conflicts or tensions?

This chapter is divided into six sections, including an introduction and conclusion. In the introduction, the background of the chapter and rationale is provided. The second section focuses on theorising borders while the third looks into the historical genesis of the Bangladesh-India border. The fourth section discusses the challenges and the fifth focuses on the possibilities in Bangladesh-India border management. The final section concentrates on the concluding remarks.

Theorising Borders

How can borders be theorised? Borders are constructed both physically and mentally. Conventionally, the border of a state refers to the external, inter-state or international borders that delimit and delineate the states as independent entities in the international system. The Bangladesh-India border separates the territoriality of these two countries and thus creates an independent identity. It is argued that 'Borders are ubiquitous in political life. Indeed, borders are perhaps even constitutive of political life. Borders are inherent to the logic of inside and outside, practices of inclusion and exclusion, and questions about identity and difference' (Vaughan-Williams, 2009, p.1). Though the neoliberals claim that the territoriality of the nation-states has been reduced due to the emergence of economic globalisation and neoliberal economies, the realists, on the contrary, argue that borders are still relevant, especially in the case of the Bangladesh-India border. According to the realist paradigm, borders are identified as a symbol of sovereignty and security. It is also identified as an essential component in the definition of the nation-state. Borders are seen as sacred, which need to be protected from external aggression. Claudia Sadowski-Smith (2011, p.273) contends that 'national borders continue to function as a means to protect state sovereignty, to delimit a specific geography, and to unite populations through territorially-bounded notions of national citizenship'.

In the case of the Bangladesh-India border, Amit Ranjan (2018, p.10) contends that 'it is the construction of identity of people, their imagination of self and about the "others" living with them or across the border that determines the character of India–Bangladesh border'. The Bangladesh-India border is a complex one where border killings by India's Border Security Force (BSF) personnel, human trafficking, and smuggling has been a common phenomenon. One also needs to take into consideration the mental border created by the national discourses over time. In this case, when the Bangladesh-India border comes to one's mind (especially a Bangladeshi), fencing, border killings, and smuggling come first. Thus, it is important to create positive narratives regarding the Bangladesh-India border by applying better border governance/management.

Historicising Bangladesh-India Border

It is argued that the history of the Bangladesh-India border dates back to the early nineteenth century 'when after the introduction of tea plantations in Assam in the province in the late 1820s and its expansion in the 1830s a large number of labourers, mainly Muslims, moved from then East Bengal to work in the plantation industry' (Ranjan, 2018, p.5). As the entire region was under British rule, there was no demarcated line between Assam and Bengal at that point of time. In fact, there is debate and disagreement on Bangladeshi immigration issues in India.

While the conventional wisdom is that illegal migration takes place only from Bangladesh to India, *The Indian Express*, in its editorial, notes that 'Indian visions of Bangladeshi hordes need to be replaced with a realisation that migrants cross in both directions' (*The Indian Express* Editorial, 2020).

Concerning demarcation of the land boundary and related matters, Bangladesh and India signed the Land Boundary Agreement (LBA) on May 16, 1974 (as mentioned in the introduction), having five articles. Article five reads that 'The Agreement shall take effect from the date of the exchange of the Instruments of Ratification'. Consequently, we see that though Bangladesh ratified the Agreement in the same year, India took almost four decades to ratify it, which demonstrated India's lack of political will to resolve the border issue. There was an Exchange of Letters dated on December 26, 1974; December 30, 1974; October 7, 1982; and March 26, 1992. Later, on September 6, 2011, during the Manmohan Singh's visit to Dhaka, Bangladesh and India signed a Protocol concerning the demarcation of the land boundary and related matters. However, the constitution amendment bill to ratify the LBA was not presented in the Rajya Sabha due to the strong opposition of the Trinamool Congress leader Mamata Banerjee and Assam Ganaparshad leaders (*The Daily Samakal*, 2013).

Mamata Banerjee opposed the ratification of the land boundary deal arguing that while Bengal will get only 7,000 acres, it will have to concede nearly 17,000 acres. Later, she agreed to exchange the enclaves (*The Daily Star*, 2014). India was home to 111 enclaves while Bangladesh had 51 enclaves. Even though there were some discord regarding the passing of the LBA Bill in the Indian Parliament, it was finally passed unanimously in the Rajya Sabha in 2015 which was repeated in the Lok Sabha, when all the 331 members present voted for the Bill that became the 100th Constitutional Amendment. Due to the ratification of the LBA, primarily three complex and sensitive issues have been resolved between Bangladesh-India border relations, i.e., i) the exchange of 162 enclaves between the countries; ii) exchange of adverse possessions of each other's territories; and iii) demarcation of 6.5 kilometres of the boundary. Many people think that it is a paradigm shift in border relations between the two immediate neighbours. Notably, prior to the 2019 Lok Sabha election, both the BJP and the Trinamool Congress sought credit for successfully exchanging the enclaves. But the question arises: Was the plight of the enclave citizens ended due to the seven decade-old issue of enclave exchanges? It is reported that the plight of the enclave citizens residing in enclave settlement camps in India is far from over. For instance, Jayprakash Roy, a resident of the Haldibari camp, notes that 'The families here have no jobs and are surviving on doles given out by the State government. This is not easy survival for us; we had come to India with a lot of hope' (Singh, 2019). Abu Taher, a 29-year-old resident of Dinhata camp in West Bengal's Cooch Behar district, contends that 'We have been here for three years, but we have not been given what we were promised. When we left Bangladesh, we thought we would get land and jobs here in India' (Singh, 2019). Thus, it appears that the exchange of enclaves could not change the fate of many people which requires enough attention from the policy and academic community to change their lives.

Additionally, the Bangladesh-India border dispute is related to the issues of smuggling, migration, drug trafficking and trans-border crimes. It is expected that LBA implementation will bring about positive outcomes through effective border management, counter-terrorism cooperation, and prevent smuggling and other border-centric crimes. Thus, it is a critical issue to engage whether the resolution of border disputes offers an opportunity to transform border relations between the two countries in order to facilitate more human interactions and peace. Adarsh Swaika, a former Deputy High Commissioner of India to Bangladesh contends that 'Settling...land boundary issues will facilitate effective border management.' (*The Daily Star*, 2016). Despite such optimism, effective border management remains a dream. Border management includes 'not only defending the border in times of war, or securing the borders in times of peace, but to ensure that there are no unauthorised movement of humans, prohibiting smuggling of arms, explosives, narcotics as well as coordinating intelligence inputs from various agencies and ensuring the socio-economic development of the border areas' (Roy, 2013, p.96). Border killings, smuggling has been a regular phenomenon in the contemporary Bangladesh-India border area. Thus, the next section focuses on the challenges in this border area.

Challenges

In 1999, Banerjee *et al.* wrote that 'After the liberation of Bangladesh it was hoped that the border would lose much of its potential for creating disputes and enmity with the improvement of bilateral relations. Sadly, even after more than 25 years of the birth of Bangladesh, almost all the outstanding issues between India and Bangladesh continue to be related to the common border' (Banerjee *et al.* 1999, p.2549). Even after almost 50 years, border problems remain key challenges in Bangladesh-India relations which are explained in the following section.

Border Killings

Despite land boundary ratification, tensions exist in the Bangladesh-India border. Border killings remain as one of the major challenges in Bangladesh-India border management. It is argued that India's Border Security Force (BSF) follows 'a shoot-to-kill policy' 'even on unarmed local villagers' [Bangladeshi] in the India-Bangladesh border area (Adams, 2011). Saleh Shahriar, Lu Qian and Sokvibol Kea (2020, p.553) contend that 'The continued culture of border killings hampers the bilateral relationships between India and Bangladesh by creating a climate of fear and mutual mistrust'. *Dhaka Tribune* writes that 'For the most part, Bangladesh has healthy bilateral relations with India. In spite of this, there is one unfortunate point of contention that rears its head time and again: Border killings of Bangladeshis at the hands of India's Border Security Force' (2020). *The Daily Star* in its editorial notes that 'The way the Indian Border Security Force has been killing Bangladeshi nationals on a regular basis makes us wonder why, despite many flag meetings between the two sides to resolve the issue, such shootings continue and lives are lost' (*The Daily Star* Editorial, 2020b).

In order to understand the brutality in the border, it is pertinent to look at a few examples of such killings. On January 15, 1999, Abdul Mannan Talukder, a 40-year-old Bangladeshi, was killed in BSF firing. He died on the spot, and they took away his body. According to the local people, he went to the frontier village for collecting paddy seeds. The BDR (Bangladesh Rifles renamed later as the Bangladesh Border Guard, BGB) protested the killing and held a flag meeting with the BSF. The BSF agreed to hand over the body (*The Daily Star*, 1999). On January 11, 2000, seven Bangladeshi fishermen along with their boats and nets were kidnapped by the Indian Border Security Force from the Bangladesh side of the river Ichhamati (*The Daily Star*, 2000). On January 7, 2011, a teenage girl, named Felani was brutally killed by the BSF on the Phulbari border in Kurigram district when she was returning home from India through the Anantapur border of the district which created huge protests in Bangladesh against India. Notably, Indian envoy in Bangladesh Rajeet Mitter was summoned by the Bangladesh foreign ministry, and a protest note on the brutal killing was handed over to him (*The Daily Star*, 2011a). Additionally, in January 2012, a 32-year old Bangladeshi named Abdul Sheikh from Chapainawabganj was brutally tortured by BSF personnel which was photographed on a mobile phone. Later several Indian TV channels broadcast that footage. *The Hindu* (2012) in its editorial titled 'Brutality on the border' asked New Delhi to make an apology to Dhaka for this. Consequently, in the inquiry, eight BSF personnel were found guilty, and they were sent to jail for 89 days (*The Daily Star*, 2012a). In June 2012, the Home Minister of India acknowledged in the Indian Parliament that 151 Bangladeshi nationals had been killed by the BSF during the first three-and-a-half years of the present (Congress-led) government tenure. *The Daily Star* in its editorial (2012b) writes that

> The mere uttering of regret by senior Indian policymakers is simply not enough. Despite several ministerial-level meetings and joint sittings of the chiefs of BSF and BGB, no substantial improvement has taken place on the ground to make the long porous border between the two countries safer. It is high time the Indian central government showed zero tolerance to border killings.

Despite promises, meetings and sittings, border killings continue. It is reported that a cowherd was brutally beaten and then killed by the BSF in July 2012 (*The Daily Jugantor*, 2012). Adams (2011) writes that 'Over the past 10 years, Indian security forces have killed almost 1,000 people, mostly Bangladeshis, turning the border area into a South Asian killing field. No one has been prosecuted for any of these killings, in spite of evidence in many cases'. *The Hindu*, in its editorial (2020), noted that 'Despite the friendship remaining solid, the border has been sensitive—at least 25 Bangladeshis were killed in the first six months of this [2020] year along the border by Indian forces'. Instead of killings, there should be other mechanisms to deal with the issue peacefully. These border killings exist as a major challenge in Bangladesh-India border governance. During the 2019 visit of Sheikh Hasina to New Delhi, she and Narendra Modi, in a joint statement 'agreed that the loss of civilian lives at the border is a matter of concern and directed the concerned border forces to enhance coordinated measures to work toward bringing such border incidents down to zero' (*The Daily Star Online*, 2019). Similarly, in the joint statement of Sheikh Hasina-Narendra Modi's December 2020 virtual summit, both the leaders agreed that 'loss of civilian lives at the border is a matter of concern and directed the border forces concerned to enhance coordinated measures to work towards bringing such border incidents to zero' (MEA, 2020). From the joint statement, it is clear that border killing remains a priority area at the highest level. One cannot rule out the role of smuggling in the case of border killings. Many Bangladeshi and Indian businessmen want to make profits illegally through smuggling along the Bangladesh-India border. One can cite the example of illegal cattle trading, which is also responsible for border killings. However, instead of border killings, there needs to be other justifiable mechanisms to deal with illegal smuggling.

Smuggling

Smuggling has traditionally been a common border crime along the Bangladesh-India border (Hussain, 1989; Maniruzzaman, 1975). Once large-scale smuggling happened from Bangladesh to India (Maniruzzaman, 1975). The smuggled products were mostly rice, wheat, jute, etc. This smuggling from Bangladesh to India is seen as one of the causes of the 1974 famine in Bangladesh, which caused 100,000 deaths (Maniruzzaman, 1975). Over the years, it has changed and smuggling is now from India to Bangladesh and vice versa. Smuggling of cattle, drugs and arms have been a common phenomenon over the decades. Table 2 notes that the volume of smuggling is increasing between Bangladesh and India.

Table 2: Data on Bangladesh-India Smuggling (in Taka)

Year	Seized illegal goods entering Bangladesh	Seized illegal goods entering India
1972	5,767,001	3,399,595
1974	14,049,568	5,664,756
1976	8,306,184	4,161,001
1980	19,916,160	62,399,773
1984	90,743,363	46,607,145
1988	363,541,629	136,734, 630
1990	420,498,212	96,969,842
1992	621,652,045	171,414,109

Source: Ahmed (1996, p. 286).

According to the data compiled by the Union Home Ministry of India, 18,132 smuggling cases along the India-Bangladesh border were recorded in 2015 which increased to 21,771 in 2016 and 29,693 in 2017 (cited in *The Daily Star*, 2018b). Tens of thousands of cattle are smuggled from India to Bangladesh, which often results in border killings. *The Hindustan Times* (2019) writes that 'Tens of thousands of cattle are estimated to be smuggled to Bangladesh annually through the porous 2,216-km India-Bangladesh border in West Bengal'. N.S. Jamwal, Commandant in the Border Security Force (BSF), writes that 'Enclaves become convenient points for smuggling, avoiding customs and excise duties, importing of contraband, and are a point of entry for illegal aliens' (Jamwal, 2004, p.9). It is also argued that the unresolved enclaves were 'dens of thugs, smugglers, terrorists, gun-runners and illegal immigration mafias. Even jihadi groups and the ISI have routinely used these as staging posts as these are permanent gaps in border surveillance' (Gupta, 2013).

The headline titled 'Drugs, arms and gold worth Tk 120 cr seized along Benapole border in 2020: 378 smugglers held' clearly shows the severity of contemporary smuggling along the Bangladesh-India border (*The Daily Star*, 2021). It is even reported that in September, October 2017, two BSF personnel were allegedly killed by cattle smugglers. Shiv Sahay Singh (2017) writes that 'The two deaths are an indication that cattle smuggling along the international border is a major challenge for security personnel guarding the border'. In a parliamentary question-answer session, it was revealed by India's Home Ministry that 109,999 head of cattle were seized in 2014, 153,602 in 2015 and 168,801 in 2016 (cited in Singh, 2017). According to a senior BSF official, 'It is impossible to stop cattle smuggling as the margin of profit is very high, and locals on both sides of the border benefit economically from it. It is like a cat-and-mouse game—you have increased surveillance at some spot, and the smugglers try other places' (cited in Singh, 2017). Notably, the smugglers get a profit of 10,000 to 15,000 rupees per animal depending on the size. This high margin works as one of the major challenges in tackling cattle smuggling. There is also a corruption-smuggling nexus as border guards on both sides 'accept and demand bribes' (Banerjee *et al.*, 1999; p. 2,549). For instance, BSF's South Bengal Frontier spokesman, S.S. Guleria contends that some state police officials cooperate with the suspects. According to Guleria, 'We have sought the help of [West Bengal] director-general of police to seize cattle-laden trucks before they reach border areas' (cited in *The Hindustan Times*, 2019). It was also reported that one Bangladeshi was brutally tortured since he was not able to pay a bribe to the BSF personnel (*The Daily Star* Editorial, 2012b). Imtiaz Ahmed (1996, pp.285-286) contends that 'Developmental protectionism, while opening up a space for the smugglers, also tends to benefit the law-enforcing agencies, who reap a share (legal or otherwise) from the inter-state illegal trading'.

Arms smuggling has also become a matter of concern. According to a report, 23 foreign pistols, 41 magazines, and 105 bullets were recovered in 2020 along the Benapole border (*The Daily Star*, 2021). Shariful Islam, a journalist of the *Daily Star,* visited Chapainawabganj, the zero line area of Bangladesh-India border, and found that arms are smuggled easily from India to Bangladesh through this route. Reportedly, criminal gangs and terrorists from Bangladesh rely on supplies of illegal arms and explosives from India through this route. In October 2016, police raided a house in Chapainawabganj town and recovered 22 foreign-made pistols, 45 magazines and 136 bullets which were brought from India (Islam, 2017). In fact, the barbed-wire fence could not deter arms smuggling. On September 14, 2017, in an interview with Islam, an arms smuggler pointed out that

> We just bring in arms when parties place orders. We do not know who is a criminal and who is a militant. Finding small firearms or bullets in the bordering areas of Malda and Murshidabad is no big deal. I just bring in the arms and hand those over to parties. There are people who would carry your arms if you pay them. After a certain distance, the goods change hands (cited in Islam, 2017).

The arms smuggler uses the hundi system, an illegal money transaction system, to pay for the arms from India. Notably, Bangladeshi smugglers get high profits by selling arms to the criminal gangs of the country (Bangladesh). According to the investigators, nine firearms that were used in the Gulshan cafe attack on July 1, 2016, were brought from India through Chapainawabganj and Jessore borders (Islam, 2017). It was also revealed that arms are smuggled from one Indian state to another through the border *haat* of Sylhet as a key transit route. Transnational syndicates are using the Gowainghat point as a new route to smuggle arms (Khan, 2019b). According to Jahangir Alam, additional deputy commissioner of the Illegal Arms Recovery Team of the Counter-Terrorism and Transnational Crime unit of Bangladesh, 'The local smugglers in guise of traders go to the Gowainghat border haat with some goods to dodge the law enforcers and received the arms from the Indian suppliers waiting inside the haat' (cited in Khan, 2019b). Those smuggled arms are also sold to the local criminal gangs of Bangladesh. For the first time, sophisticated arms like 12-chamber revolvers are found in Bangladesh which is smuggled from India. It becomes a matter of grave concern for the law and order situations of both Bangladesh and India, which needs to be strictly controlled.

It is also worthy of mentioning drugs trafficking, which has also been a common crime along the Bangladesh-India border. The issue of drug trafficking has also figured prominently in the meetings between the Border Security Force (India) and Border Guards Bangladesh (Bhattacharyya, 2019). According to the report, 23 foreign pistols, 41 magazines, and 105 bullets were recovered in 2020. Reportedly, 55,496 bottles of phensedyl, 953 kg of cannabis, 550 bottles of domestic and foreign liquor, 1,850 pieces of yaba were seized by the BGB staff along the Benapole border (*The Daily Star*, 2021). Drugs, i.e., phensedyl, are produced in laboratories in some northern states of India, which is trafficked to Bangladesh (Bhattacharyya, 2019). Reportedly, Indian Northeastern states, including Tripura, Assam, and Meghalaya, are used as transit points to smuggle drugs like yaba originating in Myanmar to Bangladesh. It is argued that 'There is no dearth of traffickers given the low income and impoverished conditions of inhabitants along the India-Bangladesh border' (Bhattacharyya, 2019). It was found recently that several Indian syndicates smuggle yaba from Myanmar and then send it to Bangladesh through using Kurigram's Rowmari border point (Khan, 2019a).

Women and Children Trafficking

Trafficking of women and children from Bangladesh to India merits serious attention. Traffickers abduct, lure, and even marry the victims and sell them to India's traffickers after crossing the Jessore border. A girl or woman is sold for Tk 25-30 lakh to India's traffickers, and then they sell the same mainly to Indian brothels. Masud Karim, officer-in-charge of Benapole Police Station, told *The Daily Star* that 'For a women, the traffickers make fake documents like a marriage certificate and a passport. Then they cross the border posing as a couple going on a trip to India. In the same way, the traffickers get passports for underage girls. They identify them as children or siblings while making fake passports and documents' (cited in Khan, 2019c). Traffickers also use many illegal routes to traffic women and girls from Bangladesh to India. The victims and the local law enforcement people claim that the traffickers use Putkhali, Sadipur, Boro Achra, and Gathipara points of Jessore to traffic the victims into India without passports (Khan, 2019c). It is also assumed that traffickers get help from the local ruling partymen, and they bribe huge amounts to the law enforcement agency personnel to be able to conduct their trafficking business smoothly (Khan, 2019c). Though there are no exact statistics, it is assumed that tens of thousands of girls and women are trafficked from Bangladesh to India. An NGO called Rights Jessore rescued 1,117 victims from India since 2009 (Khan, 2019c).

Border Tensions

Border tension also works as an impediment to Bangladesh-India border governance (Banerjee, 2001). For instance, in April 2001, there was a Bangladesh-India 'border battle' which allegedly resulted in 16 BSF and three BDR (renamed as BGB) deaths (Rashiduzzaman, 2002). With regard to the cause of the battle, there are accusations against each other. Many think that the confrontation happened over an issue in the campaign debates in the elections of Bangladesh and in West Bengal and Assam (Ahmed, 2001). Rashiduzzaman (2002, pp.189-90) contends that 'A 30-year-old dispute over enclaves on the border precipitated the clash and such border incidents during 2001 finally prompted the countries' leaders to talk about it'.

What can be Done?

Promoting Border Cooperation

Promoting Bangladesh-India border cooperation becomes essential for both states considering the growing cross-border terrorism, smuggling, trafficking, and so forth, as mentioned earlier. The former High Commissioner of India to Bangladesh, Harsh Vardhan Shringla, writes that 'The two countries also face the challenge of terrorism. Given the porous border that the two countries share, cooperation is imperative, not optional' (Shringla, 2018, p.524). On March 9, 2018, for the first time in history, Bangladesh and India's border security forces jointly declared 8.3 kilometres of their common border area as a 'Crime Free Zone' to prevent cross-border criminal activities. The area covers Putkhali and Doulatpur areas in Bangladesh and Gunarmath and Kaliyani in India (*The Daily Star*, 2018a). Additionally, another example of cooperation is a Coordinated Border Management Plan (CBMP) which is in effect since 2011. But the success of CBMP is questionable considering the level and depth of cross-border criminal activities like smuggling. In addition, in March 2011, Bangladesh and India signed an agreement not to use firearms in case of illegal activities at border area which requires changing the mentality on the ground. *The Hindu* (2012) in its editorial writes that '...such bilateral agreements on the management of their complex boundary are worth nothing unless accompanied by a change in the mindset of those responsible for it on the ground'.

Ensuring Strong Commitment

No formal arrangement or agreement on border governance will work if the border forces are corrupt. Thus, border security forces need to be honest and dedicated to preventing border crimes. In this case, the salary and other benefits of the border security forces need to be increased so that they do not get involved in corruption for material benefit. In addition, proper training incorporating the humanitarian component needs to be introduced for the border security forces. In this regard, Indian External Affairs Minister S. M. Krishna during his July 2011 Dhaka visit noted that 'We will have to deal with the border situation in a humanitarian manner. There is no justification in the killing of innocent people. But at the same time, border management is the responsibility of both the governments and border rules have to be adhered to' (*The Daily Star*, 2011b). The number of border security forces needs to be increased with proper training. Surveillance and patrolling in the border areas need to be accelerated. Similarly, India's border security forces (BSF) need to be made accountable for their brutality, torture and killings along the Bangladesh-India border. It is also argued that 'while we need our neighbour's cooperation to combat the problem, we need to address our own loopholes too and make our borders completely inaccessible to drug smugglers' (*The Daily Star* Editorial, 2020a).

Promoting Awareness

Promoting awareness among the locals on both sides of the border is also important to prevent border crimes. In this case, local NGOs, educational institutions, teachers-students and concerned citizens need to come forward. Residents in a particular society know who are involved in cross-border smuggling. In such cases, those smugglers need to be identified and properly consulted on the negative implications of their activities on society at large and consequently to lead a better life with dignity. Their socio-economic hardships also need to be addressed by the state and other non-state actors by providing them with better livelihood opportunities.

Conclusion

After analysing Bangladesh-India relations over the decades, it is observed that the border issue receives scant attention, both in policy and theory though the issue merits serious attention. For instance, border killings create huge long-term negative implications for many families in Bangladesh. In addition, news of border killings is widely covered in the media, which creates long-term negative perceptions among many people in Bangladesh. Similarly, cross-border smuggling impacts the societal order of the country. Since the Bangladesh-India border creates a conflicting negative or positive perception on the people of Bangladesh, a congenial border bears larger implications. This chapter concludes by arguing that tens of thousands of people in both Bangladesh and India living along the border areas and beyond can be benefitted by executing better border governance. Additionally, it is reiterated that to prevent cross-border crimes, i.e., smuggling, human trafficking, and arms trafficking, there is no alternative to promoting BSF-BGB cooperation, and collaboration, increased patrolling and surveillance, local support and, most importantly, a strong political will.

REFERENCES

Ahmed, I. (1996). Bangladesh-India relations: Trapped in the nationalist discourse. In A. Kalam (Ed.), *Bangladesh: Internal dynamics and external linkages* (pp. 277-296). Dhaka: UPL.

Adams, B. (2011, January 23). India's shoot-to-kill policy on the Bangladesh border. *The Guardian*. Retrieved from https://www.theguardian.com/commentisfree/libertycentral/2011/jan/23/india-bangladesh-border-shoot-to-kill-policy

Ahmed, K. (2001, April 18). Tension along the border. *BBC News*. Retrieved from http://news.bbc.co.uk/2/hi/south_asia/1283703.stm

Banerjee, P., Hazarika, S., Hussain, M., & Samaddar, R. (1999). Indo-Bangladesh cross-border migration and trade. *Economic and Political Weekly*, 34 (36), pp. 2549-2551.

Banerjee, S. (2001). Indo-Bangladesh border: Radcliffe's ghost. *Economic and Political Weekly*, 36 (18), pp. 1505-1506.

Bhattacharyya, R. (2019, May 2). India's Northeast Emerges as a Drug-Trafficking Corridor Between Myanmar and Bangladesh. *The Diplomat*. Retrieved from https://thediplomat.com/2019/05/indias-northeast-emerges-as-a-drug-trafficking-corridor-between-myanmar-and-bangladesh/

Dhaka Tribune Editorial (2020, July 10). Killings at the border need to stop. Retrieved from https://www.dhakatribune.com/opinion/editorial/2020/07/10/ed-killings-at-the-border-need-to-stop

Gupta, S. (2013, August 31). National interest: Dear Narendrabhai. *The Indian Express*. Retrieved from https://indianexpress.com/article/opinion/columns/national-interest-dear-narendrabhai/

Hussain, A. (1989). The Bangladesh-India relations, 1972-75: Seeds of future discord. In M. Ahmad, & A. Kalam (Eds.), *Bangladesh foreign relations: Changes and directions* (pp. 9-19). Dhaka: University Press Limited.

Islam, S. (2017, November 4). Arms smuggling: Just so easy. *The Daily Star*. Retrieved from https://www.thedailystar.net/frontpage/arms-smuggling-just-so-easy-1486057

Jamwal, N. S. (2004) Border management: Dilemma of guarding the India-Bangladesh border, *Strategic Analysis*, 28(1), pp. 5-36.

Khan, M. J. (2019a, August 22). Indian gangs smuggling yaba into Bangladesh. *The Daily Star*. Retrieved from https://www.thedailystar.net/backpage/news/indian-gangs-smuggling-yaba-bangladesh-1788610

Khan, M. J. (2019b, September 8). State-to-State arms smuggling in India: Syndicates using Bangladesh soil. *The Daily Star*. Retrieved from https://www.thedailystar.net/frontpage/arms-trafficking-into-india-syndicates-use-bangladesh-soil-1797079

Khan, M. J. (2019c, July 22). Trafficked into nightmares. *The Daily Star*. Retrieved fromhttps://www.thedailystar.net/frontpage/news/trafficked-nightmares-1775191

Maniruzzaman, T. (1975). Bangladesh in 1974: Economic crisis and political polarization. *Asian Survey*, 15 (2), pp. 117-128.

MEA (2020, December 17). Joint Statement on India-Bangladesh Virtual Summit. Bilateral/Multilateral Documents, Ministry of External Affairs, Government of India. Retrieved from https://mea.gov.in/bilateral-documents.htm?dtl/33306/Joint+Statement+on+IndiaBangladesh+Virtual+Summit

Ranjan, A. (2018). *India–Bangladesh border disputes: History and Post-LBA dynamics.* Singapore: Springer.
Rashiduzzaman, M. (2002). Bangladesh in 2001: The election and a new political reality? *Asian Survey,* 42(1), pp. 183-191.
Roy, N. (2013). Constraints and opportunities in the India-Bangladesh transit dispute. *Indian Journal of Asian Affairs,* 26 (1/2), pp. 93-102.
Sadowski-Smith, C. (2011). Introduction: Comparative border studies, *Comparative American Studies: An International Journal,* 9(4), pp. 273-287.
Shahriar, S., Lu Qian, L. & Sokvibol Kea, S. (2020). Anatomy of human rights violations at the Indo-Bangladesh borderlands. *Territory, Politics, Governance,* 8(4), pp. 553-578
Shringla, H. V. (2018). India–Bangladesh relations: An Indian perspective. *Strategic Analysis,* 42 (5), pp. 524-528.
Singh, S. S. (2017, October 23). Cattle smuggling goes on along Indo-Bangla border. *The Hindu.* Retrieved from https://www.thehindu.com/news/national/other-states/cattle-smuggling-goes-on-along-indo-bangla-border/article19901729.ece
Singh, S. S. (2019, April 7). Trinamool, BJP seek credit for enclave exchange. *The Hindu.* Retrieved from https://www.thehindu.com/elections/lok-sabha-2019/trinamool-bjp-seek-credit-for-enclave-exchange/article26763462.ece
The Daily Jugantar (2012, July 27). Bangladeshi cowherd was brutally beaten and killed by the BSF [in Bangla].
The Daily Samakal (2013, August 20). Land Boundary Ratification Deal was not presented in Rajya Sabha [in Bangla].
The Daily Star (1999, January 17). Bangladeshi killed in BSF firing.
The Daily Star (2000, January 13). BSF kidnaps 7 Bangladeshi fishermen.
The Daily Star (2011a, January 18). Girl Killed by BSF: Govt finally protests.
The Daily Star (2011b, July 7). Krishna meets media editors: Delhi wants more ties with Dhaka.
The Daily Star (2012a, March 15). 8 BSF men sent to jail.
The Daily Star Editorial (2012b, June 29). Minister on BSF killings.
The Daily Star (2014, June 26). Mamata now agreeable to enclaves exchange Reports Indian daily.
The Daily Star. (2016, October 8). Bangladesh-India relations: Progress made and the challenges ahead.
The Daily Star (2018a, March 10). Indo-Bangla border: 8.3 km declared 'crime free zone'.
The Daily Star (2018b, June 25). Cross-border arms smuggling on rise. Retrieved from https://www.thedailystar.net/world/asia/cross-border-arms-smuggling-rise-1594891
The Daily Star Online (2019, October 5). Loss of civilian lives at border a matter of concern: India-Bangladesh says in a joint statement. Retrieved from https://www.thedailystar.net/country/news/border-killing-matter-concern-1809709
The Daily Star Editorial (2020a, February 10). Stemming inflow of banned drugs and narcotics: Requires cooperation of our neighbours too. Retrieved from https://www.thedailystar.net/editorial/news/requires-cooperation-our-neighbours-too-1865728
The Daily Star Editorial (2020b, July 6). BSF shootings are not stopping: What about India's promise of bringing down the number of casualties to zero? Retrieved from https://www.thedailystar.net/editorial/news/bsf-shootings-are-not-stopping-1925661

The Daily Star (2021, January 1). Drugs, arms and gold worth Tk 120 cr seized along Benapole border in 2020: 378 smugglers held. Retrieved from https://www.thedailystar.net/online/news/drugs-arms-and-gold-worth-tk-120cr-seized-along-benapole-border-2020-2020841

The Hindu Editorial (2012, January 24). Brutality on the border. Retrieved from https://www.thehindu.com/opinion/editorial/brutality-on-the-border/article2826161.ece

The Hindu Editorial (2020, December 19). Friend and neighbour: On India-Bangladesh virtual summit. Retrieved from https://www.thehindu.com/opinion/editorial/friend-and-neighbour-on-india-bangladesh-virtual-summit/article33367913.ece

The Hindustan Times (2019, July 19). Cattle smuggling on India-Bangladesh border in Bengal sets off alarm bells. Retrieved from https://www.hindustantimes.com/india-news/cattle-smuggling-on-india-bangladesh-border-in-bengal-sets-off-alarm-bells/story-rYPZogt05n7MkbjGgwwBzJ.html

The Indian Express Editorial (2020, December 18). The Delhi-Dhaka bond: Sustain the partnership, reconcile domestic narratives, and manage China. Retrieved from https://www.hindustantimes.com/editorials/the-delhi-dhaka-bond-ht-editorial/story-pVlB1Yhp0J9DAHA2xyzWXJ.html

Vaughan-Williams, N. (2009). *Border Politics: The limits of sovereign power*. Edinburgh: Edinburgh University Press.

6

Understanding Water Sharing Disputes

ABSTRACT

Why have Bangladesh-India water-sharing disputes not been resolved yet? How can this dispute be resolved? This chapter investigates these questions. Bangladesh and India share 54 transnational rivers. Being an upper riparian country, India diverts water, depriving Bangladesh of her legitimate rights of a fair share. Also, there is only one water-sharing agreement, i.e., Ganga water-sharing treaty. The Treaty came into being in 1996, and it is only for 30 years. So nobody knows what will happen after 30 years. Though there was much expectation in 2011 about the Teesta Water Sharing Treaty during Manmohan Singh's visit in Bangladesh, at the last hour, it did not happen due to strong opposition by Mamata Banerjee. Notably, the Teesta is the fourth largest transboundary river of Bangladesh for irrigation and fishing. Negotiations on Teesta water sharing has been going on since 1983. India is not showing standard (expected) behaviour with Bangladesh concerning water sharing. Consequently, tens of thousands of Bangladeshi farmers and fishermen are suffering from extreme water scarcity. In this context, this chapter will look at the possibilities of resolving Bangladesh-India water sharing disputes.

Keywords: Bangladesh-India Water Dispute, Water Governance, Hydro Diplomacy, Water Cooperation.

Introduction

Bangladesh-India shares 54 transnational rivers. But there is only one water-sharing agreement, i.e., Ganga water-sharing treaty. The Treaty came into being in 1996 after almost three decades of negotiations, only for 30 years. What is going to happen in 2026 when the 30 years end? Will the treaty be renewed? What's about water-sharing agreements on the other 53 rivers including the Teesta? These are the questions that regularly arise in the minds of the people of Bangladesh. Bihar Chief Minister Nitish Kumar has also opposed the Ganga Water Treaty as he claims that it is detrimental to Bihar and the Treaty has been undertaken at the cost of Bihar's water security. And being an upper riparian country, India diverts water thus depriving Bangladesh of its legitimate rights of a fair share. Thus, the water-sharing issue has long been a matter of concern for Bangladesh.

Though there was much expectation in 2011 about the Teesta water-sharing treaty during Manmohan Singh's visit to Bangladesh, at the last hour, it did not happen due to the strong opposition of Mamata Banerjee, the West Bengal Chief Minister. Notably, the Teesta is the fourth largest transboundary river of Bangladesh for irrigation and fishing. Negotiations on Teesta water sharing have been going on since 1983. India is not showing standard (expected) behaviour with Bangladesh with regard to water sharing on the common rivers. Consequently, tens of thousands of Bangladeshi farmers and fishermen are suffering from extreme water scarcity. But in the context of contemporary Bangladesh-India relations, it is manifested that the water issue did not receive enough attention to be resolved, especially from the Indian side. Though there are unprecedented developments on the issues of connectivity, border demarcation, maritime boundary demarcation, trade and investment, the sharing of water issue has long remained an unresolved issue which merits serious attention. In fact, it is important to resolve the water-sharing disputes because water is 'an emotive issue' in Bangladesh-India relations and failure to resolve them 'will make it very difficult to mobilise public support for Indo-Bangladesh relations' (Sobhan, 2017). Against the above backdrop, this chapter investigates: Why have Bangladesh-India water sharing disputes not been resolved yet? And what are the possibilities, if any, to address water sharing disputes between Bangladesh and India?

This chapter is divided into five sections, including the introductory one. The second section focuses on a brief historical account of bilateral water-sharing, while the third section discusses the factors that led to the failure of water-sharing agreements. The fourth section focuses on the possible policy responses while the final section concentrates on a conclusion.

A Brief Historical Account

In June 1972, Bangladesh and India established the Joint River's Commission (JRC) to resolve the water sharing issues peacefully. It was a far-sighted decision by the decision-makers of Bangladesh and India to form such a mechanism to discuss transboundary water issues. But substantial progress is not manifested under this mechanism. Consequently, the world did not witness the Ganga water treaty until 1996. It is worthy to note that Bangladesh went to the United Nations to resolve its water-sharing dispute with India. But that did not work out since India was interested in a bilateral solution. The water crisis worsened in Bangladesh when India constructed the Farakka barrage in April 1975. The Farakka barrage was built to divert water from the Ganga to the Hooghly River, preventing it from silting to revive Kolkata Port. It was about 17 kilometres upstream from the western borders of Bangladesh with India. Bangladesh, the lower riparian country is dependent on the Ganga water for irrigation and inland navigation. India started withdrawing water at Farakka 'in the absence of any agreement with and to the detriment of, Bangladesh' (Islam, 1987, p.919).

The barrage has created many negative consequences for Bangladesh including severe water crises, droughts, siltation, degraded ground and surface water supplies, impeded navigation, declining fisheries, and public health risks (Nishat, 1996; cited in Giordano et al., 2002). Muhammad Zamir, a former Foreign Secretary of Bangladesh, contended in 2010 that 'Due to continuous withdrawal of waters through the Farakka Barrage for the last 31 years, a significant number of rivers of the Padma basin in Bangladesh have already turned dead' (*The Daily Star*, 2010). The former Chief Whip of the Bangladesh Parliament, A.S.M. Feroz said, 'We want to save rivers. We want to remove structures near water bodies that are negatively impacting them. But due to obstacles like the Farakka barrage, the rivers in Bangladesh are going to die soon' (quoted in Farhin, 2018).

Imtiaz Ahmed contends that the 'Farakka barrage is not solely a problem for Bangladesh. It poses a problem for the people who live in the vicinity in India, too. Such an initiative proves that development projects have been undertaken without thinking about the lives of people living near the river' (quoted in Farhin, 2018). Toriqul Islam, General Secretary of *Ganga Bhangon Protirodh Samity* (Ganges River Erosion Prevention Committee) of India, contends that 'People of Malda and Murshidabad inside India are similarly affected. People are losing their livelihoods on a daily basis because of Farakka. We wanted the barrage, but now it has become toxic for us' (quoted in Farhin, 2018). The dam has created siltation and flood problems for Bihar every year. Thus, the Bihar Chief Minister Nitish Kumar argued strongly for the decommissioning of the Farakka barrage (*Huffington Post*, 2017). Thus, on the one hand, during summer, India diverts water through the Farakka barrage which creates droughts in Bangladesh and on the other, during monsoon, India opens all the gates of Farakka, which leads to floods in Bangladesh (Nazrul, 2019). Thus, by the Farakka barrage, India creates both droughts and floods in Bangladesh, which are highly counterproductive for the country as well as for Bangladesh-India relations.

Rajkumar Singh thinks that 'the sharing of waters at Farakka had become more a matter of politics than of economy as the changeover affected the military Generals of Bangladesh, who, apart from all, faced the problem of legitimacy' (2011, p.273). Bammi notes that 'Both Prime Ministers Deva Gowda and Sheikh Hasina showed greater sagacity and leadership of a very high order and foresight by agreeing to share waters of river Ganga' (Bammi, 2010, p.92). During the visit of Sheikh Hasina to India in December 1996, Bangladesh and India signed the Ganga water treaty for 30 years. And due to the absence of the resolution of the Farakka issue for a long time, the entire southwestern part of Bangladesh was adversely affected. Consequently, this Treaty substantially improved Bangladesh-India relations. But apathy has been noticed from the Indian side. Jayanta Kumar Ray notes that 'the division of Ganga waters between India and Bangladesh remains a complex problem in dealing with which the Government of India displays neither a regard for transparency nor for expertise' (Ray, 2011, p.406). Due to the unresolved water sharing issue, Bangladesh faces severe water crisis during the dry months from December to April/May. And due to the impact of climate change, the volume of rainfall has been reduced drastically. The next section focuses on the Teesta water-sharing dispute.

Teesta Water Sharing

Notably, the Teesta is the fourth largest transboundary river in Bangladesh after the Ganga, Brahmaputra and Meghna rivers. The livelihoods of around 21 million Bangladeshis directly or indirectly depend on the Teesta, which is crucial for the agricultural and irrigation needs of the northern parts of Bangladesh (Asia Foundation, 2013). 'In 1990, the Bangladesh government constructed the Teesta barrage to provide irrigation to drought-prone districts of North-Bengal during dry seasons. However, in 1996, the Indian government established the Gajoldoba barrage, bigger than the Teesta barrage, upstream of the river, for the same purpose' (Chandan, 2019). Chandan further notes that 'As the Indian barrage withdraws water during every dry season, the Teesta River in Bangladesh turns into massive *chars* (a tract of land formed by siltation and surrounded by a river). Bangladesh's Teesta Barrage can do little to irrigate the land due to extreme water shortage'. Thus, India's massive withdrawal of Teesta waters during dry season creates a drought-like situation in the northern part of Bangladesh. According to the Department of Agriculture Extension, Rangpur, around 3,000 acres of *char* land in the Teesta have been lying unused for years since farmers do not have enough water to grow rice and other crops (*The Daily Star*, 2012). Pinaki Roy (2015) writes that 'There is no water in the irrigation canals in the region at the peak of the Boro season as the Indian authorities have blocked the water flow at Gajaldoba barrage in West Bengal'. Against India's unilateral withdrawal of waters from the Teesta River, Shakhawat Liton (2019) writes that 'Deep inside in its heart, India must know unilateral withdrawal of water from an international river goes against international law'. On the contrary, in the monsoon season, India opens the barrage which creates floods in Bangladesh swallowing croplands and village after village. So, being an upper riparian country, India creates two-way danger for Bangladesh. It is reported that the livelihoods of hundreds of fishermen are in jeopardy due to India's such behaviour concerning water sharing (Chandan, 2019).

To resolve the Teesta water dispute, Bangladesh and India made an ad hoc arrangement in 1983. According to this arrangement, Bangladesh would receive 36 per cent, while India would receive 39 per cent of the waters, and the remaining 25 per cent would remain unallocated (Ranjan, 2017). In 1996, after the Ganga water treaty was signed, the Teesta water treaty got importance in the Bangladesh-India water discussions. In 2000, Bangladesh presented its draft on the Teesta. The final draft was accepted by India and Bangladesh in 2010 (Ranjan, 2017). Consequently, in 2011, during Manmohan Singh's visit in Bangladesh, the Teesta water-sharing treaty was supposed to be signed. But Mamata Banerjee opposed the deal which led to the failure of any agreement. After that, Bangladesh has been repeatedly asking for the Agreement while the Indian government has repeatedly given assurances for the agreement. But, in reality, no progress is manifested. Thus, the question arises, what factors contribute to Bangladesh-India water cooperation to make it so complex and difficult? The next section deals with this question.

Why has Bangladesh-India Water Sharing Dispute not been Resolved yet?

Lack of India's Interest

Harsh Vardhan Shringla (2018), India's former High Commissioner to Bangladesh, published an article in *Strategic Analysis*, titled 'India-Bangladesh relations: An Indian perspective'. Though the High Commissioner focuses on the different facets of Bangladesh-India relations, including economic, energy, trade, development issues, he did not touch upon the water sharing issue. This also implies India's lack of seriousness to resolve the dispute. In fact, after almost three decades of negotiations, the Ganga water treaty was signed in 1996 for 30 years, as mentioned earlier. For many years, Bangladesh has been demanding a Teesta water-sharing agreement. But no fruitful outcome has been found yet. It is because of lack of India's interest.

In fact, Bangladesh and India have improved their ties in all dimensions except water. Now, if this water dispute can be resolved peacefully, this will create new horizons in deepening their ties. It is worthy to note that in November 2011, in a (Rajya Sabha) Parliamentary Question Answer session (Q. No. 352), the Bangladesh-India water issue was discussed. Rather than water sharing, India is more interested in inland water transit and trade. On December 18, 2002, in a Lok Sabha QA session (Question No. 4505), India's Minister of State in the Ministry of External Affairs, Digvijay Singh, answered regarding the status of the Protocol on Inland Water Transit and Trade (PIWTT) between India and Bangladesh and regarding the use of Chattogram Port for the transportation of commodities to the North East region of India. In April 2018, the status on the Protocol on Inland Water Transit and Trade (PIWTT) between India and Bangladesh was again discussed in a Rajya Sabha Parliamentary Question-Answer session. The Bangladesh-India water sharing issue was not prioritised in the Parliamentary discussions of India, which also implies India's lack of interest in resolving the case at the earliest. On October 11, 2018, the Indian High Commission in Dhaka published a detailed article on India-Bangladesh relations. Though the developments in border management, security, energy cooperation, and cultural cooperation were discussed in detail, there was no mention either of the Teesta water sharing issue or other river sharing issues except the Ganga treaty (High Commission of India, Dhaka, 2018). This implies India's lack of interest to resolve the issue.

It is even argued that the excuse of Mamata Banerjee or the federal system is used by India so that water would not be shared (Bandapaddai, 2019). If India would be sincere and serious about the issue, then the water sharing issue would have been resolved much earlier. In fact, Bangladesh showed a positive gesture to address the demand for drinking water for the people of Tripura's Sabroom town. During the official visit of Sheikh Hasina to New Delhi in October 2019, Bangladesh and India signed an MoU allowing India to withdraw 1.82 cusecs of water from Bangladesh's Feni River (Liton, 2019; *The Daily Star Online*, 2019a). On the contrary, regarding Bangladesh's water sharing, no progress is manifested in the 2019 Hasina's visit to New Delhi. Thus, Sheikh Hasina expressed her disappointment and said, 'The people of Bangladesh are awaiting an early signing and implementation of the Framework of Interim Agreement for sharing of the Teesta waters, as agreed upon by both governments in 2011' (*The Business Standard*, 2019).

Lack of Information/Knowledge of Water

Among other challenges, water has been identified as the topmost challenge in Bangladesh-India relations (Kashem and Islam, 2016). In this regard, the absence of proper water knowledge makes the issue more complicated. Himanshu Thakkar writes that amongst the challenges that India's water sector face is the lack of credible 'water information' including information about water storage, groundwater, water flows and, in some cases, even rainfall and snowfall levels that remain as the topmost challenges. This chapter contends that this lack of knowledge about the availability of water, and the absence of better water governance also works as a major challenge in Bangladesh-India water sharing disputes. In this context, Thakkar thinks that 'Access to accurate water information could help one understand the risks and urgency of the situation and steer towards informed decisions' (Thakkar, 2019, p.12).

Domestic Politics

Water is often used for political purposes in Bangladesh-India relations (Islam, 2012; Kashem and Islam, 2016). If Mamata Banerjee agrees to the water sharing agreement with Bangladesh, she thinks that people might not vote for her. Thus, in 2011, we witnessed that at the last hour, due to Mamata's opposition, the Teesta water sharing treaty was not concluded as mentioned earlier. According to Mamata Banerjee, 'Though we maintain friendship and good relations with Bangladesh, it should not be at the cost of the people of West Bengal' (*The Statesman*, 2013). On April 6, 2017, Sheikh Hasina and Mamata Banerjee had an hour-long meeting at Rashtrapati Bhavan in New Delhi on Teesta water sharing. But Mamata Banerjee refused to share Teesta waters. According to Mamata, 'The Teesta is the lifeline for the northern part of West Bengal. There will be a problem of water for drinking and irrigation purposes if Teesta water is shared' (*The Daily Star*, 2017).

Furthermore, in Bangladesh, the Bangladesh Nationalist Party (BNP) and Jamaat E Islami use water as a trump card concerning relations with India (Islam, 2012). Even when the Ganga water treaty was signed in 1996, the BNP opposed the Treaty (Subedi, 1999). According to Ainun Nisat, 'Water sharing between Bangladesh and India is not a technical matter but political' (quoted in Islam 2012, p.40). Notably, Mamata sang a song on Bangabandhu, the founding father of Bangladesh, on the occasion of a Bangladesh parliamentary members' visit to Kolkata and assured to help Bangladesh in the Teesta water-sharing agreement (*Daily Ittefaq*, 2014). In March 2015, Mamata contended that 'After my recent visit to Bangladesh, I have apprised the PM and External Affairs Minister Sushma Swaraj of the details about the Teesta water issue and Indo-Bangla relations' (*The Daily Star*, 2015). Gowher Rizvi, foreign policy adviser to Prime Minister Sheikh Hasina, in an interview with *The Hindu*, contends that the Teesta water-sharing agreement 'could not be signed because of India's domestic reasons. However, we have been repeatedly reassured by the Indian Prime Minister that the treaty will be signed soon' (Bagchi, 2018).

Creating Narratives of Water as 'Scarce' Resource and Rivers as National
How is the meaning of water created? In what ways, are international rivers perceived? Water is projected as a 'scarce resource'. When water is tagged with 'scarce' or 'resource', people/states do not become interested in sharing it. While there is a vast literature on the nexus between water and conflict, there is hardly any research on water cooperation in South Asia. Thus, the meaning of water needs to be problematised on the one hand. On the other, being an upper riparian country, until India plays a constructive role to resolve the water dispute, it will never be resolved. The Government of India decided in 2008 that the Ganga will be declared a 'national river' of India (Dhar, 2008). Such perceptions need to be problematised and changed as the Ganga is an international river. Documentary filmmaker Sourav Sarangi thinks that nationalism should not be imposed on rivers (*The Hindu*, 2019a). It is also worthy to note that Mamata Banerjee believes that Teesta water should not be shared as there is not enough to share (*The Hindu*, 2019b). In fact, Mamata Banerjee perceives the Teesta River as 'the river of West Bengal only' and thus does not bother about the international law of the rivers. Against this backdrop, it is argued that

> A radical rethink that approaches rivers as transnational waterways that connect people, facilitate agriculture, trade and economic growth in the region, rather than as limiting markers of regional interest, could help overcome the impasse in water-sharing disputes. Rivers are the lifeline of the region. Sensitive management of watersheds would be crucial to the prosperity of the millions who live in river basins in both countries [Bangladesh & India] (*The Indian Express* Editorial, 2015b).

Policy Imperatives

Still, Hope Exists

On January 4, 2000, there was a headline in the *Daily Star*, titled, 'Teesta to top agenda of water talks' (Haq, 2000). In 2021, this Teesta water sharing issue is still not resolved. But still, hope exists. Bangladesh Foreign Minister A.K. Abdul Momen thinks that there is still hope as Bangladesh-India are mentally on the same page regarding water sharing (*UNB*, 2019). In her 2019 New Delhi visit, Sheikh Hasina noted Bangladesh's expectations of an early signing of Teesta water-sharing (*The Daily Star Online*, 2019b). Regarding the water sharing issue, the Indian High Commissioner to Bangladesh, Vikram K. Doraiswami, contends that 'We've to share the waters. We're friends. We're neighbours. I think this will move very quickly' (*The Daily Star*, 2020). In order to materialise the hope, the following steps need to be taken into consideration on an urgent basis.

Addressing Domestic Politics

It can be argued that the Bangladesh-India water sharing dispute is not resolved yet due to the narrowly defined national interests of India following the realist paradigm. Islam (1987, p.919) writes that 'The crux of the Ganges water dispute lies in the conflict of national interests of the parties [Bangladesh-India]'. India needs to move out of the realist paradigm and embrace a cooperative framework. As mentioned in the earlier section, Mamata Banerjee opposed to the Teesta deal in 2011. But we argue that India needs to address its domestic politics and ensure a fair share of water for Bangladesh. Against Mamata's opposition to the Teesta water-sharing treaty, the *Indian Express* contends that 'as the Chief Minister of West Bengal, Banerjee needs to be more proactive in encouraging Delhi and Dhaka on the integrated river management projects, in order to move ahead and not back' (*The Indian Express* Editorial, 2011). The daily also thinks that it is wiser to address India's domestic politics and thus argues that 'India must resolve its own Centre-state differences to deliver on the Teesta waters deal. It wouldn't be wise to underestimate the positive impact [this] might have' (*The Indian Express* Editorial, 2015a). To provide a Bangladesh perspective, *The Daily Star* suggests that 'As for the Teesta agreement, the local factor, i.e., Mamata Banerjee's opposition to the deal, needs more robust involvement of the central government to convince the West Bengal Chief Minister of the negative fallout of a scuttled Teesta deal on the bilateral relationship' (*The Daily Star* Editorial, 2013). It is also worthy to note that in an interview with Shuprova Tasneem, Bangladesh's former High Commissioner to India, Farooq Sobhan (April 19, 2017) points out:

> [W]e needed to see tangible progress in the case of the sharing of the water of the rivers we share with India, in particular, Teesta. As a sovereign independent country, Bangladesh must deal with the central government in Delhi. It is for Delhi to sort out matters with the state governments. It is Delhi's responsibility to ensure that Bangladesh gets its fair share of water. We enjoy rights as a lower riparian. If individual states divert water to the detriment of lower riparian states or independent countries, it is incumbent on the part of the central government to prevent this from happening. Delhi could have and should have prevented the construction of the Farakka Barrage as well as the Gazaldoba dam on the Teesta, which is primarily responsible for the reduction in the availability of water in the Teesta during the dry season. It is unacceptable that vast tracts of land in Bangladesh bordering West Bengal are now left without water during the dry season; this has had a huge impact on the lives of millions of people and there is no light at the end of the tunnel. India today is loudly protesting the building of hydroelectric projects on the Brahmaputra within China; and has been very vocal in defending its rights as a lower riparian in its negotiations with Nepal, but it seems the same rights that it claims for itself as a lower riparian are not applicable to Bangladesh.

Hydro-diplomacy Pedagogy and Water Cooperation

Notably, political engagement is pertinent to promote water cooperation. In that regard, hydro-diplomacy will be an important catalyst to promote water cooperation. The IUCN defines hydro-diplomacy as '...a critical tool to ensure that shared water resources are managed efficiently, sustainably and equitably...' (IUCN, 2012). It also prescribes that water cooperation 'requires creating a "hydro-diplomacy culture" where dialogue, knowledge sharing and deliberations are an integral part of any development initiative'. Notably, water cooperation has also been recognised by the United Nations by dedicating 2013 as the International Year of Water Cooperation. In this context, hydro-diplomacy will be imperative to promote water cooperation between Bangladesh and India.

Regarding the hydro-diplomacy pedagogy, it is essential to note that pedagogy plays a vital role to shape intellectual ground and to take appropriate steps to resolve water-sharing problems. Hence, the development of pedagogy on water diplomacy is crucial in Bangladesh's and India's universities. The long-standing Bangladesh-India water disputes are due to the lack of knowledge of proper water and ignorance about the positive outcome of water dispute resolution, one can argue. Therefore, developing hydro-diplomacy curricula is crucial.

Promoting Joint Research

Knowledge over water is pertinent to deal with water issues. Thus, the academic community and researchers need to come forward with joint studies to investigate the challenges and possibilities to resolve the water dispute. There is hardly any collaborative research conducted by Bangladeshi and Indian academics on water issues. In addition, organising regional and international seminars, conferences on water diplomacy and water cooperation needs to be promoted.

Constructive Role of Academics and Media

In order to address the water crisis, Asim Mukhopadhyay (1980) suggests that Bangladesh exploit its 'enormous stock' of groundwater and replace Boro rice by wheat. Mukhopadhyay also contends that the impacts of the Farakka barrage on Bangladesh as claimed by Bangladeshi scholars is exaggerated. Such scholarship needs to be problematised. To resolve Bangladesh-India water sharing disputes, it is desirable to have a constructive role of academics and media who can play an essential role through creating debates and discussions, to inform and influence policies. In resolving Bangladesh-India water sharing disputes, Indian and Bangladeshi media need to play a constructive role.

Is Statist Approach Enough?

We have seen that engineers dominate Bangladesh-India water negotiations, and thus the technical solution to reach a consensus on sharing the quantity of water becomes desirable. In the case of Bangladesh-India water negotiations, Asia Foundation (2013, p.1) notes that:

> Bilateral negotiations are reductionist in nature, centred on arriving at a technical formula to determine the quantity of water that both countries can claim. This narrow approach has excluded a range of

economic, social, and cultural interests from bilateral discussions and prevented the development of a basin-wide, integrated approach to planning, management, and conservation of the Teesta River Basin.

Thus, it is crucial to involve social scientists who bring multiple meanings of water and seek an integrated approach to resolve the Bangladesh-India water sharing issue. Also, the role of the media and other non-state actors needs to be promoted to address the water-sharing issue.

Conclusion

This chapter has shown the contours of Bangladesh-India water sharing disputes. Water remains a contested issue between Bangladesh and India for a long time that needs to be resolved for the benefits of all. The existing discourse of water, i.e., 'water war', 'water conflict' needs to be problematised. New thinking needs to be developed. In this context, the introduction of a hydro-diplomacy course in the region will be imperative. In addition, promoting cooperation over water and proper water information and governance also becomes essential. Since Bangladesh and India share international rivers, India should not treat water as its national resource/issue. The long-standing Bangladesh-India maritime and land boundary disputes have been resolved peacefully through international regimes. It is also possible to resolve the water dispute amicably. If necessary, Bangladesh should go to international organisations to resolve the water dispute. This chapter concludes by arguing that there is less cooperation over water than challenges. And for this, India cannot avoid its responsibility.

REFERENCES

Asia Foundation (2013, March). *Political economy analysis of the Teesta River basin*. New Delhi: Asia Foundation.

Bagchi, S. (2018, December 25). No question of re-negotiating the Teesta agreement: Gowher Rizvi. *The Hindu*. Retrieved from https://www.thehindu.com/news/international/no-question-of-re-negotiating-the-teesta-agreement-gowher-rizvi/article25828468.ece

Bammi, Y. M. (2010). *India-Bangladesh relations: The way ahead*. New Delhi: United Service Institution of India and Vij Books India Pvt. Ltd.

Bandapaddai, S. (2019, October 2). [In Bangla] (US Federal system is only for Teesta). *Daily Prothom Alo*.

Chandan, M.S.K. (2019, April 7). The vanishing fishermen of Teesta. *The Daily Star*.

Daily Ittefaq (2014, November 23). Mamata sang a song on Bangabandhu [in Bangla].

Dhar, A. (2008, November 5). Ganga to be declared a national river. *The Hindu*. Retrieved from http://www.Thehindu.com/todays-paper/tp-national/Ganga-to-be-declared-a-national-river/article15335757.ece

Farhin, N. (2018, February 11). Farakka Barrage key factor in Bangladesh's water crisis. *Dhaka Tribune.*

Giordano, M., Giordano, M., & Wolf, A. (2002, December). The geography of water conflict and cooperation: Internal pressures and international manifestations, *The Geographical Journal,* 168 (4), pp. 293-312.

Haq, M. A. (2000, January 4). Teesta to top agenda of water talks. *The Daily Star.*

High Commission of India, Dhaka (2018). India-Bangladesh relations. Bilateral relations. Retrieved from https://www.hcidhaka.gov.in/pages?id=eyJpdiI6Iklx T20xUnFVbFlMaElNeHg0WmhNT1E9PSIsInZhbHVlI joiRFV3MWs5 UjNRVD ZiakhtZ0I0XC9tc0E9PSIsIm1hYyI6ImZhN2RlMWQ0NjAwYjd jOTUzNWYz ZDNiOWRiYzIyNTZmODU5MTBiODVmNGEzNjl iMjA3MmRiZmE5ODMy OTE4NWIifQ==&subid=eyJpdiI6IjBkQThFNnoxTVlueWx BejJzUEI 1S Gc9PSIsInZhbHVl IjoiUHEzdFwvdkxkMUtlS0E2c1JRaWh4RXc9 PSIsIm1hYyI6Ij I5YzQxNzdkYmJkYzBmOWRkZGEwZWMxMmM4ZDY3MTc0YW RiZjlmYjll Z Dg0MGYyNmMyYTEwNDlmMTc4MzE2NmEifQ==

Huffington Post. (2017, February 20). Bihar Chief Minister Nitish Kumar demands decommissioning of Farakka Barrage. Retrieved from https://www.huffington post.in/2017/02/20/bihar-chief-minister-nitish-kumar-demands-decommission ing-of-far_a_21717674/

Islam, M. R. (1987). The Ganges water dispute: An appraisal of a third party settlement. *Asian Survey,* 27 (8), pp. 918-934.

Islam, M. S. (2012). Bangladesh-India water sharing disputes: Possible policy responses. *Journal of Bangladesh Studies,* 14 (1), pp. 38-49.

IUCN (2012, October 30), Hydro-diplomacy: sharing water across borders. Retrieved from: http://www.iucn.org/?11378/Hydro-diplomacy-sharing-water-across-borders

Kashem, M. A. and Islam, M. S. (2016). Narendra Modi's Bangladesh policy and India–Bangladesh relations: Challenges and possible policy responses. *India Quarterly,* 72(3), 250–267.

Liton, S. (2019, October 6). Pledge after pledge flows down the Teesta. *The Business Standard.* Retrieved from https://tbsnews.net/analysis/pledge-after-pledge-flows-down-teesta

Mukhopadhyay, A. (1980, April 26). River of contention. *Economic and Political Weekly,* 15 (17), pp. 766-768.

Nazrul, A. (2019, October 2). [In Bangla] (Who is responsible for Unexpected floods?), *Daily Prothom Alo.*

Ranjan, A. (2017, March 29). Why India and Bangladesh need a resolution on Teesta water sharing. *The Wire.* Retrieved from https://thewire.in/diplomacy/teesta-water-india-bangladesh

Ray, J. K. (2011). *India's Foreign Relations, 1947-2007.* New Delhi: Routledge.

Roy, P. (2015, March 8). Teesta woes for farmers. *The Daily Star.*

Singh, R. (2011). *Contemporary India with controversial neighbours.* New Delhi: Gyan Publishing House.

Shringla, H. V. (2018). India–Bangladesh relations: An Indian perspective. *Strategic Analysis,* 42 (5), pp. 524-528.

Srivastava, A. (2011, September 30). Nitish Kumar accuses Lalu Prasad of compromising Bihar's interest in the Farakka Water treaty. *India Today.* Retrieved from https:// www.indiatoday.in/magazine/nation/story/20111010-bihar-cm-nitish-kumar-lalu-prasad-yadav-farakka-water-treaty-747879-2011-09-30

Sobhan, F. (2017, April 19). Interview taken by Shuprova Tasneem. *Dhaka Tribune*. Retrieved from https://www.dhakatribune.com/bangladesh/foreign-affairs/2017/04/19/water-highly-emotive-issue

Subedi, S. P. (1999). Hydro-diplomacy in South Asia: The conclusion of the Mahakali and Ganges River Treaties. *The American Journal of International Law*, 93 (4), pp. 953-962.

Thakkar, H. (2019). Challenges in water governance: A story of missed opportunities. *Economic & Political Weekly*, 54 (15), pp. 12-14.

The Business Standard (2019, October 6). No headway on Teesta, Rohingya: Dhaka, Delhi sign seven deals on use of Chattogram, Mongla ports, withdrawal of Feni river water. Retrieved from https://tbsnews.net/bangladesh/no-headway-teesta-rohingya

The Daily Star (2010, January 10). Mistrust must go to open new era of ties. Retrieved from https://www.thedailystar.net/news-detail-121241

The Daily Star (2012, February 23). Steep decline in Teesta water flow. Retrieved from https://www.thedailystar.net/news-detail-223577

The Daily Star Editorial (2013, February 19). Indian Foreign Minister's visit: Yet more assurances.

The Daily Star (2015, March 10). Mamata talks Teesta, LBA.

The Daily Star (2017, April 9). Teesta has no water to share: An adamant Mamata tells Hasina at the Rashtrapati Bhavan.

The Daily Star Online (2019a, October 5). Bangladesh allows India to withdraw Feni river water. Retrieved from https://www.thedailystar.net/politics/sheikh-hasina-narendra-modi-talks-begin-in-new-delhi-prioritises-bangladesh-india-relation-1809646

The Daily Star Online (2019b, October 5). Bangladeshi people waiting to see early signing of Teesta deal: Hasina. Retrieved from https://www.thedailystar.net/country/sheikh-hasina-says-people-of-bangladesh-waiting-for-teesta-water-deal-1809679

The Daily Star (2020, December 27). Delhi wants to move quickly on water sharing issues: Indian envoy. Retrieved from https://www.thedailystar.net/country/news/delhi-wants-move-quickly-water-sharing-issues-indian-envoy-2018061

The Hindu (2019a, February 25). Don't impose nationalism on rivers, says film-maker. Retrieved from https://www.thehindu.com/todays-paper/tp-national/tp-karnataka/dont-impose-nationalism-on-rivers-says-film-maker/article26360137.ece

The Hindu (2019b, July 3). Not enough water in Teesta to share: Mamata. Retrieved from https://www.thehindu.com/news/national/other-states/not-enough-water-in-teesta-to-share-mamata/article28265532.ece

The Indian Express Editorial (2011, September 6). Being Mamata. Retrieved from http://archive.indianexpress.com/news/being-mamata/842119/0

The Indian Express Editorial (2015a, February 26). Dhaka's war within. Retrieved from https://indianexpress.com/article/opinion/editorials/dhakas-war-within/

The Indian Express Editorial (2015b, August 1). Mapping the future. Retrieved from https://indianexpress.com/article/opinion/editorials/mapping-the-future/

The Statesman (2013, August 25). Indo-bangla ties not at Bengal's cost: CM. Retrieved from https://www.thestatesman.com/bengal/indo-bangla-ties-not-at-bengal-s-cost-cm-11955.html

UNB (2019, April 27). Dhaka, Delhi mentally on same page over water sharing: FM.

7

NARRATIVES ON CONNECTIVITY

ABSTRACT

The partnership between Bangladesh and India has reached a new height by forging connectivity in rail, roads, and waterways. This chapter analyses the recent hallmark development in Bangladesh-India relations, i.e., connectivity. After two decades of the beginning of their ties, a Dhaka-Kolkata direct bus service was opened in 1999, which created the foundation in building connectivity in Bangladesh-India relations. In addition, direct train service and connectivity in inland waterways has also added new impetus in deepening Bangladesh-India relations which is beneficial to people across the borders. This chapter argues that increasing Bangladesh-India connectivity results in increasing people-to-people contacts and greater cultural intimacy.

Keywords: *Connectivity, Northeast India, water connectivity, people-to-people contacts, cultural intimacy.*

Introduction

'The transport network centring around Bangladesh was once an integrated system radiating outwards from international seaports to Kolkata and Chattogram. The inland water transport system also served parts of undivided India, particularly the northern and eastern parts, with connections to the ports of Kolkata and Chattogram. The benefits from a restoration of such transport linkages can be measured both in terms of savings in the form of reduced transport costs as well as in terms of the new economic opportunities such restoration would open up. If traffic could have moved freely through the transport systems in India, Bangladesh, and Myanmar, it would have produced huge cost saving thereby creating an impetus for exploring new opportunities. Similar benefits would have accrued to Nepal and Bhutan if their traffic could use the shorter route across Bangladesh to the seaports of Chattogram and Mongla' (Rahmatullah, 2003, p.295).

The above quotation from Rahmatullah provides a strong rationale of connectivity both at the bilateral and sub-regional levels. Unfortunately, though Bangladesh became an independent nation in 1971, and shared a strong cultural similarity with West Bengal, it took two decades to open the Dhaka-Kolkata direct bus service due to political reasons (Anam, 1999). After coming to power in 1996, the Awami League government in Bangladesh under Sheikh Hasina wanted to improve the connectivity between India and Bangladesh. Consequently, the Sheikh Hasina government decided to introduce the direct Dhaka-Kolkata bus service which was strongly opposed by the opposition party, the Bangladesh Nationalist Party (BNP) by giving some economic reasons that the domestic market of the country will be negatively affected. In this context, A.H. Jaffor Ullah writes that 'it would be simply foolish to oppose the bus service from Dhaka to Kolkata only on the ground that too much merchandise would seep into Dhaka from W. Bengal' (Ullah, 1999). Consequently, the Dhaka-Kolkata direct bus service began its trial in April 1999, which had been cited by the opposition in Bangladesh, the BNP, as another example of selling out the country to India (Anam, 1999). Anam argued that the bus link should also help to forge closer Bangladesh-India trade cooperation. This is how Bangladesh-India connectivity began. Under the Sheikh Hasina government (2009-present), the world witnessed a well-developed Bangladesh-India connectivity by road, air, and waterways which has already impacted the lives of tens of thousands of people across the borders.

Connectivity matters as it directly impacts the lives of the people. It promotes growth and bridges the gaps, whether developmental or psychological. It is recognised that enhancing multimodal connectivity is a 'win-win' situation for both Bangladesh and India (Chaudhury, 2020). For instance, it is argued that 'multi-modal connectivity would also improve transport connectivity between Northeast India and Bangladesh'

(CUTS, 2019, p.19). Bangladesh former High Commissioner to India Syed Muazzem Ali in a seminar titled 'Political Economy of Bangladesh' at Jawaharlal Nehru University (JNU) points out that 'Connectivity offers a game-changing opportunity' in Bangladesh-India relations (*The Daily Star*, 2018b). Pinak Ranjan Chakravarty, a former High Commissioner of India to Bangladesh, emphasises the importance of connectivity in deepening Bangladesh-India ties (Chakravarty, 2019). Against the above backdrop, this chapter examines the connectivity narratives between Bangladesh and India, focusing on the emerging developments, the necessity of having more robust connectivity, and the problems and possibilities in Bangladesh-India connectivity.

This chapter is divided into six sections, including an introduction and conclusion. The first section discusses the background and rationale of Bangladesh-India connectivity. The second focuses on the conceptualisation of connectivity, while the third explains the different dimensions in Bangladesh-India connectivity. The fourth section discusses the implications of forging Bangladesh-India connectivity, while the fifth section examines the challenges. The final section concentrates on the concluding remarks.

Conceptualising Connectivity

Connectivity has become a global phenomenon today. It is also central to the globalisation process, which is often defined as a precondition for growth, prosperity, and development. Connectivity can be both physical and intangible. One can argue that physical, institutional, economic, and people-to-people linkages become pertinent in the conceptualisation of Bangladesh-India connectivity. The recent developments in Bangladesh-India connectivity have become a successful example for many in the region and beyond. Bangladesh Commerce Minister Tipu Munshi opines that 'Now-a-days connectivity is a must to remain engaged with the global and regional trade and I hope all the agreements between Bangladesh and India related to connectivity will be implemented successfully' (*New Age*, 2020).

According to India's External Affairs Minister, Sushma Swaraj, connectivity is defined as 'DNA' of India. India is the inheritor of two powerful connectivity legacies: the message of Buddha and the Spice

Route (MEA, 2016). Swaraj adds that 'Where India itself is concerned, whether it is domestic, external or regional, connectivity will determine how we meet our promise of growth, employment and prosperity' (MEA, 2016). Harsh V. Pant (2020) writes that 'For Modi, the development of India's East and Northeast is a top priority and a strategic imperative for New Delhi. And that region can only achieve its full potential if it's better integrated with Bangladesh, thereby ensuring that India-Bangladesh connectivity projects will continue to be at the top of the agenda'.

As 'the 3C Mantra', i.e., Commerce, Culture and Connectivity, are the primary objectives of India's foreign policy under Narendra Modi, the issue of connectivity remains a priority area in Bangladesh-India relations. Veena Sikri writes, 'mutually beneficial and forward-looking collaborative programmes of connectivity are essential for transforming our four-thousand-kilometre common land border from its present hubris of poverty and illegal activity into centres of shared prosperity and growth' (Sikri, 2015).

Beyond physical connectivity, Bangladesh and India need to focus on inculcating intangible connectivity, e.g., connectivity through hearts and minds among the people of these two nations. In this context, winning hearts and minds becomes necessary through deepening cultural connectivity and broadly by pro-people foreign policy formulations and execution towards each other.

Dimensions of Connectivity

Physical Connectivity: Connectivity by Road

It is worthy to note that an agreement was signed between the Indian railways and Bangladesh railway in July 2000 to restore a third broad gauge rail link between Petrapole (India) and Benapole (Bangladesh). The BJP led National Democratic Alliance (NDA) government came to power in 2001. On the other hand, Begum Khaleda Zia took over as the Prime Minister on 10 October 2001. The NDA government tried to develop India-Bangladesh ties. For instance, as a personal envoy of Prime Minister Vajpayee, Brajesh Mishra was sent to Bangladesh on 26-27 October 2001 to felicitate Begum Zia for her party's victory. Notably, the protocol and agreement to operate a passenger bus service between Agartala and Dhaka was signed on 10 July 2001, and an agreement on facilitating a passenger train service between India and Bangladesh was signed on 12 July 2001. But it was delayed due to the political differences between Dhaka and New Delhi.

Bangladesh and India initiated trial runs of passenger train services between Dhaka and Kolkata in July 2007 in preparation for regular train services. Consequently, the world witnessed the revival of the Dhaka-Kolkata passenger train service, the 'Maitree' Express, after 43 years on 14 April 2008. This was a milestone to deepen Indo-Bangla people-to-people contacts. In October 2014, an inter-railway meeting between Bangladesh and India was held in Kolkata in which it was agreed to increase the frequency of the Maitree Express from two to three days which was implemented from January 2015. In fact, the introduction of the Maitree train between Dhaka and Kolkata has added a new impetus in Bangladesh-India connectivity. In April 2014, in a joint meeting between Bangladesh and Indian Railways held in Dhaka, India sought increased rail links (Khan, 2014).

The operationalisation of connectivity is already visible. For instance, according to the 2014-2015 Annual report of the Ministry of External Affairs, India 'the movement of 10,000 MT of rice to Tripura from Kolkata through the Protocol Routes by barges up to Ashuganj and subsequently by road to Agartala was undertaken in two phases of 5000 MT each and was completed in November 2014' (Ministry of External Affairs, 2015, p.6).

In June 2015, speakers at a seminar held in Dhaka emphasised on promoting railway connectivity in the context of South Asian connectivity (*The Daily Star*, 2015). In July 2016, Mazibul Hoque, Minister of Bangladesh railway, visited Agartala for laying the foundation stone of a new rail link connecting Tripura with Bangladesh. 'The process of laying the 15 km long railway tracks to connect Agartala with Akhaura in Bangladesh will be completed in two-and-a-half years time after laying of tracks begin. Of the 15-km track, 5 km would be on the Indian side and the rest in Bangladesh' (*The Indian Express*, 2017). Pinak Ranjan Chakravarty writes that 'the Akhaura-Agartala rail link will dramatically change connectivity' between Bangladesh and India (Chakravarty, 2019). If implemented, it will connect West Bengal with Tripura through Bangladesh. It is expected that this will improve India-Bangladesh connectivity as well as trade.

In February 2018, the Executive Committee of the National Economic Council, Bangladesh, approved Tk 1683 crore to transform about 67 kilometres of metre gauge rail line into the dual gauge to provide railway transit to India, Nepal and Bhutan and increase trade among the countries (*The Daily Star*, 2018a). India would finance 81 per cent of the cost under a Line of Credit. According to the Indian Foreign Secretary, Harsh Shringla, rail links between Akhaura-Agartala and Chilahati-Haldibari and Khulna-Mongla rail line are expected to be completed by 2021 (*Hindustan Times*, 2020). When implemented, this will boost Bangladesh-India connectivity by rail.

In August 2019, during Bangladesh Railway Minister Nurul Islam Sujan's New Delhi visit, Bangladesh and India agreed to increase railway connectivity following the growing demand of the passengers. Both sides agreed that the frequency of the Kolkata-Dhaka Maitree Express and the Kolkata-Khulna Bandhan Express would be increased following passenger's demands. Bangladesh had proposed the frequency of journeys of the Maitree Express be increased to six days a week from the existing four and the frequency of the Bandhan Express from the present one day in a week to three days a week (*New Age*, 2019b). In their December 2020 virtual summit, Sheikh Hasina and Narendra Modi inaugurated the Chilahati-Haldibari rail link after 55 years to boost railway connectivity between Bangladesh and India. The rail link was halted due to the 1965 India-Pakistan war. It is expected that the opening of the rail link will strengthen the movement of people and goods between Bangladesh and West Bengal and north-eastern Indian states (*The Daily Star*, 2020).

Another development is that the Phulbari-Banglabandha immigration check post was inaugurated in February 2016 to facilitate cross-border movement of people and goods between Bangladesh and India. Trans-shipment of goods to the Northeastern states of India through the Ashuganj river port and Akhaura-Agartala by road commenced in June 2016 under the PIWTT. In addition, Bangladesh and India have agreed to operate the Benapole-Petrapole Integrated Check Post at 24x7 level with effect from August 1, 2017, which is imperative to intensify Bangladesh-India trade.

Though railway connectivity is emphasised, the operationalisation of buses is also highlighted. For instance, the Kolkata-Khulna-Dhaka bus service commenced operations from April 2017. The Bandhan Express between Kolkata and Khulna was inaugurated in November 2017. To boost connectivity further, Bangladesh and India have agreed and established internet bandwidth to Tripura from Bangladesh and supply of 100 MW power from Tripura to Comilla in March 2016. Bangladesh has provided internet connectivity to Agartala through the gateway at Cox's Bazar.

Connectivity through Waterways

In South Asia, inland water transport (IWT) links prevailed only between Bangladesh and India. It is argued that inland water transport connectivity 'has great potential for development since it is the cheapest mode of transportation' (Rahmatullah, 2006, p.381). Bangladesh-India IWT cooperation can be traced back to the 1980 Trade Agreement. According to Article VIII of the Agreement, 'The two Governments agree to make mutually beneficial arrangements for the use of their waterways, railways and roadways for commerce between the two countries and for passage of goods between two places in one country through the territory of the other'. From this provision, Bangladesh and India signed a protocol on 'Inland Water Transit and Trade' in October 1999. This was 'the only transit facility for India through Bangladesh for serving the requirements of North-East Indian states' (Rahmatullah, 2006, p.381).

IWT facility was underutilised due to the difficulties of round-the-year navigation, draft limitation of certain major routes, lack of sufficient ports of call, absence of night navigation facilities, etc. (Rahmatullah, 2006, p.381). The Inland Water Transit and Trade Protocol expired on October 3, 2001. While India asked for five years' renewal of the Protocol, Bangladesh agreed to one, two and three-month extensions.

Bangladesh and India signed the Coastal Shipping Agreement in 2015 to facilitate inland water connectivity. On October 25, 2018, they signed another agreement on the use of Chattogram and Mongla ports for movement of goods to and from India. According to the Article 6 of the Agreement, the routes that will be used for the transmission of goods from India through Chattogram and Mongla ports are: i) Chattogram port/Mongla port to Agartala via Akhaura; ii) Chattogram port/Mongla port to Dawki via Tamabil; iii) Chattogram port/Mongla port to Sutarkandi via Sheola; iv) Chattogram port/Mongla port to Srimantapur via Bibirbazar; v) Agartala to Chattogram port/Mongla port via Akhaura; vi) Dawki to Chattogram port/Mongla port via Tamabil; vii) Sutarkandi to Chattogram port/Mongla port via Sheola; viii) Srimantapur to Chattogram port/Mongla port via Bibirbazar; ix) Any other route as approved by the Inter-Governmental Committee. Article 8 of the Agreement reads that the movement of cargo under the agreement shall be exempted from Customs duties or any other taxes other than administrative and operational fees. Against the exemption of duties and taxes, Khandaker R. Zaman (2019) writes that 'The ports in Bangladesh that will be used as gateways for the transit of Indian goods need to recover their costs and expenses by imposing a levy to be able to sustain and continue to provide the services of a transhipment port'.

In July 2019, in a meeting with the Indian High Commissioner to Bangladesh, Riva Ganguly Das, Bangladesh Prime Minister Sheikh Hasina emphasised on promoting waterway connectivity between Bangladesh and India (*New Age*, 2019a). Consequently, during Sheikh Hasina's October 2019 India visit, Dhaka and New Delhi signed Standard Operating Procedures (SOPs) for the use of Chattogram and Mongla ports for movement of goods to and from India, particularly to and from Northeast India through waterways, rail, road or multi-modal transport. In May 2020, Bangladesh and India signed the second Addendum on Protocol on Inland Water Transit, Trade to facilitate more trade (*UNB News*, 2020). In the Addendum, the number of India-Bangladesh Protocol (IBP) routes have been increased from eight to 10, and new locations are also added to the existing routes. It is noted that 'Inclusion of the Sonamura-Daudkhandi stretch of the Gumti River (93 km) as IBP routes No. 9 & 10 in the Protocol will improve the connectivity of Tripura and adjoining States with India and Bangladesh's economic centres and will help the hinterland of both the countries' (*UNB News*, 2020). It is further argued that 'The connectivity provided by the existing and the newly added protocol routes is all the more pertinent in the present Covid-19 scenario as it will be instrumental in providing economical, faster, safer and greener mode of transport for traders and business communities of both the countries and will also have environmental benefits for the region' (*UNB News*, 2020).

In July 2020, the first trial of a container ship from Kolkata to Agartala through Chattogram Port of Bangladesh was successfully completed. Though there is mixed opinion in Bangladesh regarding transit to Northeast India, Dipanjan Roy Chaudhury (2020), from India, views it as a 'win-win' situation. Chaudhury writes that

> trial run assumes significance as this will lead to development of the North East region and enhance India's connectivity with Bangladesh. Once this gets fully implemented, it will reduce distance, time and logistical cost for transportation of goods from India to north eastern states and will be a win-win for both the economies. Job creation, spurring investment in the logistics sector, integration of supply chain, promotion of business services, e.g., finance, transport, insurance and revenue are the major advantages that will accrue to Bangladesh.

In August 2020, another milestone on connectivity was the first-ever export consignment from Daudkandi, Bangladesh, reached Tripura, India, through waterways. Notably, Bangladesh vessel *MB Premier* carried 50 metric tonnes of cement and arrived at Sonamura of Tripura, after a 93-km journey on the Gumti River. The initiative is vital in the case of Bangladesh-India connectivity. It is noted that 'The ambitious project has already been projected by Tripura's incumbent BJP-IPFT government as a major catalyst to catapult Tripura into a gateway to the North-East' (Deb, 2020). According to the Ministry of Foreign Affairs, Bangladesh, 'This initiative will greatly boost our connectivity and bilateral trade with India. Enhanced connectivity through inland waterways, particularly in this Covid-19 scenario, is significant because it provides for economical, faster, safer, and cleaner modes of transportation for traders and business communities of both countries'.

Connectivity at Sub-Regional Level

BBIN Motor Vehicles Agreement

Bangladesh always emphasises regional and sub-regional connectivity to accelerate the well-being of the people in the country, region and beyond (*The Daily Star*, 2019b). The role of Bangladesh in the BBIN Motor Vehicles Agreement that connects Bangladesh, Bhutan, India and Nepal; in the South Asian Association for Regional Cooperation (SAARC) which connects eight SAARC countries; in the Bay of Bengal Initiative for Multi-Sectoral Technical and Economic Cooperation (BIMSTEC) which connects Bangladesh, India, Maldives, Sri Lanka, Thailand, Nepal and Bhutan in a forum for multilateral cooperation is widely recognised. Bangladesh is often identified as a champion of regional and sub-regional cooperation. Mohammad Mohiuddin Abdullah (2011) opines that 'Bangladesh could emerge as a transport hub for the sub-region comprising Bangladesh, Bhutan, Nepal and India if it opens up its transport system to provide regional connectivity. Transport connectivity with India alone will not create a win-win situation for all countries involved, i.e., Nepal and Bhutan'. Gowher Rizvi, the international affairs advisor to the Prime Minister of Bangladesh, contends that 'We are lagging behind in realising the benefits from regional connectivity. There is no escape from regional connectivity. The time has come to take bold steps to recreate the vision towards building a South and Southwest Asian community. We have already squandered time and resources and we will be answerable to our next generation for the delay' (*The Daily Star*, 2013). Considering the failure of SAARC as a regional organisation, C. Raja Mohan (2020) suggests that 'Instead of merely praying for the revival of SAARC, Delhi could usefully focus on promoting regionalism among Bangladesh, Bhutan, India and Nepal'.

There is also a possibility of regional aviation connectivity. Bangladesh proposed that Bhutan use its Syedpur airport as the Bangladesh government has a plan to establish a regional aviation hub centring around that airport. Bhutan is only around a few hundred miles from Syedpur. According to A.K. Abdul Momen, the Foreign Minister of Bangladesh, 'Our Prime Minister says – connectivity is productivity – so we proposed to Bhutan to use our seaports and to establish road and railways connectivity with us' (*The Daily Star*, 2019a). It is also found that there is a possibility of regional and sub-regional railway connectivity in South Asia to boost trade and people-to-people contacts (Hoque, 2020). To materialise such projects, a visionary leadership along with strong political will, especially from India is necessary.

Implications

India sought connectivity from Bangladesh, which was earlier known as a transit point for a long time to connect with its Northeastern states. Notably, Northeast India shares 98 per cent of its borders with its neighbouring countries with only 2 per cent with mainland India. It is argued that 'For several decades, the geographical isolation of the region has been viewed as one of its key development constraints. Connecting the Northeast with the neighbouring countries by land and sea will increase economic activity and generate jobs' (Yhome, 2015, p.1223). The *Times of India* (2015), in its editorial contends that 'Transit through Bangladesh will help India bring its northeast closer and resolve some of the problems of that region even as Bangladesh gains access through India to markets in Bhutan and Nepal. If Bangladesh can become India's land bridge to Southeast Asia, moribund economies of India's eastern and northeastern states can be revitalised'.

Due to being landlocked, North-East Indian states would pay a high price for conducting trade. According to a report of the Committee on Clause Seven of the 1990 Assam Accord, Assam was spending almost as much in transporting essential commodities such as foodgrains, fish, and edible oils from 'mainland' India as the costs of the commodities (cited in Subramanian, 2001). Uma Subramanin (2001, pp.84-86) found that 'Tea from Assam is shipped to Europe via Kolkata port. The transportation cost includes a trucking distance of more than 1,400 kilometres through the land corridor around Bangladesh to Kolkata port. The traditional tea route for Assamese tea via Chattogram port would cut the distance by almost 60 percent'. Subramanian (2001, pp.93-94) notes that

> it takes 45 days to move a container from Delhi to Dhaka: the container is moved via Tughlakabad to Mumbai and then shipped to Singapore, where it is brought by feeder ships to Chattogram port and then to the Dhaka inland container depot (ICD) by rail. The 2,000 kilometres between Dhaka and Delhi could be covered in two to three days according to estimates from the railways, but a bilateral protocol between the two countries would be needed.

Thus, physical connectivity reduces distances which lessen transport costs. For instance, M.L. Debnath, president of the Tripura chamber of commerce, told the BBC that 'We are now paying 80,000 rupees (US$ 16,00) for each truck to bring goods from Kolkata to Agartala. If the trucks can come through Bangladesh, then the cost will be only 20,000 rupees' (cited in Roy, 2013, p.99). This will directly impact the consumers as the price of the products would be reduced. The Bangladesh business community views the necessity of multi-modal connectivity with India to tap business potentials. The Federation of Bangladesh Chambers of Commerce and Industry president Sheikh Fazle Faim contends that 'Although 80 per cent of India-Bangladesh business takes place through land route, reaching the next tier of multimodal connectivity through air, rail and waterways would increase business' (*New Age*, 2020). Mahbubul Alam, president of the Chattogram Chamber of Commerce and Industry, opines that 'Though India is one of the largest trading partners for Bangladesh, still we have a huge opportunity to enhance the volume of trade through connectivity' (*New Age*, 2020). Many believe that connectivity brings a win-win situation for both Bangladesh and India. For instance, Dipanjan Roy Chaudhury (2020) writes that both Bangladesh and India recognise that 'increasing connectivity through air, water, rail and road offers mutually beneficial opportunity for enhancing economic cooperation between Bangladesh and the North Eastern States of India and beyond'.

In addition, one can also argue that Bangladesh-India connectivity leads to increased people-to-people contacts. People in Bangladesh and India can travel by land, rail, and air to each other's country for medical, trade, investment, and education purposes. Thus, it is argued that improved Bangladesh-India connectivity leads to increased people-to-people contacts. People-to-people contact can help to reduce differences. Besides, when physical connectivity gets simplified, many Bangladeshi medical patients seeking treatment in India would benefit immensely. Thus, improved connectivity benefits people at the grassroots level directly.

Better connectivity would also bring greater cultural intimacy. In fact, people's (negative) perceptions in these two countries need to be changed for the betterment of all. In this case, improved connectivity would help. Though Bangladesh and India are close neighbours, there are vast differences between how Indians construct about Bangladesh and its people and Bangladeshis against India and its people. Thus, increased connectivity would work to lessen the differences.

Challenges

Domestic Politics

To a more considerable extent, domestic politics determines the nature and level of Bangladesh-India ties. Zaglul Ahmed Chowdhury writes that 'Indo-Bangladesh ties have a particular character dating from 1971, but they also vary depending on which government is in the seat of power in New Delhi and in Dhaka' (Chowdhury, 2010). M. Serajul Islam writes that 'Unfortunately, it is Bangladesh's partisan politics that could stand in the way of effecting a paradigm shift in Bangladesh-India relations' (Islam, 2010). In fact, domestic politics in Bangladesh played a crucial role in delaying the beginning of Bangladesh-India connectivity. For instance, from the very beginning, the BNP opposed this concept, which was earlier known as transit. In January 2010, with regard to Prime Minister Sheikh Hasina's forthcoming official visit to India, BNP chairperson Khaleda Zia warned that 'If you give consent to...transit facilities, and if the maritime boundary dispute is not resolved, then we will go for a movement. Allowing India-to-India corridor in the name of the Asian Highway will also not be acceptable' (*The Daily Star*, 2010).

Poor Infrastructure
Poor infrastructure remains a key challenge in improving Bangladesh-India connectivity. Rehman Sobhan, Chairman, Centre for Policy Dialogue (Dhaka), contends that:

> One of the main goals of promoting transit was that they should become an opportunity for the transport sector of Bangladesh, and they should become the principal carriers of whatever goods come from India or go across Bangladesh to other parts of India. But to do so, investment is needed. Unfortunately, the Ashuganj Port is still somewhat in the primitive stage. Similarly, the road connection between Ashuganj and the Tripura border is still in an unfit condition to carry the intense traffic (*The Daily Star*, 2016).

There are also challenges in waterway connectivity. Ensuring navigability throughout the year becomes a significant challenge. In this case, regular river dredging and preventing river bank erosion, both in Bangladesh and India, becomes essential.

Lack of Political Will
Strong political will is a must to implement any project, whether at the bilateral or sub-regional level. With regard to the connectivity at the sub-regional level, lack of political will, especially from Nepal and Bhutan, remains a key challenge. There is enough scope of sub-regional connectivity, as mentioned earlier, which needs to be utilised for the benefit of the people of these countries and beyond.

Conclusion

Bangladesh-India connectivity matters for tens of thousands of people across the borders. Increased air, road or water connectivity would intensify bilateral trade, people's movements, and socio-cultural exchanges and linkages. People will be directly benefitted when it impacts on the volume of the bilateral trade and the prices of the products. Most importantly, India sought transit facilities to Bangladesh for decades. The Awami League government under Sheikh Hasina has shown a positive gesture towards India's connectivity needs which is recognised from all corners in India. For instance, the Indian Minister of State for External Affairs points out that 'We appreciate the cooperation rendered by our Bangladeshi friends in understanding India's connectivity needs via Bangladesh' (MEA, 2020). The former Indian High Commissioner in Dhaka, Pankaj Saran, contends that 'I don't believe that countries which are so close geographically cannot live without connectivity. It is time for India and Bangladesh…to find a new development cooperation where we can help each other and not exploit each other's weaknesses' (Zaman, 2014). Thus, it becomes crucial to ensure the win-win situation in promoting Bangladesh-India connectivity, where people would be the ultimate beneficiaries.

REFERENCES

Abdullah, M. M. (2011, September 21). Regional connectivity: Problems and prospects. *The Daily Star*. Retrieved from https://www.thedailystar.net/news-detail-203266

Anam, M. (1999, April 19). Though late, Dhaka-Kolkata bus link likely to help Indo-Bangla trade. *India Today Magazine*. Retrieved from https://www.indiatoday.in/magazine/neighbours/story/19990419-though-late-dhaka-calcutta-bus-link-likely-to-help-indo-bangla-trade-780740-1999-04-19

Chaudhury, D. R. (2020, July 17). India-Bangladesh multi-modal connectivity: A win-win proposition for both nations. *The Economic Times*. https://economictimes.indiatimes.com/news/politics-and-nation/india-bangladesh-multi-modal-connectivity-a-win-win-proposition-for-both-nations/articleshow/77023135.cms?utm_source=contentofinterest&utm_medium=text&utm_campaign=cppst

Chakravarty, P. R. (2019, January 2). The bilateral transformation. *The Hindu*. Retrieved from https://www.thehindu.com/opinion/lead/the-bilateral-transformation/article25884055.ece

Chowdhury, Z.A. (2010, January 9). Sheikh Hasina's New Delhi visit: A trip full of curiosity and hope. *The Daily Star*.

CUTS (2019). Role of multi-modal connectivity in fostering value chains in the BBIN sub-region.

Deb, D. (2020, September 7). Explained: What the opening of waterway with

Bangladesh means for Tripura. *The Indian Express*. Retrieved from https://indianexpress.com/article/explained/explained-what-the-opening-of-waterway-with-bangladesh-means-for-tripura-6584061/

Hindustan Times (2020, August 21). India, Bangladesh to create new mechanism to monitor bilateral projects. Retrieved from https://www.hindustantimes.com/india-news/india-bangladesh-to-create-new-mechanism-to-monitor-bilateral-projects/story-I1f7uV1GrTKpFuD4m4onHM.html

Hoque, M. (2020, September 8). Bangladesh-India-Nepal to widen regional rail connectivity. *Daily Asian Age*. Retrieved from https://dailyasianage.com/news/240646/bangladesh-india-nepal-to-widen-regional-rail-connectivity

Islam, M. S. (2010, January 9). Will India reciprocate Bangladesh moves? *The Daily Star*.

Khan, A. R. (2014, April 22). India wants increased rail link. *The Independent*.

Ministry of External Affairs, Government of India (2015). Ministry of External Affairs Annual Report 2014-2015, New Delhi: Policy Planning and Research Division, Ministry of External Affairs.

MEA (2016, March 1). Speeches & Statements: Speech by External Affairs Minister at the inauguration of Raisina Dialogue in New Delhi. Retrieved from https://www.mea.gov.in/SpeechesStatements.htm?dtl/26432/Speech_by_External_Affairs_Minister_at_the_inauguration_of_Raisina_Dialogue_in_New_Delhi_March_01_2016

MEA, Government of India (2020, June 30). Speeches & Statements: Keynote Address by Minister of State for External Affairs at Digital Conference on Doing Business with Bangladesh. Retrieved from https://www.mea.gov.in/Speeches-Statements.htm?dtl/32800/keynote+address+by+minister+of+state+for+external+affairs+at+digital+conference+on+doing+business+with+bangladesh

Mohan, C. R. (2020, October 20). Explained Ideas: Five main strategic implications of Bangladesh's economic rise. *The Indian Express*. Retrieved from https://indianexpress.com/article/explained/india-bangladesh-per-capita-gdp-c-raja-mohan-6799038/

New Age (2019a, July 15). PM for boosting waterway connectivity with India. Retrieved from https://www.newagebd.net/article/78574/pm-for-boosting-waterway-connectivity-with-india

New Age (2019b, August 7). Dhaka-Delhi agrees to increase rail connectivity. Retrieved from https://www.newagebd.net/article/80939/dhaka-delhi-agree-to-increase-rail-connectivity

New Age (2020, August 20). Bangladesh, India need multimodal connectivity to tap trade potentials. Retrieved from https://www.newagebd.net/article/114054/bangladesh-india-need-multimodal-connectivity-to-tap-trade-potentials

Pant, H. V. (2020, August 27). Delhi-Dhaka ties: India is doing well in the region. *Hindustan Times*. Retrieved from https://www.hindustantimes.com/analysis/delhi-dhaka-ties-india-is-doing-well-in-the-region/story-5TOwex1XXEtncjv306a0QI.html

Rahmatullah, M. (2003). Cooperation between Bangladesh and the Indian bordering states in transport, including port facilities. In M. A. Mubeen, & M. H. Kabir (Eds.), *25 Years of BIISS: An Anthology* (pp.288-320). Dhaka: Academic Press and Publishers Limited.

Rahmatullah, M. (2006). Promoting transport cooperation in South Asia. In *Regional Cooperation in South Asia: A Review of Bangladesh's Development 2004*, (pp. 373-396). Dhaka: Centre for Policy Dialogue and The University Press Limited.

Roy, N. (2013). Constraints and opportunities in the India-Bangladesh transit dispute. *Indian Journal of Asian Affairs*, 26 (1/2), pp. 93-102.

Sikri, V. (2015, June 6). The Modi factor. *The Daily Star*.
Subramanian, U. (2001). Transport, logistics, and trade facilitation in the South Asia subregion. In T. R. Lakshmanan, U. Subramanian & W. P. Anderson, (Eds.), F. A. Leautier. *Integration of transport and trade facilitation: Selected regional case studies* (pp.. 81-110). Washington DC: The World Bank.
The Daily Star (2010, January 2). Protect country's interest: Khaleda warns govt against failure in talks with India.
The Daily Star (2013, June 28). Focus on regional connectivity: Analysts say better connectivity will accelerate economic growth. Retrieved from https://www.thedailystar.net/news/focus-on-regional-connectivity
The Daily Star (2015, June 21). Rail must get priority for connectivity. Retrieved from https://www.thedailystar.net/business/rail-must-get-priority-connectivity-100438
The Daily Star (2016, October 8). Bangladesh-India relations: Progress made and the challenges ahead.
The Daily Star (2018a, February 28). Tk 1,683cr project to transform rail connectivity with India. Retrieved from https://www.thedailystar.net/business/tk-1683cr-project-transform-rail-connectivity-india-1541218
The Daily Star (2018b, June 22). Bangladesh for greater economic ties with India.
The Daily Star (2019a, April 12). Bangladesh eyes better connectivity with Bhutan: FM. Retrieved from https://www.thedailystar.net/country/news/bangladesh-eyes-better-connectivity-bhutan-fm-1728988
The Daily Star (2019b, October 3). Bangladesh for enhancing South Asian connectivity. Retrieved from https://www.thedailystar.net/city/news/bangladesh-enhancing-south-asian-connectivity-1808557
The Daily Star (2020, December 17). Bangladesh 'significant pillar' of India's Neighbourhood First policy: Modi. Retrieved from https://www.thedailystar.net/world/south-asia/news/bangladesh-significant-pillar-indias-neighborhood-first-policy-modi-2012889
The Indian Express (2017, July 30). Land acquisition for Agartala-Akhaura railway project begins. Retrieved from https://indianexpress.com/article/india/land-acquisition-for-agartala-akhaura-railway-project-begins-indian-railways-bangladesh-railways-4774051/
Times of India Editorial (2015, June 8). Opening doors: Modi's successful Dhaka trip raises hopes of subcontinent's Berlin Walls coming down. Retrieved from https://timesofindia.indiatimes.com/blogs/toi-editorials/opening-doors-modis-successful-dhaka-trip-raises-hopes-of-subcontinents-berlin-walls-coming-down/
Ullah, A.H. Jaffor (1999, January 7). Dhaka-Kolkata Bus Route: Why is BNP So Perturbed? *The Daily Star*.
UNB News (2020, May 20). Trade & Transit: Dhaka, Delhi take steps to facilitate more trade. Retrieved from http://unb.com.bd/category/Bangladesh/trade-transit-dhaka-delhi-take-steps-to-facilitate-more-trade/51891
Yhome, K. (2015). The Burma roads: India's search for connectivity through Myanmar. *Asian Survey*, 55(6), pp. 1217-1240.
Zaman, S.S. (2014, May 4). Dhaka, Delhi working to establish links with northeast. *Dhaka Tribune*.
Zaman, K.R. (2019, December 31). Connectivity: a bilateral agenda. *New Age*. Retrieved from https://www.newagebd.net/article/95094/connectivity-a-bilateral-agenda

8

Unfolding the Role of Civil Society

ABSTRACT

Civil society plays a crucial role in deepening or sometimes disrupting Bangladesh-India relations. The scholarship on Bangladesh-India relations has been dominated by state-centric analysis marginalising the role of civil society. In creating and disseminating knowledge on the Bangladesh-India partnership that transcends from generation to generation in the classroom and beyond, the role of scholars and scholarship becomes essential. In addition, in shaping public opinion, the role of the media becomes critical. Business lobby groups also influence the formulation of state's trade and economic policies and, thus, foreign policy more broadly. Against this backdrop, this chapter asks: How does civil society play a role in deepening or disrupting Bangladesh-India relations? It argues that in the discourse of Bangladesh-India relations, one needs to take into account civil society's role seriously to realise the full potential of the partnership.

Keywords: *Bangladesh-India Ties, Civil Society, Media, Think Tanks, Business Lobby Groups, Scholars & Scholarship.*

Introduction

The contemporary nature of Bangladesh-India relations can be defined as a 'role model' for other countries and regions. The partnership has expanded from traditional political and diplomatic ties to a development partnership. In the process of the partnership, alongside state actors, non-state actors, including civil society, play an essential role. The role of civil society in Bangladesh-India relations dates back to the 1971 Liberation War of Bangladesh (Azad, 2008). In fact, Indian civil society, including the media, played a crucial role to create public opinion at home and abroad in favour of Bangladesh's independence. Later, business lobby groups, think tanks, academia, and the media played an important role sometimes to disrupt and sometimes to deepen Bangladesh-India relations. Ironically, the scholarship on Bangladesh-India relations has been dominated by state-centric analysis sidelining civil society's role, which needs to be problematised. This chapter argues that the role of civil society becomes essential in boosting Bangladesh-India relations. In fact, the untapped potential of the partnership can only be realised if the contributions of civil society are recognised and thus utilised. This chapter suggests that in the discourse of Bangladesh-India relations, one needs to take into account the role of civil society seriously. Therefore, this chapter investigates: How does civil society play a role in Bangladesh-India relations? Under the civil society domain, this chapter investigates the role of the media, i.e., the print media, scholars and scholarship, business lobby groups, and think tanks.

This chapter is divided into four sections. The first discusses the rationale and background of the chapter. The second explains the theoretical understanding of civil society while the third investigates civil society's role in Bangladesh-India relations. The final section focuses on the concluding remarks.

Understanding Civil Society

The idea of civil society can be traced from the works of Cicero, and other Romans to the ancient Greek philosophers. In classical usage, 'civil society was equated with the state' (Carothers and Barndt, 1999-2000, p.18). Scottish and Continental Enlightenment of the late 18th century contributed to the emergence of the modern idea of civil society. Scholars like Thomas Paine to Georg Hegel contributed to the development of civil society 'as a domain parallel to but separate from the state—a realm where citizens associate according to their own interests' (cited in Carothers and Barndt, 1999-2000, p.18). For John Locke, civil society becomes imperative for people to organise their public life of freedom and prosperity (cited in Ehrenberg, 2017). In the post-Second World War,

Antonio Gramsci revived the term to 'portray civil society as a special nucleus of independent political activity, a crucial sphere of struggle against tyranny' (cited in Carothers and Barndt 1999-2000, p.18).

In the 1990s, civil society became a 'mantra' both for political leaders and political scientists. When the former dictatorial countries started to embrace the idea of democracy, civil society also received substantial space around the world. It is mostly viewed as a 'social renewal' when the people became tired of the party systems in the USA and Western Europe. In the case of the developing world, it is argued that 'privatisation and other market reforms offered civil society the chance to step in as governments retracted their reach' (Carothers and Barndt, 1999-2000, p.19). The Information Revolution plays a key role in 'forging connections and empowering citizens. Civil society became a key element of the post-cold-war zeitgeist' (Carothers and Barndt, 1999-2000, p.19).

Civil society is defined as a voluntary, apolitical, non-profitable actor/organisation where it works as a bridge between the state and its people. Thus, civil society provides space. Non-governmental organisations, media, academia, the business community, religious, cultural and sports organisations and research institutions are seen as major elements of civil society. The initiatives that civil society takes to bring together concerned individuals outside the government to address the bilateral, regional and global issues, 'which have proved intractable to formal diplomacy at the inter-governmental level' is known as Track II diplomacy (Sobhan, 2002, p.xiii). Thus, in the case of bilateral relations, civil society plays a role at the Track II level to sensitise mutual concerns and prescribe policy imperatives and so forth.

Civil Society and Bangladesh-India Relations

Bangladesh and India are enriched with civil society organisations. Though civil society's role is largely analysed from the perspective of domestic spheres, in the case of Bangladesh-India relations, civil society plays a vital role. Shristi Pukhrem (2011), for instance, writes in *The Daily Star* that 'better relations between India and Bangladesh could be established only if the two countries emphasise a "people-to-people" approach. Here, the role of civil society, academic institutions, NGOs, media and information technology are noteworthy in formulating and shaping policies'. Indeed, civil society can better inform policymakers and the public about the nature, scope, rationale, opportunities and challenges in Bangladesh-India relations through its policy of advocacy, arranging dialogues and debates, education and research, and lobbying.

Role of the Media

It is argued that 'The media are increasingly a part of the process (if not the entire process) in the communications between governments and publics about international politics' (Karl, 1982, p.144). In foreign-policy making, the role of the media becomes important (Craig, 1976; Carroll, 1997; Karl, 1982; *Great Decisions* 1991, Knecht and Weatherford, 2006). In fact, 'Media diplomacy is conditioning the formulation and execution of foreign policy and the public's understanding of international affairs' (Karl, 1982, p.152). Raymond Carroll (1997, p.7) contends that 'The unprecedented power of the news media has caused many to worry about their influence over the country's foreign policy'. Karl further (1982, p.149) notes that:

> Governments today talk not so much to each other as at each other through the media. The use of the media to pre-empt governments may often delay normal diplomatic relations or create foreign-policy crises largely unanticipated by governments. Government misuse of the media has also led to a number of dangers that mislead domestic public opinion and foreign publics and governments.

The role of the media becomes essential for two specific reasons, e.g., the incredible reach of the media and its credibility among the people (Sinha, 2005, pp.67-68). It is argued that the media 'popularise an issue, explain it and communicate pedagogically its various complex dimensions, stakes and origins. Being visible brings credibility and legitimacy' (Martens and Naether, 2009, p.21). It also creates 'pressure, increasing the receptivity of institutions by making them aware of the existence of a conflict or international problem' (Martens and Naether, 2009, p.21). In fact, 'common people tend to believe what is communicated by the media' (Sinha, 2005, p.68).

The role of the media in Bangladesh-India relations is also recognised by both the policy and academic community. For instance, section 27 of the Joint Statement on the Sixth Meeting of the India-Bangladesh Joint

Consultative Commission held on September 29, 2020, states that 'Both Ministers underscored the value of positive media reporting on the bilateral engagements between the two countries and agreed to call upon their respective media communities to play more responsible roles in this regard' (MOFA, Dhaka 2020). In addition, Indian High Commissioner to Bangladesh Riva Ganguly Das points out that the 'Media plays an important role in highlighting the immense potential and opportunities that exist for all the stakeholders' (*The Daily Star*, 2019). Regarding the role of print media in Bangladesh-India relations, Sitara Parvin and Mofizur Rahman (2001-2002) note that:

> Items that can be considered to be promotive (sic) of bilateral relationships did not receive the kind of attention they deserved in the newspapers of India and Bangladesh. Stories on trade and finance, cultural activities could have received better treatment. Similarly, the newspapers also neglected items on agriculture, education and various development-oriented activities (cited in Sinha, 2005, p.68).

Role of the Indian Media

The Indian media is primarily interested in the domestic affairs of the country while ignoring regional or global events. Even leading English language news channels and newspapers 'focus to an extraordinary degree on domestic events, personalities and phenomena' (Malik and Medcalf, 2011, p.3). Bangladesh is poorly covered in the Indian media. It is argued that instead of positive news, negative stories on Bangladesh affairs are primarily dominated in the Indian media (Sinha, 2005; Anam, 2017). Though Bangladesh is a close neighbour, its concerns are hardly written in the Indian media. For instance, the construction of the Farakka barrage by India and its resulting negative consequences on Bangladesh have not been adequately addressed in the Indian media. In addition, water-sharing issues, border killings, trade imbalance, maritime boundary disputes, and enclaves are barely covered in the Indian media. In a dialogue on Role of Media in Strengthening Relations between Bangladesh and India, Indian journalists recognised Bangladesh's contributions to addressing India's security concerns and admitted India's failure to reciprocate. Indian journalists also acknowledged that the Indian media failed to positively portray the opportunities created and opened up by Bangladesh (*The Daily Star*, 2013). Sinha (2005, pp.69-70) contends that:

Bangladesh is a marginal entity in the mainstream print and electronic media in India. But when it finds any mention its dominant representations in the Indian national media, both the mainstream print and electronic variety, pertain to its image as a 'wasteland' marked by utter poverty, natural disasters like flood, religious bigotry, and fundamentalism, den of anti-Indian forces,...and 'official sponsorship of infiltration. The images being mentioned here are not fictional but are real images of events. But the more important point is that if they are the only ones, selected to depict a close neighbour, with little reference to images that would also provide some positive account, the question arises as to how would the mainstream media contribute to the promotion of good neighbourly relations between India and Bangladesh.

Mahfuz Anam (2011), the editor and publisher of *The Daily Star*, Bangladesh, writes that 'For 18 unrelenting years, the economic and ecological devastation that Farakka wrought on large parts of Bangladesh remained unnoticed in India. Unbelievably, no mainstream Indian newspaper, magazine or TV station bothered to cover this great human tragedy occurring just next door'. Anam (2017) further observes that:

> As a media person, I have never been able to understand the indifference of the Indian media towards Bangladesh's issues, especially those affecting bilateral relations. The saddest example is the Farakka barrage, which, in my view, was the first major cause of the rise of grassroots-level anti-Indianism in the late eighties. This lasted for decades and still lingers—but this was never reported in-depth in India by any mainstream print or audiovisual media. In fact, water sharing of our common rivers remains a blotch in our relations. The failure to even talk about Teesta, when a deal was ready to be signed in September 2011, has greatly disappointed us in Bangladesh. The rationale for Bangladesh's position on this crucial water sharing issue has almost never found adequate space in the Indian media. There are many other issues that can be cited. Nothing about Bangladesh is covered except for occasional instances of communal violence—which is endemic to the subcontinent—and the so-called rise of terrorism that Bangladesh is waging a frontal onslaught against.

Some media reports in India created discomfort in Bangladesh regarding contemporary Bangladesh-India relations. For instance, against the backdrop of China's zero-tariff announcement for 97 per cent of

Bangladeshi products in the Chinese market, in June 2020, the *Ananda Bazar Patrika*, a leading Bengali daily in India, described it as *'Khoyraati'* (charity) to Bangladesh. Bangladesh has responded critically to the news report. *The Times of India* reports that against the backdrop of the India-China clash at Galwan Valley in Ladakh, 'Beijing seems to be aggressively wooing Bangladesh, a strong ally of India in the neighbourhood, with a host of sops' (Chatterjee, 2020). In addition, *The Hindu* (Bhattacherjee, 2020) ran a story which is also discussed critically in Bangladesh. Bangladesh Foreign Minister Abdul Momen points out that Indian media reports highlighting the Bangladesh-China trade relations in a demeaning manner are 'unacceptable' (*Dhaka Tribune*, 2020a). Later, the *Ananda Bazar Patrika* apologised for the news.

During the COVID-19 global pandemic, while some media portals based in Northeast India spread misinformation about the reduction of warmth in Bangladesh-India relations, Bangladesh Foreign Minister A.K. Abdul Momen described Bangladesh-India ties as 'blood relationship', 'rock solid' while India described its ties with Bangladesh as 'exceptionally close' (*The Business Standard*, 2020). Echoing the warm sentiments, Indian External Affairs Minister S. Jaishankar claims that 'very few countries in the world share such close fraternal ties as those of ours...our partnership today stands out as a role model in the region for good neighbourly relations' (Kumaraswami, 2020). Thus, Bangladesh Foreign Minister Abdul Momen defines media reports on Bangladesh-India-China relations as 'rubbish', 'nonsense' (*Dhaka Tribune*, 2020b). The role of the Indian media in Bangladesh-India relations has been described critically by many in Bangladesh (Arafat, 2020; Khan, 2020; *Dhaka Tribune*, 2020a, 2020b). The *Dhaka Tribune* (2020c) writes that 'Using The Eastern Link, Bhaumik is now apparently working in full swing to serve the interest of a vested group that evidently does not want Indo-Bangla ties to remain strong and free of tension'. Shahab Enam Khan (2020) contends that 'It has always been quite distressing to see the reactions of the Indian media regarding Bangladesh, in any matter, be it economy, military, politics, or cricket. The Indian media, often regarded as a wild propaganda machine, has kept on attempting to stain the sovereign entity called Bangladesh'.

Against such reporting in the Indian media, Indian scholar Joyeeta Bhattacharjee (2020) writes that 'In Bangladesh, the Indian media is closely observed, especially, any mention about the country or bilateral ties between the neighbours. A positive mention about the country in the Indian media results in a feeling of joy and a negative mention evokes public displeasure, which often gives leeway to some vested quarters to encourage anti-India rhetoric'. Therefore, Bhattacharjee (2020) suggests that the Indian media 'be conscious' and 'adopt a more nuanced approach while reporting about the bilateral relationship'. Against the conventional wisdom regarding the role of the Indian media in Bangladesh-India relations, this chapter also looks into some positive examples of constructive engagement of the Indian print media (see Table 3).

Table 3: Editorial Coverage of Indian Print Media on Bangladesh-India Relations

Name of the newspaper	Title of the editorial	Date & year
Hindustan Times	India opens heart, purse to Bangladesh	January 12, 2010
The Indian Express	Railroading ties	January 12, 2010
The Indian Express	Eastward momentum	September 5, 2011
The Indian Express	Being Mamata	September 6, 2011
The Indian Express	The Eastern obligation	February 18, 2013
The Indian Express	Last bus to Dhaka	July 29, 2013
Hindustan Times	Why Sushma Swaraj is in Dhaka and what India can do for Bangladesh	June 25, 2014
Times of India	Don't politicise LBA: India-Bangladesh boundary deal must be passed without exclusions	May 4, 2015
The Hindu	Local politics in foreign policy	May 5, 2015
The Indian Express	Delhi's turn: India must keep its word to Bangladesh and push through the Land Boundary Agreement	May 6, 2015
Times of India	Border breakthrough: Ratification of LBA paves the way for enhanced India-Bangladesh ties and regional growth	May 8, 2015
Times of India	Only connect: Modi's Bangladesh visit can trigger India's integration with its northeast as well as Southeast Asia	June 3, 2015
The Indian Express	Taking the leap: Prime Minister Modi's Bangladesh visit affirms a more purposeful and problem-solving neighbourhood policy	June 8, 2015
The Indian Express	Mapping the future: India and Bangladesh bury a Partition legacy. Now, both countries must focus on trade and connectivity	August 1, 2015
The Indian Express	1971 in 2016: India's relations with Bangladesh have gone well, but countries sharing centuries of history need to be much closer	December 15, 2016

Name of the newspaper	Title of the editorial	Date & year
Hindustan Times	India's best regional partnership: Delhi must allay Dhaka's apprehensions on the NRC process	October 6, 2019
The Indian Express	Good going: But with Dhaka something's missing: Economic policy making in Delhi needs to be more sensitive to the regional dimension	October 7, 2019
The Economic Times	For better India, Bangladesh relations	October 7, 2019
The Hindu	Best friends for now: On New Delhi-Dhaka ties	October 7, 2019
The Indian Express	At great cost: New citizenship law is taking a toll on ties with Dhaka	December 16, 2019
Hindustan Times	Reassure Dhaka; bring ties back on track: With yet another minister calling off his visit to India, Bangladesh's unease is clear	January 14, 2020
The Indian Express	In plain Bangla: It may be diplomatically imprudent to alienate a friendly neighbour with CAA premise —persecution within	January 21, 2020
Hindustan Times	Focus on Bangladesh: Delhi must not let ties with Dhaka dip	July 30, 2020

Source: Author.

Table 3 demonstrates that Indian mainstream print media wrote several editorials addressing Bangladesh's concerns and interests. Until 2008, the Indian media ran stories on Bangladesh that is primarily negative. Since 2009, due to the Sheikh Hasina government in power, there is a paradigm shift in Bangladesh-India relations, which is also reflected in the Indian print media as Table 3 shows. Indeed, the Indian print media ran a number of constructive editorials on Bangladesh-India relations which merit a degree of analysis. Thus, after analysing the editorials, it is concluded that Bangladesh's role in addressing India's security concerns, addressing Northeast India's connectivity needs, the importance of India's reciprocal actions especially in the context of addressing Bangladesh's water-sharing concerns are emphasised in Indian print media editorials. More specifically, Indian print media wrote several editorials on the rationale behind the ratification of LBA that needs to be appreciated. The contemporary NRC issue and its negative implications on Bangladesh-India relations are also highlighted. It is also found that the importance of Bangladesh for India's long term interest in the context of security, economic and socio-cultural dimension is emphasised in those editorials. Thus, it is argued that India cannot afford to lose its partnership with Bangladesh. Consequently, it is suggested that India needs to deepen its relations with Bangladesh based on a win-win situation and reciprocity for the well-being of the people of both India and Bangladesh.

In fact, Bangladesh received better attention in the Indian print media coverage particularly since 2010, though the coverage was limited largely to the official visits of the heads of states. Despite such constructive editorial coverage in the Indian print media, this chapter argues that Bangladesh merits much more attention than it usually receives in the Indian print media given the nature, scope and current height of contemporary Bangladesh-India relations. For instance, though one can cite the issue of border killings as a major concern for Bangladesh, it is rarely covered in the Indian print media editorials. It is also argued that water sharing issues and trade imbalance deserve much more attention in the Indian print media. The Rohingya crisis, which is a primary concern for Bangladesh and the role of India in the resolution of the crisis, also deserves better attention. It is also worthy to note that the impressive socio-economic development of Bangladesh and the potential in accelerating bilateral investment also needs to be highlighted in the Indian print media editorials.

Role of Bangladeshi Media

To a more considerable extent, Bangladeshi media constructively engage with Bangladesh-India relations. Compared to the Indian print media, the Bangladeshi print media gives more space to Bangladesh-India relations. Consequently, many editorials are written on deepening Bangladesh-India relations (Table 4). One can argue that the Bangladeshi media promotes/advocates a win-win partnership between Bangladesh and India. It is noted that bilateral trade imbalance, Free Trade Agreement, transit facility for India, inter-regional cooperation and water sharing disputes are the dominant features in the Bangladeshi media on Bangladesh-India relations (Sinha, 2005).

Table 4: Editorial Coverage of Bangladeshi Media on Bangladesh-India Relations

Name of the Newspaper	Title/headline	Date & year
The Daily Star	Expectations from Indo-Bangla summit: Taking the relationship on to a new plane	January 10, 2010
The Daily Star	Delhi summit a sign of productive bilateralism: We look forward to quick progress on water-sharing issue	January 13, 2010
The Daily Star	A new phase ushered in Indo-Bangla relations: Commitments will have to be fulfilled for mutual gains	January 14, 2010

Name of the Newspaper	Title/headline	Date & year
The Daily Star	Why this claim game? No visit can be a hundred percent success or a hundred percent failure	January 18, 2010
The Daily Star	Border killings: Why can't the BSF be reined in by its government?	September 7, 2010
The Daily Star	Dhaka-Delhi deal on border trade: The move could lead to wider economic cooperation	October 25, 2010
The Daily Star	Business prospects with North-eastern India: Removal of trade barriers and enhanced connectivity are key	November 12, 2010
The Daily Star	Bangladesh-India Secretary level meeting: Peaceful border requires more than mere expression of intent	January 22, 2011
The Daily Star	Economic ties with India: Sharma visit injects dynamism	April 25, 2011
The Daily Star	India needs to deliver: Pranab's statement very welcome	May 9, 2011
The Daily Star	High level Indo-Bangla interactions: The historic opportunity shouldn't be lost	July 7, 2011
The Daily Star	Krishna visit proves useful: A boost to Dhaka-Delhi ties	July 10, 2011
The Daily Star	Honouring Indira Gandhi: Recognition was long overdue	July 26, 2011
The Daily Star	Sonia Gandhi's visit to Dhaka: An opportunity to tackle critical issues	July 27, 2011
The Daily Star	BD-India Home Ministers' meet: India needs to deliver	August 1, 2011
The Daily Star	Indian premier's visit: Our expectations	September 5, 2011
The Daily Star	Welcoming Manmohan: We are shocked but still hopeful	September 6, 2011
The Daily Star	We have been let down: However, we remain hopeful	September 7, 2011
The Daily Star	Mamata let-down most unfortunate: Trust in negotiation process diluted	September 7, 2011
The Daily Star	Lessons from Dhaka summit: It's the process that comes under question	September 8, 2011
The Daily Star	Visit by neighbouring Indian CMs: We need to strengthen our relations with them	September 8, 2011
The Daily Star	India's pro-active response: Hopefully it will lead to deterrence	February 2, 2012
The Daily Star	BSF chief's statement regrettable: An authentic clarification called for	February 12, 2012
The Daily Star	Pranab's visit proves forward-looking: Some positive assurances given	May 8, 2012
The Daily Star	Foreign secretary-level talks in Delhi: Resolving bilateral issues must acquire urgency	July 26, 2012
The Daily Star	Khaleda Zia's India visit: We hope the rapprochement is real	November 5, 2012
The Daily Sun	Treaties to strengthen bond of friendship	January 30, 2013
The Daily Star	Indo-Bangladesh treaties: They augur well	January 31, 2013
The Daily Star	Indian Foreign Minister's visit: Yet more assurances	February 19, 2013
The Daily Star	Indian president's visit: Promise of progress	March 5, 2013

Name of the Newspaper	Title/headline	Date & year
The Daily Star	Foreign Minister's futile trip: Disappointing for Bangladesh	July 29, 2013
The New Age	Yet another pointer, incumbents' appeasement policy to India	September 1, 2013
The Daily Star	Modi-Hasina talks: Let the Indian PM's assurances have a timeframe	September 29, 2014
The Daily Star	Revisiting Indo-BD issues: Call for greater commitment from India	November 16, 2014
The Daily Star	Warm welcome to PM Modi: Heightened expectations, matching outcome hoped for	June 6, 2015
The Independent	Taking India-Bangladesh relations to a new height	June 7, 2015
The Independent	No change in Teesta related woes of Bangladesh	June 8, 2015
The Daily Star	Modi's action-packed visit ends: Stage set for a huge impetus to Indo-Bangla relations	June 8, 2015
The Financial Express	The Modi visit: Envisioning an era of change	June 9, 2015
The Independent	Gains from Modi's visit	June 9, 2015
The Daily Star	Prime minister's visit to India: Hope the bottlenecks are resolved	April 7, 2017
The Daily Sun	PM's Delhi visit	April 9, 2017
The Independent	Dhaka-Delhi ties get a boost	April 10, 2017
The New Age	Delhi's crude selfishness to a 'friendly' Dhaka	April 10, 2017
The New Age	India's friendship fraught with unfriendliness	April 14, 2017
The Daily Star	Fast implementation of Indian loans: Joint panel for better project monitoring	October 7, 2017
The Daily Star	Sushma's message: More substantive action needed	October 25, 2017
The Daily Star	Jaishankar's visit: Vague responses to two crucial issues	August 22, 2019
The Daily Star	Is the NRC exclusion really India's internal issue?	September 2, 2019
The Daily Star	An apt appraisal worthy of note: PM's remarks on India's CAA reflect wider concerns	January 21, 2020
The Daily Star	BSF shootings are not stopping: What about India's promise of bringing down the number of casualties to zero?	July 6, 2020
The Daily Star	Bangladesh and India's relations must go to the next level: Stumbling blocks in the friendship have to be removed	December 19, 2020

Source: Author.

Table 4 shows that Bangladesh's partnership with India is a priority area for the print media in Bangladesh. The issue of economic cooperation, water sharing, border killings, connectivity, security and defence cooperation, and energy cooperation, Citizenship Amendment Act/National Register of Citizens of Assam are some dominant issues in the Bangladeshi print media editorials. The importance of an improved Bangladesh-India relationship is also highlighted. For instance, prior to

Sheikh Hasina's 2010 New Delhi visit, while addressing a rally at Paltan Maidan of Dhaka, Begum Khaleda Zia, the opposition leader of Bangladesh Nationalist Party, prejudiced the New Delhi outcome. On the day after Khaleda Zia's address, *the Daily Star*, in its editorial (2010a), argued that using such language that might prejudice the Delhi outcome is counterproductive for Bangladesh. With an expectation on promoting Bangladesh-India relations to a new height, *The Daily Star*, in its editorial (2010b) wrote that 'India's short-, medium-and long-term interests are in a way tied with economic progress of Bangladesh. In fact, invigorated two-way street of a bilateral relationship paradigm freed of tension and underpinned by connectivity to Nepal and Bhutan can be the cornerstone of robust regional cooperation within the SAARC umbrella'. On January 13, 2010, *The Daily Star* wrote another editorial appreciating the New Delhi summit as a 'productive sign of bilateralism' and urged to resolve the water sharing issue (*The Daily Star* Editorial, 2010c). On the next day, the daily wrote another editorial describing the outcome of the summit as a 'new phase' in Bangladesh-India relations while emphasising the execution of the commitments for mutual benefit. Most importantly, Bangladesh's concerns are particularly highlighted repeatedly in those editorials. However, in those editorials, it is argued that Bangladesh has done its part, i.e., addressed India's security and connectivity concerns. It is on India's part now to deliver on its repeated promises, i.e., Teesta water-sharing agreement. Thus, the editorials suggest that India needs to address its domestic issue with West Bengal and thus the water sharing issue with Bangladesh. The point of border killings is also highlighted in the Bangladeshi print media editorials repeatedly and therefore it is suggested that instead of repeated promises, India truly needs to stop its 'shoot-to-kill' policy in the Bangladesh-India border area.

Role of Scholars and Scholarship

Scholars and the scholarship play a vital role in producing and disseminating knowledge on Bangladesh-India relations which is transmitted from generation to generation in classroom exercises and beyond. If one surveys, there is a lack of serious scholarship in Bangladesh-India relations. This aspect is relatively marginal among academic communities in Bangladesh. Except for some popular media pieces, serious scholarship on the country's relations with India is absent in

Bangladesh. Therefore, expertise in Indian affairs in Bangladesh is limited. Similarly, Partha S. Ghosh (2011, p.207) contends that 'By and large, India's academic expertise on Bangladesh is rather limited'. Thus, it is argued that 'If India–Bangladesh relations are to move beyond the routine demands of existential politics, there is no escape from investing more time and money to know each other better. Deeper appreciation of the social and political dynamics of each country is needed in at least one specialised centre of learning in the other country' (Ghosh, 2011, p.208).

Academic exchanges, joint research projects, field work in each other's country becomes essential. But it is challenging to get a research and conference visa. Ghosh (2011, p.208) reflects that 'it is much easier for an American or European scholar to stay in Bangladesh or India for a long period of research on that country than for a Bangladeshi or an Indian'. This issue needs to be taken into consideration very seriously by the policymakers of these two countries. In fact, promoting more academic interaction becomes necessary for better Bangladesh-India relations. As theory translates into practice, this neglected area of study needs to be accelerated, and there must be several joint research projects between Bangladeshi and Indian scholars.

The role of the academic community is critically important to elevate Bangladesh-India relations or to resolve bilateral disputes. In an increasing water conflict, hydro-diplomacy has emerged as a major tool to address water issues. Hence, the introduction, development and expansion of hydro-diplomacy courses and curricula at the university level and the role of academics is a crucial one. And effective hydro-diplomacy can be imperative to resolve India-Bangladesh water sharing disputes (Islam, 2015). In addition, it is observed that in both countries some academics, for the sake of narrowly defined 'national interests' help to sustain such disputes through their 'hawkish' stance in their writings. In fact, such types of academic work sometimes influence the policies of the decision-makers. Such academic practice is a significant hindrance to the consolidation of Bangladesh-India ties. Hence, the role of academics needs to be redefined, focusing on constructive engagements.

In the context of academic practice, it is argued that Bangladesh, being surrounded on three sides by India and with strong trade and economic ties with India, having sound knowledge about each other is imperative to elevate their bilateral relations. Better theory, in fact, translates into better policies. But in the case of India-Bangladesh ties, there is a shortage of academic practice. Very few scholars concentrate on India-Bangladesh scholarship. Besides, 'South Asia' as an academic area of inquiry is a neglected area in the academic world which also merits serious food for thought. Needless to say, this lack of academic practice works as a significant challenge to uplift Bangladesh-India relations to a more considerable extent in one way or the other.

The Memorandum of Understanding (MoU) signed between Dhaka University (DU) and Jawaharlal Nehru University (JNU) during the Indian Prime Minister Manmohan Singh's September 2011 visit in Bangladesh is imperative to promote academic cooperation between these two friendly nations. According to AAMS Arefin Siddique, the former Vice-Chancellor of Dhaka University, 'graduates of DU and JNU, as expected, serve in key positions of different sectors in their own countries. A good personal relationship among them from early on will help them deal with different bilateral issues in the future' (Ahammed, 2011). In October 2011, Dhaka University, Assam University, and Burdwan University jointly organised a two-day international conference on 'Bangladesh Liberation War and Indo-Bangla Relations' at Dhaka University. Notably, 24 scholars from India participated in the conference (*The Daily Star*, 2011b). Such intellectual interaction is necessary for uplifting Bangladesh-India relations.

Many Indian scholars suggest changing Indian policy towards Bangladesh realising the importance of the country and thus addressing mutual concerns. Kanti Bajpai (2011), for instance, writes that 'We in India have failed to appreciate just how important Bangladesh is to our well-being' especially in the context of peace and development. Bajpai also notes that 'Bangladesh is crucial for India because it represents opportunities and lessons worth learning. If we were not so arrogant, we might learn something from our great neighbour to the east. In short, Bangladesh matters. If only we could see'. Considering the importance of Bangladesh for India, Deb Mukharji (2019) writes that 'Delhi needs to do more to protect and deepen ties with Dhaka'. Thus, scholars and scholarship play an essential role in Bangladesh-India relations, which needs to be appreciated and promoted.

Role of Business Lobby Groups and Others

Economic cooperation remains a key priority area in the foreign policy formulation of both Bangladesh and India. In this context, business lobby groups play a crucial role. Thus, it is also worthy to note the role of business lobby groups in Bangladesh-India relations. Malik and Medcalf (2011) provide a detailed account of the role of business lobby groups in Indian foreign policy. Indian business lobby groups play a vital role in the formation of Indian policy towards Bangladesh. The Federation of Bangladesh Chambers of Commerce and Industry (FBCCI) in Bangladesh and the Confederation of India Industry (CII) and the Federation of Chambers of Commerce and Industry (FICCI) in India, are critical private business lobby groups, respectively. Representatives of these groups join Prime Ministerial and other business delegations abroad and thus influence policymaking.

The Bangladesh-India Friendship Society (BIFS), India-Bangladesh Chamber of Commerce & Industry (IBCCI), Bangladesh-India Friendship Dialogue, Bangladesh Chapter of India Foundation and Bangladesh Foundation for Regional Studies are some examples of institutions that are playing a crucial role in promoting Bangladesh-India relations. For instance, the Metropolitan Chamber of Commerce and Industry, Bangladesh, supported the proposal of giving transit facility to India, and they contended that this would help to increase Bangladesh-India bilateral trade and investment (*The Daily Star*, 2000).

In February 2010, the Indian Chamber of Commerce (ICC) and the India-Bangladesh Chamber of Commerce and Industry (IBCCI), signed the Dhaka Declaration for promoting Bangladesh-India economic cooperation focusing on the Northeastern states of India. Notably, both the ICC and IBCCI agreed to jointly pursue eight specific priorities to strengthen Bangladesh-India economic cooperation with special emphasis on India's Northeastern states, i.e., strengthening Bangladesh-India trade infrastructure with special focus on Assam, Meghalaya, Tripura, and Mizoram; connectivity through Chattogram port, improving the navigability of the waterways through dredging; implementing night navigation system; removing tariff and non-tariff barriers; promoting tourism between Bangladesh and India's Northeastern states; establishing road connectivity between commercially viable locations and exchanging business and government delegations between Bangladesh and India's Northeastern states (*The Daily Star*, 2010d). In addition, the India-Bangladesh Chamber of Commerce and Industry (IBCCI) and the High Commission of India in Bangladesh organised, on 29 March 2014 at Ruposhi Bangla Hotel, Dhaka, a seminar entitled 'Foreign Investment in Bangladesh: Opportunities and Prospects' with a special session on power sector. Such practices need to be increased to exploit the full potential in India-Bangladesh relations.

It is found that the Bangladesh business community is more interested in deepening Bangladesh-India economic cooperation. The former FBCCI president, Yousuf Abdullah Harun, contends that 'Although Bangladesh and India are situated in a region endowed with vast resources; in reality they could not convert these resources into productive and collective wealth in an accelerating manner. The trade intensity indicates that there is scope for mutual trade and cooperation' (*The Daily Star*, 2010a). Similarly, Annisul Huq, former president of the Federation of Bangladesh Chambers of Commerce and Industry (FBCCI), notes that making ports and railway accessible to neighbours will naturally benefit Bangladesh and help increase intraregional economic activities (*The Daily Star*, 2010b).

On the other hand, it is noted that 'The Tamil Nadu textile lobby, in particular, based around Coimbatore and Salem, has been particularly vocal in demanding continued protection from Bangladeshi imports, and seems to be able to twist India's trade policy—and its foreign policy—around its little finger' (Sharma, 2011). These domestic lobby groups in India play a crucial role in imposing various tariffs and non-tariff barriers in the context of India's imports from Bangladesh, which need to be addressed. Thus, one needs to understand the role of domestic lobby groups either in deepening or disrupting Bangladesh-India relations.

Role of Think Tanks

Though minimal, think tanks also play a role in shaping Bangladesh-India relations through their policy reports, workshops, dialogues, seminars and conferences. Though the role of think tanks could be influential in shaping policies, it is minimal in the case of Bangladesh-India relations as policymakers hardly care to them. In the case of India, foreign policy think tanks are limited in number with inadequate funding and minimal influence in shaping policies (Baru, 2013). K. Subramanian, who ran a government-funded think tank, Institute of Defence Studies and Analyses (IDSA), remarked that 'Our senior bureaucrats have burdened themselves with so much of trivia because of the lack of a culture of delegation that they have no time to read such outside studies. Therefore, they have no use for them' (cited in Baru, 2013). Despite this, it is found that a few think tanks based in New Delhi and Dhaka took initiatives to remove the decades-long stalemate in Bangladesh-India relations. For instance, to promote Bangladesh-India relations, the Centre for Policy Research (CPR), New Delhi and the Centre for Policy Dialogue (CPD), Dhaka, initiated the India-Bangladesh Dialogue at non-official/ Track II level. The inaugural dialogue was held in February 1995 in New Delhi in the issue of economic cooperation. The CPR and CPD jointly organised eight rounds of discussions in different dimensions, including economic relations, water resources, political and security relations and social and cultural issues between 1995 and 2001 (Table 5).

Table 5: India-Bangladesh Dialogue at Track II Level (1995-2001)

Theme	Place	Date & Year
Economic Relations	New Delhi	February 1-2, 1995
Economic Relations	Dhaka	May 20-22, 1995
Water Resources	New Delhi	August 27-29, 1996
Water Resources	Dhaka	June 23-25, 1997
Political and Security Relations	New Delhi	December 1-2, 1997
Political and Security Relations	Dhaka	June 29-July 1, 1998
Social and Cultural Issues	New Delhi	March 22-23, 1999
Concluding Review Dialogue	Dhaka	January 15-16, 2001

Source: Sobhan, 2002, p. xv.

Inculcating bilateral issues, creating sensitivity towards each other's problems, and in policy advocacy, e.g., preparing policy papers to resolve bilateral issues to progress the ties, India-Bangladesh Dialogue at Track II level between 1995 and 2001 played a vital role. In addition, Bangladesh Enterprise Institute (BEI), Dhaka and Observer Research Foundation (ORF), New Delhi, jointly organised Bangladesh-India Security Dialogue to promote security cooperation. Between 2009 and 2014, six rounds of dialogue were held both in Dhaka and New Delhi. Regarding the relevance of such dialogues, it is argued that:

> The Indo-Bangladesh dialogue process, in some measure, did influence Track-I negotiations. Dialogue participants who crossed over into government had been sufficiently exposed to the concerns either side through these dialogues. This exposure contributed to making them more receptive towards finding solutions to particular issues in such areas as water sharing or market access for Bangladesh's exports. Those who did not move into office, but who were in positions of public influence, were also left more aware of the concerns of the other country and could draw upon this in relevant areas of policymaking (Sobhan, 2002, p.xviii).

There are some limitations of Track II level initiatives as Ghosh (2011, p.208) notes: 'most of them tread only marginally beyond the boundaries of existential politics because largely these efforts are managed by former politicians, bureaucrats or those with close linkages to present or past governments'. In addition, as mentioned earlier, the funding issue also becomes a significant challenge for think tanks.

Besides, through research, policy advocacy and interviews, experts from think tanks also play a crucial role in forming an opinion on Bangladesh-India relations. For instance, the former executive director of the CPD, Mostafizur Rahman, in an interview with *The Daily Star*, argues for improved Bangladesh-India relations (*The Daily Star*, 2010c). Rehman Sobhan from the CPD argued for greater connectivity and economic cooperation with India's Northeastern states. According to Sobhan, 'The moment you open up the transport and communication and economic links with the north-eastern parts of India, Bangladesh will emerge as the natural trading partner of the neighbouring country, as it will become a hinterland and the point of access to north-eastern India and the rest of the world' (*The Daily Star*, 2011a).

On the other hand, Joyeeta Bhattacharjee (2012) from the ORF writes that 'The West Bengal chief minister's stand on the sharing of waters with Bangladesh of the two common rivers passing through both countries, the Teesta and the Ganga, was governed by an extremely narrow objective that put at stake the overall national interest'. Bhattacharjee (2012) further notes that 'The non-signing of the Teesta agreement has substantially hampered ties between the two countries'.

Conclusion

Improved Bangladesh-India relations matter for more than 170 million people in Bangladesh and 1.3 billion people in India. In the context of realising the full potential in Bangladesh-India ties, civil society plays a crucial role through providing information and expertise, recommendations, constructive opinions, informed analysis, and lobbying. Since the existing role of civil society is marginalised, given the dominance of state-centric analysis in the Bangladesh-India partnership, it becomes important to acknowledge and embrace civil society's role by the governments of these two nations. In addition, civil society in both Bangladesh and India need to play a constructive role in deepening Bangladesh-India relations.

This chapter suggests that the media needs to play a constructive role in resolving long-standing disputes, i.e., water sharing dispute, border killings, and trade imbalance. The media, especially the Indian media, needs to be more sensitive and constructive on Bangladesh affairs. In fact, it is widely recognised in the Indian media that Bangladesh, under the Sheikh Hasina regime, has addressed India's key concerns, i.e., security and connectivity. Simultaneously, it is also admitted in the Indian media that India failed to reciprocate to Bangladesh in the context of water sharing issue and trade imbalance which requires substantial political will from the Indian side. In this context, this chapter suggests that the Indian media needs to cover Bangladesh's concerns on a regular basis so that India's policy community becomes more sensitive and thus take up effective policies to address those issues for mutual gain.

It is also argued that developing in-depth expertise on Indian affairs in Bangladesh and vice versa becomes necessary for proper understanding and thus exploring Bangladesh-India relations for the greater interest of the people of these countries. In this context, developing dedicated research institutes on Indian Affairs in Bangladesh and vice versa becomes essential. In addition, collaboration between Bangladeshi and Indian scholars on research in various dimensions of Bangladesh-India ties becomes critical. Also, the role of think tanks needs to be appreciated and promoted.

Finally, this chapter concludes by arguing that domestic business lobby groups play a crucial role in shaping policies on Bangladesh-India economic relations. This domestic lobby group, especially in India, needs to come out from its narrowly defined interest and embrace more comprehensive India's economic cooperation with Bangladesh. Civil society also needs to be constructive and dedicated to improving Bangladesh-India relations, considering the long-term benefit of the people of these two countries and beyond. Similarly, it is also crucial 'to initiate activities to strengthen civil societies, which would not only empower and benefit the people of South Asia but would also put Bangladesh-India relations on a newer and fresher grounds' (Ahmed, 1996, p.291).

REFERENCES

Ahmed, I. (1996). Bangladesh-India relations: Trapped in the nationalist discourse. In A. Kalam (Ed.), *Bangladesh: Internal dynamics and external linkages* (pp. 277-296). Dhaka: UPL.

Ahammed, R. (2011, October 7). DU-Jawaharlal Nehru University MoU: Move to establish long term Indo-Bangla relations. *The Daily Star.*

Anam, M. (2011, September 6). A chance to make history. *The Indian Express.* Retrieved from http://archive.indianexpress.com/news/a-chance-to-make-history/842124/0

Anam, M. (2017, January 5). Despite history, geography. *The Indian Express.* Retrieved from https://indianexpress.com/article/opinion/columns/india-bangladesh-relations-treaty-terrorism-despite-history-geography-4459231/

Arafat, M. A. (2020, August 5). Bangladesh-India ties are not a zero-sum game. *The Daily Star.* Retrieved from https://www.thedailystar.net/opinion/news/bangladesh-india-ties-are-not-zero-sum-game-1939865

Azad, S. (2008). *Role of Indian people in Liberation War of Bangladesh.* New Delhi: Bookwell.

Bajpai, K. (2011, September 17). Why Bangladesh should matter to us. *Times of India.* Retrieved from https://timesofindia.indiatimes.com/edit-page/Why-Bangladesh-should-matter-to-us/articleshow/10009443.cms

Baru, S. (2013, January 21). Sanjaya Baru: Indian minds, foreign funds. *Business Standard.* Retrieved from https://www.business-standard.com/article/opinion/sanjaya-baru-indian-minds-foreign-funds-110080900083_1.html

Bhattacharjee, J. (2012, February 23). Pouring cold water on neighbourly ties. *Hindustan Times.* Retrieved from https://www.hindustantimes.com/india/pouring-cold-water-on-neighbourly-ties/story-AxIXoYRa2ybp3pIOOMaQcO.html

Bhattacharjee, J. (2020, August 7). India-Bangladesh relations: A different stroke. ORF Online. Retrieved from https://www.orfonline.org/expert-speak/india-bangladesh-relations-different-stroke/

Bhattacherjee, K. (2020, July 25). Sheikh Hasina did not meet Indian envoy despite requests: Dhaka daily. *The Hindu.* Retrieved from https://www.thehindu.com/news/national/sheikh-hasina-did-not-meet-indian-envoy-despite-requests-dhaka-daily/article32187068.ece

Carroll, R. (1997). Today's media: what voice in foreign policy? *Great Decisions,* 7-16.

Carothers, T. & Barndt, W. (1999-2000). Civil society. *Foreign Policy*. No. 117, pp. 18-24 + pp. 26-29

Chatterjee, M. (2020, June 20). Nepal on its side, China now woos Bangladesh. *The Times of India*. Retrieved from http://timesofindia.indiatimes.com/articleshow/76475086.cms?utm_source=contentofinterest&utm_medium=text&utm_campaign=cppst

Craig, A. (1976). The media and foreign policy. *International Journal*, 31 (2), News and Nations, 319-336.

Dhaka Tribune (2020a, June 25). Momen: Indian media comments about Bangladesh not acceptable. Retrieved from https://www.dhakatribune.com/bangladesh/government-affairs/2020/06/25/india-our-biggest-friend-but-indian-media-comments-not-acceptable

Dhaka Tribune (2020b, July 31). Foreign Minister: Media reports on Bangladesh-India-China relations are rubbish. Retrieved from https://www.dhakatribune.com/bangladesh/foreign-affairs/2020/07/31/foreign-minister-media-reports-on-bangladesh-india-china-relations-are-rubbish

Dhaka Tribune (2020c, July 31). Is Subir Bhaumik's 'The Eastern Link' trying to ruin Indo-Bangla ties? Retrieved from https://www.dhakatribune.com/bangladesh/2020/07/31/is-subir-bhaumik-s-the-eastern-link-trying-to-ruin-indo-bangla-ties

Ehrenberg, J. (2017). *Civil society: The critical history of an idea*, Second Edition, NYU Press. Retrieved fromhttps://www.jstor.org/stable/j.ctt1bj4rhv.7

Ghosh, P. S. (2011). Changing frontiers: Making deeper sense of India-Bangladesh relations. *South Asia Research*, 31 (3), pp. 195-211.

Great Decisions (1991). Media's role in shaping foreign policy. pp. 87-96.

Islam, M. S. (2015, March 4). Troubled waters: Discussing hydro-diplomacy and water cooperation in South Asia. *The Daily Star*. Retrieved from https://www.thedailystar.net/op-ed/politics/troubled-waters-4921

Karl, P. A. (1982). Media diplomacy. *Proceedings of the Academy of Political Science*, 34 (4), The Communications Revolution in Politics, pp. 143-152.

Khan, S. E. (2020, August 19). Wildly inappropriate views on Bangladesh in Indian foreign relations discourse and media. *NIICE*. Retrieved from https://niice.org.np/archives/5835

Knecht, T. & Weatherford, M. S. (2006). Public opinion and foreign policy: The stages of Presidential decision making. *International Studies Quarterly*, 50 (3), pp. 705-727

Kumaraswami, S. (2020, July 27). Relationship with India rock solid: Bangladesh. *Deccan Chronicle*. Retrieved from https://www.deccanchronicle.com/nation/in-other-news/270720/relationship-with-india-rock-solid-bangladesh.html

Malik, A. & Medcalf, R. (2011). India's new world: Civil Society in the making of foreign policy. Lowy Institute for International Policy. Retrieved from http://www.jstor.com/stable/resrep10152

Martens, Q. & Naether, M. (2009). NGOS' advocacy in European foreign policy: A new civil society. *Studia Diplomatica*, 62 (1), pp. 17-29.

MOFA, Dhaka (2020, September 29). Joint Statement on the Sixth Meeting of the India-Bangladesh Joint Consultative Commission. Retrieved from https://mofa.gov.bd/site/page/947fae98-5490-4700-a2cd-7b304de3eaf2

Mukharji. D. (2019, October 8). Delhi needs to do more to protect and deepen ties with Dhaka. *The Indian Express*. Retrieved from https://indianexpress.com/article/opinion/columns/india-bangladesh-relations-shiekh-hasina-narendra-modi-6058161/

Pukhrem, S. (2011, November 12). Need to broaden scope of India-Bangladesh engagement. *The Daily Star*.

Sharma, M. S. (2011, July 5). The Delhi-Dhaka distance. *The Indian Express*. Retrieved from http://archive.indianexpress.com/news/the-delhidhaka-distance/812740/0

Sinha, D. (2005). India and Bangladesh: Media and mediation in strengthening partnership. In S. Haidar (Ed.), *India-Bangladesh: Strengthening the Partnership* (pp. 65-78). Chandigarh, India: Centre for Research in Rural and Industrial Development.

Sobhan, R. (2002). Preface. In R. Sobhan (Ed.), *Bangladesh-India relations: Perspectives from civil society dialogues*, (pp. xiii-xxi). Dhaka: CPD & UPL.

The Business Standard (2020, August 18). Indian FS Harsh Vardhan arrives in Dhaka to boost ties. Retrieved from https://tbsnews.net/bangladesh/indian-fs-harsh-vardhan-arrives-dhaka-boost-ties-120973

The Daily Star (2000, January 20). MCCI supports transit facility to India.

The Daily Star (2010a, January 10). Mistrust must go to open new era of ties: Professionals hope for a fruitful India visit of PM.

The Daily Star (2010b, January 15). Analysts back opening ports to neighbours.

The Daily Star (2010c, January 28).'If north-east India develops, exports from Bangladesh will go up'. Interview with Dr. Mustafizur Rahman.

The Daily Star (2010d, February 26). Trade bodies vow to deepen ties: Dhaka declaration adopted on connectivity with northeastern states of India.

The Daily Star Editorial (2010a, January 3). Begum Zia must not prejudge Delhi outcome.

The Daily Star Editorial (2010b, January 10). Expectations from Indo-Bangla summit: Taking the relationship on to a new plane.

The Daily Star Editorial (2010c, January 13). Delhi summit a sign of productive bilateralism: We look forward to quick progress on water-sharing issue.

The Daily Star (2011a, February 6). Economist stresses deeper links with India.

The Daily Star (2011b, October 23). Regular contact for more Indo-Bangla ties urged.

The Daily Star (2013, August 18). Indo-Bangla Relations: Historic opportunity missed: Say senior journalists of the two countries. Retrieved from https://www.thedailystar.net/news/historic-opportunity-missed

The Daily Star (2019, April 14). Media linkage important for Bangladesh-India relations. Retrieved from https://www.thedailystar.net/city/news/media-linkage-important-bangladesh-india-relations-1729642

9

CHINA FACTOR IN BANGLADESH-INDIA TIES

ABSTRACT

How does the 'China factor' impact Bangladesh-India relations? This chapter investigates this question. Bangladesh enjoys warm relations with both China and India, which are important development partners of Bangladesh. But considering the growing Sino-Indian rivalry, India views improved Bangladesh-China relations sceptically. This chapter argues that neither India nor China should be worried about Bangladesh as the country follows 'friendship to all, and malice to none' policy on the one hand. And on the other, it believes that it is essential to maintain good relations with India and China for its continued growth, prosperity, and development.

Keywords: *China factor, Bangladesh-China relations, Bangladesh-India relations, Sino-Indian rivalry, 'Friendship to all and malice to none'.*

Introduction

From commerce to culture, institution to investment/infrastructure, energy to education, science and technology to socio-economy, Bangladesh-China relations have touched upon every aspect of human society that matters to the people of Bangladesh and China and beyond. The policy community in Bangladesh defines China as an 'all-weather friend'. The former foreign affairs advisor, Iftekhar Ahmed Chowdhury, contends that 'If there is anything constant in international relations, it is the friendship between China and Bangladesh' (*The Daily Star*, 2007). Similarly, China sees Bangladesh as a 'good neighbour and good partner'. In the popular discourse of Bangladesh, China is seen as a friend and development partner of Bangladesh due to increasing Chinese cooperation and less Chinese interference in the domestic affairs of the country. During the 1971 Liberation War of Bangladesh, China opposed the political settlement, and thus tilted towards Pakistan given the Cold War realities and China's close partnership with Pakistan. China also used its veto power against Bangladesh in the United Nations. But China and Bangladesh have overcome this hurdle and uplifted their bilateral relations to a new height. According to a 2015 Pew survey, for instance, 77 per cent Bangladeshis expressed a favourable view towards China (Smith, 2017). October 4, 2020, marked the 45th anniversary of their bilateral relations. Currently, both Bangladesh and China are enjoying a robust and comprehensive partnership which is often described as the 'trusted ally'. In addition, the declaration and celebration of 2005 as the 'China-Bangladesh Friend Year' and the formation of 'Closer Comprehensive Partnership of Cooperation' in 2010 by the leaders of China and Bangladesh demonstrates the consolidated level of China-Bangladesh relations. It can also be mentioned that Bangladesh is often identified by China as a 'close neighbour' (Ministry of Foreign Affairs, People's Republic of China, 2008). Besides, the visit of Prime Minister Sheikh Hasina to China in June 2014 and the return visit by China's President Xi Jinping in October 2016 elevated the Bangladesh-China bilateral relations to a new height. Bangladesh and China have turned their relationship into a strategic partnership in 2016. The growing Bangladesh-China partnership in the economic, security, strategic, and development realm has created concerns for India. On the one hand, there is growing Sino-Indian rivalry and the other, India wants to ensure its influence in Bangladesh. Thus, India views the growing Bangladesh-China relations sceptically. Against this backdrop, this chapter investigates: How does the China factor impact Bangladesh-India relations? And what is Bangladesh's response in countering Indian perceptions in the growing Bangladesh-China relations?

This chapter is divided into five sections, including an introduction and conclusion. The first section focuses on the background and aim of the chapter. The second discusses contemporary developments in Bangladesh-China relations. The third section explains the Chinese factor in Bangladesh-India relations, while the fourth focuses on Bangladesh's response. The final section concentrates on concluding remarks.

Contemporary Developments in Bangladesh-China Relations

In June 2014, during the official visit of Bangladesh Prime Minister Sheikh Hasina to China, Bangladesh and China entered into 'Deepening the Closer Comprehensive Partnership of Cooperation' comprising 20 paragraphs. Both sides agreed to 'intensify cooperation on trade, investment, finance, agriculture, science-technology-innovation, health, education, transportation and infrastructure development based on equitable mutual benefits' (Joint Statement of the People's Republic of China and the People's Republic of Bangladesh on Deepening the Closer Comprehensive Partnership of Cooperation, 2014). China's President Xi Jinping's return visit to Bangladesh in October 2016 resulted in 27 deals worth US$ 24.45 billion and was a milestone in boosting Bangladesh-China economic partnership. Consequently, the year 2017 has been designated as the 'Year of Friendship and Exchanges' between China and Bangladesh. In July 2019, Sheikh Hasina paid a five-day official visit to China during which Bangladesh and China signed nine instruments for further strengthening cooperation on power, water resources, culture, and tourism sectors as well as providing 2,500 tonnes of rice for the displaced Rohingyas. During her keynote speech at a roundtable with Chinese business leaders at the China Council for the Promotion of International Trade (CCPIT), Sheikh Hasina invited the Chinese business community to explore and harness the full trade potential with Bangladesh given the country's impressive economic growth over the past several years (*The Daily Star*, 2019a).

Bangladesh-China economic cooperation is growing rapidly. Article 5 of the 2014 Joint Statement between China and Bangladesh reads that 'economic cooperation and trade constitute an important part in forging closer comprehensive cooperative partnership between China and Bangladesh' (Joint Statement, 2014). Article 5 also states that both sides 'agreed to take further concrete measures to increase bilateral trade, widen economic cooperation and augment investment flow, with a view to reducing widening bilateral trade imbalance' (Joint Statement, 2014). Li Jiming, Chinese Ambassador in Bangladesh, contends that 'deepening cooperation in bilateral trade between China and Bangladesh is an inevitable choice to benefit the national economies and livelihoods, enhance the friendship between the two countries' (*UNB News*, 2020). The Ambassador noted that the volume of Bangladesh-China bilateral trade had grown rapidly. For instance, the bilateral trade volume was only US$ 3.06 million in 1975, which reached US$ 18.33 billion in 2019 (*UNB News*, 2020). China is the largest trading partner of Bangladesh, while Bangladesh is the second-largest trading partner of China in South Asia. Zhang Zuo, a former Chinese Ambassador to Bangladesh, notes that approximately 200 large Chinese companies and 200 Chinese SMEs are operational in Bangladesh.

There are some exciting developments in Bangladesh-China relations under the Sheikh Hasina regime (2009-present). For instance, in June 2020, China announced that 97 per cent products (a total of 8,256 products) from Bangladesh would be exempted from tariffs, as mentioned in chapter 8. Tariff exemption has been operational since July 1, 2020. Li Jiming contends that 'It will be a win-win cooperation for China and Bangladesh to fully explore China's import capability, catch up with the demand of the Chinese market, and strengthen bilateral trade' (*UNB News*, 2020). The Ambassador also noted that Bangladesh can immensely benefit from China's growing import market, which is expected to exceed US$ 30 trillion in the next 15 years.

Bangladesh has traditionally been supporting China with on its 'one China' policy which is also reaffirmed under the Sheikh Hasina regime (2009-present). Over the decades, India was Bangladesh's largest trading partner but has been replaced by China from 2004 onward. Bangladesh joined China's Belt and Road Initiative (BRI) in 2016, which has been viewed critically in India. Chinese Ambassador Jiming notes that Bangladesh-China economic cooperation has been further deepened under the BRI project (*UNB News*, 2020). Sheikh Fazle Fahim, president of the Federation of Bangladesh Chambers of Commerce and Industry, notes that 'For Bangladesh, BRI-related investment is spread across multiple sectors which will contribute to Bangladesh's rapid GDP growth, including infrastructure, connectivity and shipping' (Lingqing, 2019). The Bangladesh Power System Upgrade and Expansion Project is one of the key projects under BRI which has benefitted more than seven million Bangladeshis, providing electricity connections to over 2.5 million rural people (Hassan, 2019).

Chinese Investments in Bangladesh

In the fiscal year (FY) 2019 (ended June 30, 2019), China replaced the USA and became the top source of inflow of foreign direct investments in Bangladesh amounting to US$ 1,159.42 million ($1.16 billion), recording 130 per cent growth over US$ 506.14 million in FY18 (Kibria, 2019). For the first time, Chinese investment exceeded US$ 1 billion. Notably, China invested US$ 960.59 million in power sector development. China's Yabang Group, a leading dye and paint manufacturer, is set to invest US$ 300 million in establishing a textile and chemical industry on 100 acres at Bangabandhu Sheikh Mujib Shilpanagar (BSMSN), a flagship project of the Bangladesh Economic Zones Authority (Uddin, 2020).

Bangladesh has sought US$ 6.4 billion investments for nine development projects including the construction of the first phase of the Pyra seaport, and the construction of Bangladesh's longest bridge linking Barisal with the island district of Bhola (Rahaman, 2020a). According to Bangladesh government officials, there is the possibility that China might invest around US$ 50 billion in the next 15 years in Bangladesh (*The Daily Star*, 2019b). In August 2020, it was confirmed that China would provide US$ 970 million of loans to upgrade the electricity grids in Bangladesh. It is reported that out of the loan, US$ 690 million will be provided under preferential buyers' credit and US$ 280 million under the concessional government loan. A consortium of Chinese companies, including CCC Engineering Ltd., Jiangsu ETERN Co. Ltd., and Fujian Electric Power Company are contractors of the project of strengthening the power grid in Bangladesh (Rahaman, 2020b). Sheikh Fazle Fahim, president of the Federation of Bangladesh Chambers of Commerce and Industry, notes that around 400 Chinese companies are operational in Bangladesh in different sectors including power, textiles, weaving, leather, footwear, construction, engineering and non-banking financial institutions, with a net investment of US$ 1.03 billion in 2018 (Lingqing, 2019). In 2019, Bangladesh set-up a US$ 400 million joint venture with a Chinese company to build renewable energy projects to provide a total of 500 megawatts of power by 2023 (*The Financial Express*, 2019).

Defence Cooperation

Bangladesh and China signed a defence cooperation agreement in December 2002 during the visit of Khaleda Zia in China. Under the agreement, Bangladesh buys military hardware from China. Bangladesh has also bought two submarines from China. Bangladesh-China defence cooperation has also reached a new height (*bdnews24.com*, 2017). For instance, China is the major military hardware supplier to Bangladesh. Between 2011 and 2015, Bangladesh was the second-largest buyer of Chinese arms after Pakistan. In 2008, Bangladesh faced naval tensions in the Bay of Bengal with Myanmar. Thus, after assuming power in 2009, Sheikh Hasina decided to purchase submarines and consequently ordered two Type-035G Ming class submarines from China in 2013 at a cost of US$ 203 million (Jha, 2016). Finally, in November 2016, Bangladesh received the two submarines from China (*The Diplomat*, 2017).

There is a regular exchange of visits of military personnel between Bangladesh and China. In August 2013, General Iqbal Karim Bhuiyan, Chief of Army Staff of the Bangladesh Army, visited China. In August 2013, the Chinese Navy hospital ship 'Peace Ark' visited Chattogram. In September 2013, Chief of Air Staff of the Bangladesh Air Force Muhammad Enamul Bari visited China. In March 2015, China launched a new frigate for Bangladesh which will augment the coastal defence capability of the Bangladesh Navy. In the areas of detection, identification and destruction of surface and aerial targets, maritime monitoring and patrols, and search and rescue missions, the frigate will be useful (*The Daily Star*, 2015).

In October 2018, Bangladesh and China signed three documents in Dhaka on security cooperation titled 'Plan of Action on Law Enforcement Training Cooperation,' Cooperation document on the establishment of a joint working group and a Letter of exchange on police equipment. Both sides agreed to cooperate on Intelligence sharing and to fight terrorism and transnational crime together (*The Independent*, 2018). In October 2020, Bangladesh procured seven Chinese-made K-8W training aircraft under an agreement to modernise its Air Force. Thus, Bangladesh and China have entered into a new development and security partnership which is mostly viewed by India as a matter of concern. The next section discusses India's concerns on the Bangladesh-China partnership.

India's Concerns and Responses

The geostrategic location of Bangladesh makes it an important country for both India and China. In this regard, Arafat Kabir (2014) writes that

'Bangladesh, sitting between two heavyweights – India and China – faces an intriguing challenge to balance its relationships with Beijing and Delhi. However, India, which engulfs Bangladesh on three sides, has more leverage on Dhaka than any other nation has'. It is argued that 'in recent years China has made significant gains in countries such as Myanmar, Nepal, and Bangladesh. In so doing it has eroded some of the historic advantages that India enjoyed in these countries' (Datta, 2008, p.756). Bangladesh's growing partnership with China is viewed critically from the Indian side. *Firstpost* (2020), for instance, notes that 'Although Bangladesh under Sheikh Hasina has broadly had warm relations with India, New Delhi has a good reason to view the involvement of Dhaka in the BRI with concern'. Thus, the daily concludes that 'As China forges closer ties with Bangladesh through the BRI, India needs to work both on maintaining good ties with Dhaka and also countering the influence of the initiative through strategic alliances' (*Firstpost*, 2020). Also, Constantino Xavier, fellow (Foreign Policy Studies), Brookings India and the Brookings Institution, Washington DC, contends that 'China has always been present in Bangladesh, including in the defence sector, but India's sensitivity has naturally increased after the Ladakh standoff. Delhi is now pushing Dhaka to reduce its relations with China, and Dhaka is naturally pushing back so it can receive maximum benefits from China without upsetting India' (cited in Basu, 2020a). It is reported that 'India is concerned that China, which has been "targeting all of India's friendly neighbours" such as Nepal and Sri Lanka, will now focus on turning Bangladesh against New Delhi, at a time when Dhaka is already unhappy over the National Register of Citizens (NRC) and a host of other issues' (Basu, 2020a). Rouhin Deb (2020) argues that 'China has started to woo Bangladesh to expand its influence in the region'. P.R. Kumar (2020) writes that

> Since the LAC standoff with India, China has begun courting India's neighbours even more vigorously, especially Bangladesh and Nepal. Beijing has granted duty-free access to 97 percent of Bangladeshi products from July 1 and is examining a request for $64 billion through the Investment Cooperation Working Group with China, which was established in 2019. With this move, as many as 8,256 Bangladeshi items will enjoy duty-free access to Chinese markets. All these moves have made the Modi government even (more) concerned about President Xi's growing influence in Bangladesh, which at present is the closest to India in the neighbourhood.

Shantanu Mukharji (2020) writes that:

> In fact there appears to be a strong pro-China lobby active in Bangladesh influencing public opinion to gradually abandon India and give a fresh look to Sino-Bangladesh relations. Soon after the Chinese misadventures in Ladakh, Bangladesh newspapers, in very provocative tenor, carried columns questioning India on its 'silence' and refraining from retaliation as seen with the Balakot strikes in the wake of the Pulwama terror attack of 2019. The language used in these narratives could easily be interpreted as anti-India and pro-China. Similarly, debates were generated in popular Bangladesh TV channels with many showing a tilt towards China.

Thus, there is an apparent concern raised by the Indian academic community over China's growing partnership with Bangladesh. One can also note that there is growing Sino-Indian rivalry in the maritime domain. Notably, Bangladesh cooperates with both India and China in the case of maritime cooperation. For instance, Bangladesh signed a blue economy and maritime cooperation agreement with both of them. India views Bangladesh's naval cooperation with China sceptically. It is argued that due to the Sino-Indian rivalry, port development in Bangladesh was delayed and the Bangladeshi expert community believes that due to India's concern, the China-funded Sonadia deep-sea port project was cancelled by the Bangladesh authority which pleased India.

Against the backdrop of India's concerns over the growing Bangladesh-China partnership, one can ask: How should India respond to the ever-increasing Bangladesh-China relations? The Indian academic community provides some suggestions to the Indian government. Deb (2020) suggests that India needs to be 'more accommodating on various matters of international affairs' with Bangladesh and thus develop its relations with Bangladesh based on trust and well-being rather than short term financial gains. Mozammil Ahmad (2020) concludes that 'At a time when India is losing its relations with neighbouring countries, instead of mocking Dhaka's relations with another country, India must double its efforts to sustain the long friendship with Bangladesh'. Rouhin Deb (2020) prescribes that

> India cannot match China in terms of investment, so it better carve its own niche to be in the game. As far as Bangladesh is concerned, it shares lot of cultural and linguistic similarities with the States of Assam,

West Bengal and Tripura. India might therefore rather build on these similarities and strengthen ties through various cultural and intellectual exchanges with Bangladesh, which would rather have long-term positive implications.

Indian investment in Bangladesh is about US$ 3 billion while China's investment is US$ 26 billion, with a funding commitment of about US$ 38 billion. The volume of Bangladesh-China trade was worth US$ 18 billion in 2019, while the Bangladesh-India trade volume amounted to about US$ 10 billion (Singh, 2020). Given the growing partnership between Bangladesh and China, India is also trying to reach out to Bangladesh at its maximum level to counter China's influence. The visit of India's Foreign Secretary Harsh Shringla in Bangladesh in August 2020 during the COVID-19 pandemic underscores the importance that India attaches to Bangladesh. Notably, it was the first visit of Shringla as Indian Foreign Secretary since the COVID-19 outbreak. It is argued that 'as China backs Bangladesh more aggressively', the Narendra Modi government sent its Foreign Secretary to Dhaka even during travel restrictions (Basu, 2020b). According to the Statement of the Visit published in the Indian Ministry of External Affairs official website, 'India's proposal to launch a travel air bubble between the two countries opening limited flights for official, business and medical travellers was appreciated by the Bangladesh side. There were discussions relating to the cooperation in the areas of security, including fencing and joint efforts to prevent trans-border crimes. The issue of safe repatriation of internally displaced persons from the Rakhine state also came up for discussion' (MEA, 2020). It is argued that the visit has boosted India's relations with Bangladesh (Bhattacharjee, 2020). Notably, the travel air bubble became operational in October 2020. Thus, one can conclude that India needs to be more engaging and constructive concerning its relations with Bangladesh instead of critiquing Bangladesh's growing partnership with China.

Bangladesh's Response

One can ask: How is Bangladesh responding to the Sino-Indian rivalry and its impact on Bangladesh? Bangladeshi experts believe that India should not be worried about Bangladesh-China relations (*The Business Standard*, 2020). In fact, Bangladesh has been able to maintain good relations with all countries, including India and China, due to the 'friendship to all, malice to none' foreign policy principle of Sheikh Hasina. According to Sheikh Hasina,

> [W]hat's the problem with it (maintaining ties with both China and India)? We have ties with all our neighbours. Bangladesh has no animosity with anyone because we are following the lesson taught by the Father of the Nation Bangabandhu Sheikh Mujibur Rahman. We are also moving forward internationally by following a policy of – 'friendship to all, malice to none'. We have friendly ties with all. That's why Bangladesh is receiving more investment now (*bdnews24.com*, 2019).

Bangladesh believes in peaceful coexistence and its 'friendship to all and malice to none' policy. Against the backdrop of June 2020, the Sino-Indian border clash in Ladakh, Bangladesh Foreign Minister, A.K. Abdul Momen told the *Dhaka Tribune* that 'Our position is always clear. We want peace, not conflict. Both China and India are our friends. We do hope both China and India will de-escalate the situation immediately and resolve all issues through negotiations. We believe in peaceful coexistence among neighbours in the interest of development' (cited in Bhuiyan, 2020). The Minister also notes that 'Bangladesh's relations with India are rock-solid and historic while Bangladesh has economic ties with China. We must not compare' (*The Daily Star*, 2020). So, there is nothing to be worried for India.

Conclusion

The transformation of Bangladesh-China relations has impacted millions of people in Bangladesh and China in one way or the other. Behind the economic success story of Bangladesh, the role of China and India is undeniable. Bangladesh-China cooperation also has broader regional implications. As the current Chinese Ambassador to Bangladesh, Li Jiming, writes: 'The cooperation between China and Bangladesh not only benefits the peoples of the two countries but also benefits regional development and stability' (Jiming, 2020). Thus, this chapter suggests that instead of critiquing Bangladesh-China relations, India needs to address Bangladesh's concerns, i.e., the water sharing issue, trade imbalance, and the NRC issue. This chapter also argues that India should not be worried about Bangladesh-China relations as Bangladesh values its partnership with both India and China. In fact, if Bangladesh develops, it will be of interest to both India and China. Thus, India and China need to think about whether India-Bangladesh-China trilateral cooperation can be forged and whether it will be imperative to the benefit of the people of these countries and beyond. This chapter also suggests that in developing trilateral cooperation, the role of the media and academics needs to be constructive.

REFERENCES

Ahmad, M. (2020, July 8). Bangladesh and the China-India Conflict. *The Diplomat*. Retrieved from https://thediplomat.com/2020/07/bangladesh-and-the-china-india-conflict/

Basu, N. (2020a, July 31). China takes Bangladesh into its embrace now as Delhi-Dhaka ties go downhill. *The Print*. Retrieved from https://theprint.in/diplomacy/china-takes-bangladesh-into-its-embrace-now-as-delhi-dhaka-ties-go-downhill/471769/

Basu, N. (2020b, August 18). Modi govt rushes FS Shringla to Dhaka today as China backs Bangladesh more aggressively. *The Print*. Retrieved from https://theprint.in/diplomacy/foreign-secretary-harsh-shringla-to-visit-bangladesh-today-set-to-meet-pm-hasina/483881/

bdnews24.com (2017, July 31). China-Bangladesh defence relations reach 'unprecedented heights'. Retrieved from: http://bdnews24.com/bangladesh/2017/07/31/china-bangladesh-defence-relations-reach-unprecedented-heights

bdnews24.com (2019, July 4). Friendly foreign policy increasing investment in Bangladesh, says PM Hasina. Retrieved from https://bdnews24.com/bangladesh/2019/07/04/friendly-foreign-policy-increasing-investment-in-bangladesh-says-pm-hasina

Bhattacharjee, J. (2020, September 8). Bangladesh: Indian Foreign Secretary's visit boosts bilateral ties. Observer Research Foundation. Retrieved from https://www.orfonline.org/expert-speak/bangladesh-indian-foreign-secretarys-visit-boosts-bilateral-ties/

Bhuiyan, H. K. (2020, June 17). Bangladesh wants China, India to de-escalate situation. *Dhaka Tribune*. Retrieved from https://www.dhakatribune.com/bangladesh/2020/06/17/bangladesh-wants-china-india-to-de-escalate-situation

Datta, S. (2008). Bangladesh's relations with China and India: A comparative study. *Strategic Analysis*, 32:5, pp. 755-772, DOI: 10.1080/09700160802309134

Deb, R. (2020, September 1). Will India lose Bangladesh as an ally? *The Hindu Business Line*. Retrieved from https://www.thehindubusinessline.com/opinion/will-india-lose-bangladesh-as-an-ally/article32498065.ece#

Hassan, M. E. (2019, November 15). Bangladesh can walk a long way thanks to BRI. *People's Daily Online*. Retrieved from http://en.people.cn/n3/2019/1115/c90000-9632652.html

Jha, S. (2016, December 30). The Bay of Bengal naval arms race. *The Diplomat*. Retrieved from https://thediplomat.com/2016/12/the-bay-of-bengal-naval-arms-race/

Jiming, L. (2020, June 7). Building a China-Bangladesh community of public health through solidarity and cooperation. *UNB News*. Retrieved from http://www.unb.com.bd/category/Opinion/building-a-china-bangladesh-community-of-public-health-through-solidarity-and-cooperation/52694

Joint Statement between the People's Republic of China and the People's Republic of Bangladesh on Deepening the Closer Comprehensive Partnership of Cooperation (2014, June 10). Embassy of the People's Republic of China in the People's Republic of Bangladesh. Retrieved from http://bd.china-embassy.org/eng/zmgx/zywj/t1165885.htm

Kabir, A. (2014, April 7). Modi-fying our strategy. *Dhaka Tribune*.

Kibria, A. (2019, November 3). China top source of FDI in BD. *The Financial Express*. Retrieved from https://thefinancialexpress.com.bd/economy/china-top-source-of-fdi-in-bd-1572769449

Kumar, P. R. (2020, September 1). China specter over South Asia impacting India-Bangladesh ties. *South Asia Monitor*. Retrieved from https://southasiamonitor.org/spotlight/china-specter-over-south-asia-impacting-india-bangladesh-ties

Lingqing, Z. (2019, July 5). BRI-related investments bring substantial benefits for Bangladesh. *China Daily*. Retrieved from https://www.chinadaily.com.cn/a/201907/05/WS5d1e9fa7a3105895c2e7bceb.html

MEA, Government of India (2020, August 26). Statement on Foreign Secretary's Visit to Dhaka on 18–19 August 2020. Retrieved from https://www.mea.gov.in/press-releases.htm?dtl/32913/Statement+on+Foreign+Secretarys+Visit+to+Dhaka+on+18++19+August+2020

Ministry of Foreign Affairs, People's Republic of China (2008, October 20). Ambassador Zheng Qingdian Gave Lecture at Bangladesh National Defence College.

Mukharji, S. (2020, August 4). Delhi must preserve ties with Dhaka. *The Statesman*. Retrieved from https://www.thestatesman.com/opinion/delhi-must-preserve-ties-with-dhaka-1502914090.html

Rahaman, M. M. (2020a, June 29). BD seeks $6.4b Chinese fund for new projects. *The Financial Express*. Retrieved from https://thefinancialexpress.com.bd/economy/bd-seeks-64b-chinese-fund-for-new-projects-1593400758

Rahaman, M. M. (2020b, August 8). BD gets $1.0b China loan to improve power grid. *The Financial Express*. Retrieved from https://thefinancialexpress.com.bd/economy/bangladesh/bd-gets-10b-china-loan-to-improve-power-grid-1596857911

Singh, A.I. (2020, October 21). Is India slipping behind? Bangladesh reveals India's challenged pre-eminence in the Bay of Bengal. *Times of India*. Retrieved from https://timesofindia.indiatimes.com/blogs/toi-edit-page/is-india-slipping-behind-bangladesh-reveals-indias-challenged-pre-eminence-in-the-bay-of-bengal/

Smith, J. M. (2017, January 20). Why China's submarine deal with Bangladesh matters. *The Diplomat*. Retrieved from http://thediplomat.com/2017/01/why-chinas-submarine-deal-with-bangladesh-matters/

The Business Standard (2020, August 30). India should not be worried about Bangladesh-China relationship: Experts. Retrieved from https://tbsnews.net/foreign-policy/india-should-not-be-worried-about-bangladesh-china-relationship-experts-125917

The Daily Star (2007, April 12). Sino-Bangla ties to grow further. Retrieved from http://archive.thedailystar.net/2007/04/12/d70412060767.htm

The Daily Star (2015, January 1). China launches new frigate for Bangladesh navy. Retrieved from https://www.thedailystar.net/china-launches-new-frigate-for-bangladesh-navy-57961

The Daily Star (2019a, July 5). Explore full trade potential with Bangladesh: PM urges

Chinese businesses. Retrieved from https://www.thedailystar.net/business/news/explore-full-trade-potential-bangladesh-1766893

The Daily Star (2019b, December 19). Better China-Bangladesh connectivity a must. Retrieved from https://www.thedailystar.net/city/news/better-china-bangladesh-connectivity-must-1842458

The Daily Star (2020, August 9). Relations with Delhi, Beijing must not be compared: Says foreign minister.

The Diplomat (2017, January 20). Why China's submarine deal with Bangladesh matters. Retrieved from https://thediplomat.com/2017/01/why-chinas-submarine-deal-with-bangladesh-matters/

Firstpost (2020, October 5). As China draws Bangladesh closer into BRI embrace, India must step up efforts to secure its regional interests. Retrieved from https://www.firstpost.com/india/as-china-draws-bangladesh-closer-into-bri-embrace-india-must-step-up-efforts-to-secure-its-regional-interests-8880531.html

The Financial Express (2019, August 29). Chinese firm to build renewable power projects in Bangladesh. Retrieved from https://thefinancialexpress.com.bd/public/trade/chinese-firm-to-build-renewable-power-projects-in-bangladesh-1567062123

The Independent (2018, October 26). Bangladesh, China sign 3 docs on security cooperation: Dhaka, Beijing agree on Intel sharing; fight terrorism together. Retrieved from http://www.theindependentbd.com/post/171994

Uddin, S. (2020, July 27). Chinese Yabang set to invest $300m. *The Financial Express*. Retrieved from https://thefinancialexpress.com.bd/trade/chinese-yabang-set-to-invest-300m-1595822263

UNB News (2020, June 30). Economic ties with China set to enter 'significant new stage' of cooperation: BD to remain most dynamic economy in South Asia, says Beijing. Retrieved from https://unb.com.bd/category/Bangladesh/economic-ties-with-china-set-to-enter-significant-new-stage-of-cooperation/53917

10

COVID-19, POST-COVID-19 WORLD AND BANGLADESH-INDIA COOPERATION

ABSTRACT

The COVID-19 global pandemic has serious foreign policy consequences including for Bangladesh-India relations. For instance, Bangladesh-India bilateral visits, trade, investment, travel, and various projects halted or slowed down due to the pandemic on the one hand and on the other, while many countries stopped cooperating with each other, the world witnessed Bangladesh-India cooperation on many grounds, including medical cooperation and cooperation over connectivity. It is often argued that the 'new normal' brought about by the pandemic would prevail everywhere, even in the conduct of the state's foreign relations. Thus, this chapter asks: How does the COVID-19 global pandemic affect a state's foreign policy in general and Bangladesh-India relations in particular? What would be the nature of Bangladesh-India relations in the post-COVID-19 world? What would be the future course of action for Bangladesh and India in the post-COVID-19 world to deepen the bilateral partnership?

Keywords: *COVID-19, Bangladesh-India Relations, Post-COVID-19 World Order, Medical Cooperation.*

Introduction

The COVID-19 global pandemic is also known as coronavirus disease, which began at the end of 2019 in China and has spread all over the world and thus impacted both states and people. The pandemic has shaken the world with broader implications at the domestic, regional and global scale in the domain of economy, security, foreign policy, and diplomacy. Itty Abraham (2020) writes that 'There have been remarkably few truly global turning points in the last century and a half, so calling the COVID-19 coronavirus pandemic a historic turning point is no small matter'. The coronavirus crisis created not only a health crisis but also an economic crisis and affected normal relations between people and states. Thus, normal bilateral relations, whether by bilateral visits, trade, investment, and people-to-people contacts have been affected severely. One can argue that the novel coronavirus has serious foreign policy consequences (Fuchs, 2020). In addition, the rise of extreme nationalism and a protectionist policy during the coronavirus pandemic has also been observed globally. Armando Barucco, director of the Policy Planning Unit of the Italian Ministry of Foreign Affairs and International Cooperation, writes that 'There is little doubt that the extreme forms of nationalism and isolationism that have pervaded public discourse and foreign policy in recent years will become even stronger and more vocal' because of COVID-19 (Barucco, 2020). It is often argued that the 'new normal' brought about by the pandemic would prevail everywhere, even in the conduct of a state's foreign relations. Thus, this chapter asks: How does the COVID-19 global pandemic affect Bangladesh-India relations? What would be the nature of Bangladesh-India relations in the post-COVID-19 world? What would be the future course of action for Bangladesh and India in the post-COVID-19 world to deepen the bilateral partnership?

This chapter has three main sections, excluding the introduction and conclusion. The first discusses COVID-19 impacts on foreign policy while the second section focuses on the pandemic's implications on Bangladesh-India ties. The final section maps Bangladesh-India relations in the post-pandemic era while it is argued that there is no alternative to promoting Bangladesh-India cooperation in the post-pandemic era.

Implications of COVID-19 on Foreign Policy

Impact on State Behaviour
Scholars are divided regarding the impacts of COVID-19 on the state's behaviour. The pro-state progressive school of thought thinks that the pandemic has brought the end the of so-called Washington Consensus

that promoted Neo-liberalism based on free market and privatisation. It is argued that the pandemic has demonstrated the necessity for a well-resourced and responsive state. However, there is another school of thought, called end-of-globalisation pessimists, who argue that the COVID-19 global health crisis has brought about the end of the current globalisation era and a return of inter-state competition. They further argue that the inter-connected world under contemporary economic globalisation has been imperative to spread the disease. The end-of-globalisation pessimists additionally show the limits of international cooperation, multilateral institutions and global supply chains that made the states more vulnerable to the pandemic. Pessimists further argue that the states of the world could take lessons from the pandemic and thus embrace 'relative international autarky' (cited in Abraham, 2020). Joseph S. Nye notes that 'More likely, however, the new coronavirus will simply accelerate existing trends toward nationalist populism, authoritarianism, and tense relations between the United States and China' (Harvard Kennedy School, 2020). Stephen Walt points out that:

> COVID-19 is more likely to reinforce divisive trends that were underway before the first case was detected. In particular, it will accelerate a retreat from globalisation, raise new barriers to international trade, investment, and travel, and give both democratic and non-democratic governments' greater power to track and monitor their citizens' lives. Global economic growth will be substantially lower than it would have been had the pandemic not occurred. Relations among the major powers will continue the downward trend that was apparent before the pandemic struck (Harvard Kennedy School, 2020).

Robin Niblett contends that

> It seems highly unlikely in this context that the world will return to the idea of mutually beneficial globalisation that defined the early 21st century. And without the incentive to protect the shared gains from global economic integration, the architecture of global economic governance established in the 20th century will quickly atrophy. It will then take enormous self-discipline for political leaders to sustain international cooperation and not retreat into overt geopolitical competition (Allen *et al.*, 2020).

In fact, empirical evidence supports the pessimists' view as the COVID-19 global pandemic has shown the world that many countries including the developed ones closed doors of cooperation and followed protectionist policies with regard to exporting medical equipment including personal protective equipment (PPE) and food items. It is reported that by March 2020, nearly 60 countries, including the European Union, restricted exporting medical equipment, i.e., personal protective equipment, including face shields, surgical masks and gowns (Boykoff 2020). And by the first week of April 2020, the USA restricted export of critical medical gear (Bade 2020; Toosi 2020). Some countries, including the United Kingdom, banned the export of essential medicines for COVID-19 patients (Rees, 2020). In a joint study by the European University Institute, Global Trade Alert, and World Bank Group (2020) it was found that since the beginning of 2020, nearly 86 jurisdictions were reported which executed a total of 157 export controls of medical supplies and medicines. Export curbs on food are also manifested (see Table 6). Notably, 27 jurisdictions are reported executing a total of 39 export controls since the beginning of 2020 (European University Institute *et al.* 2020).

Table 6: Total Number of New Export Controls and Import Eeforms in Sensitive Sectors since January 2020, by Month (updated on May 22, 2020)

Month of implementation	No. of new cases	Type	Sector
January	2	Export curb	Medical sector
February	16	Export curb	Medical sector
March	96	Export curb	Medical sector
April	41	Export curb	Medical sector
May	2	Export curb	Medical sector
February	1	Export curb	Food
March	16	Export curb	Food
April	22	Export curb	Food
January	3	Import reforms	Medical sector
February	5	Import reforms	Medical sector
March	84	Import reforms	Medical sector
April	56	Import reforms	Medical sector
May	5	Import reforms	Medical sector
January	1	Import reforms	Food
February	-	Import reforms	Food
March	10	Import reforms	Food
April	19	Import reforms	Food
May	2	Import reform	Food

Source: EUI *et al.* (2020).

Against the claim of the end or decline of globalisation, Kishore Mahbubani argues that 'The COVID-19 pandemic will not fundamentally alter global economic directions. It will only accelerate a change that had already begun: a move away from U.S.-centric globalisation to a more China-centric globalisation' (Allen *et al.*, 2020). Shivshankar Menon thinks that 'this is not yet the end of an interconnected world. The pandemic itself is proof of our interdependence' (Allen *et al.*, 2020). In the context of Bangladesh-India relations, we see that though the border was closed to contain the spread of the disease, both nations cooperated on the issue of addressing the crisis. The next section explains the implications of the COVID-19 global pandemic on Bangladesh-India relations.

COVID-19 and Bangladesh-India Ties

In addressing COVID-19 global pandemic impacts, Bangladesh-India cooperation is manifested at the regional level. Bangladesh, along with other South Asian nations, responded positively when India convened a video conference on March 15, 2020, with other South Asian leaders to craft a regional response to address the coronavirus crisis. In the conference, several decisions were taken to combat the novel coronavirus, e.g., Creation of SAARC COVID 29 Emergency Fund, Rapid Response Teams for COVID-19, Online Training Capsules, Video Conference of Trade Officials, COVID Website, Integrated Health Platform for Disease Surveillance, and Creation of Research Platforms. India pledged US$ 10 million, Bangladesh pledged US$ 1.5 million, Afghanistan, US$ 1 million, Bhutan US$ 1 lakh, Maldives US$ 2 lakh, Nepal, US$ 8.31 lakh and Sri Lanka US$ 5 million. It was decided that the fund will be owned and operated by respective member states. Bangladesh also proposed hosting a research institute to fight future public health threats in the SAARC Region (MOFA, Dhaka, 2020a).

During the COVID-19 global pandemic, while some media portals based in Northeast India spread misinformation about the reduction of warmth in Bangladesh-India relations, Bangladesh Foreign Minister Abdul Momen describes Bangladesh-India ties as 'blood relationship', 'rock solid' while India described its relations with Bangladesh as 'exceptionally close' (*The Business Standard*, 2020a). Echoing the warm sentiments, Indian External Affairs Minister S. Jaishankar claims that 'very few countries in the world share such close fraternal ties as those of ours...our partnership today stands out as a role model in the region for good neighbourly relations' (Kumaraswami, 2020). Indian scholar, Joyeeta Bhattacharjee (2020), writes that 'The cooperation between the two countries has deepened in areas of tackling disasters like the Covid-19 pandemic and connectivity' (Bhattacharjee, 2020). Notably, during the pandemic, India has provided 10 Broad Gauge (BG) locomotives to Dhaka to boost railway connectivity between Bangladesh and India. In the Joint Statement on the Sixth Meeting of the India-Bangladesh Joint Consultative Commission, held on September 29, 2020, it is noted that

> The first trial movement of cargo from Kolkata to North East India through roads and waterways of Bangladesh, signing of the second addendum to the Protocol on Inland Water Transit and Trade, export of goods from India using rail route, including container and parcel trains, are initiatives which could be taken successfully despite the COVID induced constraints, reflecting the excellent understanding shared between the two countries (MOFA, Dhaka 2020b).

On August 18, 2020, during the COVID-19 global pandemic, Indian Foreign Secretary Harsh Vardhan Shringla visited Bangladesh to discuss the progress and prospects of Bangladesh-India relations which demonstrate the importance that New Delhi attaches to Dhaka. In this regard, Masud Bin Momen, the Foreign Secretary of Bangladesh, contends that 'When countries around the world have been stagnant in terms of diplomatic relations amid the ongoing pandemic, Indian Foreign Secretary has come to our country to discuss and take forward cooperation on matters of mutual interest' (*The Business Standard*, 2020b). The Indian Foreign Secretary reiterated that Bangladesh comes first in the context of India's 'neighbourhood first' policy. Both sides discussed ways to address issues arising out of the COVID-19 situation (Chaudhury, 2020).

During the pandemic, various dimensions in the bilateral ties were halted, including trade, investment, and people's movement. In addition, the June 2020 Sino-Indian border clash and the Chinese announcement of zero-tariff benefits for the 97 per cent of Bangladeshi products to China created concern in different corners of India which motivated India to reinforce its relations with Bangladesh. Thus, Bangladesh received priority in Indian foreign policy formulation which prompted the Indian Foreign Secretary's visit during COVID-19. After the meeting, the Indian Foreign Secretary contends that 'The bilateral relations between Bangladesh and

India are far better now than before. India gave much importance in strengthening relations with Bangladesh in Covid' (*The Business Standard*, 2020b). Notably, it was Shringla's first trip abroad since the COVID-19 global pandemic outbreak. The Indian Foreign Secretary also assures that Bangladesh would get priority in getting the COVID-19 vaccine once it is produced in India (*The Daily Star*, 2020). Consequently, an MoU was signed in November 2020 between the Serum Institute of India and Beximco Pharma of Bangladesh for priority delivery of 30 million doses of COVID-19 vaccine to Bangladesh.

The COVID-19 global pandemic had some direct impact on Bangladesh-India relations. **First,** Bangladesh-India bilateral trade has halted due to the COVID-19 global pandemic. From March 2020 until the first week of June, India suspended all trade activity with Bangladesh through land ports which severely impacted bilateral trade. According to Bangladesh Bank, the volume of bilateral trade was worth US$ 2 billion during April-May in 2019 which decreased to US$ 421 million for the same period in 2020 due to the pandemic (Noyon, 2020). In addition, in the 2020 budget, India announced protectionist policies focusing on increasing tariffs and non-tariff barriers. Against the backdrop of Indian External Affairs Minister, S. Jaishankar's criticism of free trade and globalisation and India's move towards embracing the ideology of 'swadeshi', Prabhas Ranjan (2020) writes that 'Trade protectionism seems to be the official policy, with the government following the path of its ideological leanings'. While India-Bangladesh economic cooperation would be imperative against the backdrop of protectionist policies in other parts of the world in the pandemic and post-pandemic world, India's protectionist policy will negatively impact Bangladesh-India trade relations.

Second, due to the lockdown, regular flights were stopped, and the border was closed. As a result, regular Bangladeshi patients were not able to visit Indian doctors and hospitals which hampered their medical treatment. Later, Bangladesh and India established air connectivity under an 'air bubble arrangement' amid the pandemic.

Post-COVID-19 World and Bangladesh-India Cooperation

If one looks at it theoretically, Stephen Walt contends that 'the post-COVID-19 world will be less open, less free, less prosperous, and more competitive than the world that many people expected to emerge only a few years ago' (Harvard Kennedy School, 2020). Syed Sharfuddin (2020, p.249) contends that 'It is most likely that countries will adopt greater protectionist policies and impose high tariffs on imports to support their local industries. Until the economies of major industrialised countries stabilise, there could also be tariff wars on selected manufactured goods to protect national economies'. It is argued that in the post-pandemic world, poorer nations will be hard hit due to the global economic fallout. In this context, it becomes important to map the nature and scope of Bangladesh-India relations in the post-COVID-19 world.

Economic diplomacy, Rohingya repatriation diplomacy, regional and sub-regional cooperation, global health cooperation, blue economy diplomacy and international organisations would be dominant area in the post-pandemic diplomacy of Bangladesh. On the contrary, while addressing (virtual) the inaugural session of a course on 'India and the reshaping of the world order' at St Stephen's College, India's Foreign Secretary Harsh Shringla, outlines India's foreign policy priorities in the post-pandemic world. According to Shringla, 'neighbourhood first', BIMSTEC, 'Act East' policy, Think West', India's outreach to the Gulf and West Asian countries, multilateralism, 'global order based on rules in post-Covid-19 world' would be prioritised in the foreign policy formulations of India in the post-COVID-19 world (*Hindustan Times*, 2020). The Foreign Secretary also claims that 'We would like a new form of globalisation, based on fairness, equality and humanity in the post-COVID world' (*Hindustan Times*, 2020).

This chapter argues that Bangladesh and India need to promote cooperation in certain areas in the post-pandemic world. **First**, in the post-COVID-19 world, one can contend that India will go for more protectionist policies as it is already reflected in its 2020 budget. Instead of embracing protectionist policies, this chapter argues for increasing economic cooperation in order to face the post-pandemic world.

Second, Bangladesh and India need to promote cooperation on human security issues. The COVID-19 global pandemic has caused insecurity to millions of people in Bangladesh and India, including health, food, and economic insecurity (Chaudhary *et al.*, 2020; Hossain and Islam, 2020). Due to long lockdown measures for many months to contain the pandemic, and because of global supply chain shock, thousands of people in Bangladesh and India have lost their jobs/livelihood. Many Bangladeshi and Indian expatriates have lost their jobs abroad, which has impacted the food security of those affected families directly. Also, the loss of remittances to the national economy of these nations has implications for national food security. Besides, due to the global supply chain shocks, many international buyers have cancelled their orders in ready-made garments in Bangladesh and India. As a result, many garments workers have lost their jobs. This has resulted in acute food insecurity for them as well as for their family. Thus, in the post-COVID-19 world, Bangladesh and India need to promote cooperation in the broader human security areas, including health and food security. It is wise to be prepared to face any future pandemic which requires cooperation both at the regional and global level. Along with promoting bilateral cooperation, Bangladesh and India need to work together to deepen health cooperation at the regional and international level for the benefit of the people of these two countries and beyond.

Third, it is found that the coronavirus crisis might 'affect the state of contemporary terrorism. In...10 different ways...the pandemic could impact the terrorism landscape in the short, medium and long terms. These range from terrorists leveraging an increased susceptibility to radicalisation and inciting a rise in anti-government attitudes, even reconsidering the utility of bioterrorism' (Ackerman & Peterson, 2020, p.59). It is also argued that 'the pandemic responses have created opportunities for armed actors and left civilians more exposed to violence' (Mustasilta, 2020, p.1). Therefore, alongside economic and human security cooperation, Bangladesh and India need to deepen security cooperation against terrorist activities arising due to the COVID-19 crisis.

Finally, the global South, including Bangladesh and India, is severely affected due to the coronavirus crisis. In this context, McCann and Matenga (2020, p.161) argue that 'The impact of the COVID-19 pandemic on the global South will be formidable and will take decades to recover from'. Against such a backdrop, Bangladesh and India need to collaborate on the international platforms to ensure fair treatment by the global North to the global South in the areas of climate change, free trade, global health governance, food security, and global inequality.

Conclusion

This chapter examines the narratives on Bangladesh-India relations during the COVID-19 global pandemic and maps the direction of bilateral ties in the post-pandemic era. This chapter finds that there is a positive sign of cooperation between India and Bangladesh in the COVID-19 era in the areas of health cooperation, cooperation over air connectivity, and political interaction. But it is ironic that India's move towards a protectionist policy might seriously impact Bangladesh-India economic ties. As a result, the Bangladeshi business community will be the largest sufferer. There is also India's promise of providing COVID-19 vaccine to Bangladesh on a priority basis. This chapter suggests that Bangladesh and India need to promote health and economic cooperation in the post-pandemic era instead of embracing protectionist policies. This chapter concludes by arguing that, in the post-pandemic world, Bangladesh and India need to work together to advance the wellbeing, security and prosperity of the people of these two countries, the region of South Asia and beyond.

REFERENCES

Abraham, I. (2020, May 1). Four future scenarios, or, What's different about the Covid-19 crisis? *The India Forum*. Retrieved from https://www.theindiaforum.in/article/what-s-different-about-covid-19-crisis

Ackerman, G. & Peterson, H. (2020). Terrorism and COVID-19: Actual and potential impacts. *Perspectives on Terrorism*, 14 (3), pp. 59-73.

Allen, J., Burns, J., Garrett, L., Haass, R. N., Ikenberry, G. J., Mahbubani, K., Menon, S., Niblett, R., Nye Jr., J.S., O'Neil, S. K., Schake, K., &Walt, S. M. (2020, March 20). How the world will look after the coronavirus pandemic. *Foreign Policy*. Retrieved from https://foreignpolicy.com/2020/03/20/world-order-after-coroanvirus-pandemic/

Bade, G. (2020, April 3). Despite expanded DPA, confusion reigns over coronavirus industrial response. *Politico*. Retrieved from https://www.politico.com/news/2020/04/03/trump-dpa-medical-goods-164036

Barucco, A. (2020, May 20). Foreign policy after covid: A checklist for a new world. European Council on Foreign Relations. Retrieved from https://www.ecfr.eu/article/commentary_foreign_policy_after_covid_a_checklist_for_a_new_world

Bhattacharjee, J. (2020, August 7). India-Bangladesh relations: A different stroke. *ORF Online*. Retrieved from https://www.orfonline.org/expert-speak/india-bangladesh-relations-different-stroke/

Boykoff, P. (2020, March 28). In the race to secure medical supplies, countries ban or restrict exports. *CNN*. Retrieved from https://edition.cnn.com/2020/03/27/business/medical-supplies-export-ban/index.html

Chaudhary, M., Sodani, P.R., & Das, S. (2020). Effect of COVID-19 on economy in India: Some reflections for policy and programme. *Journal of Health Management*, 22(2) pp. 169–180.

Chaudhury, D. R. (2020, August 19). Highest importance for Bangladesh in India's 'neighbourhood first' policy. *The Economic Times*. Retrieved from https://economictimes.indiatimes.com/news/politics-and-nation/highest-importance-for-bangladesh-in-indias-neighbourhood-first-policy/articleshow/77638216.cms?utm_source=contentofinterest&utm_medium=text&utm_campaign=cppst

European University Institute, Global Trade Alert, and World Bank Group (2020). The COVID-19 pandemic: 21st century approaches to tracking trade policy responses in-real time. Retrieved from https://www.globaltradealert.org/reports/54

Fuchs, M. H. (2020, July 23). A foreign policy for the post-pandemic world: How to prepare for the next crisis. *Foreign Affairs*. Retrieved from https://www.foreignaffairs.com/articles/2020-07-24/foreign-policy-post-pandemic-world

Harvard Kennedy School (2020, June 24). How COVID-19 has changed public policy. Retrieved from https://www.hks.harvard.edu/faculty-research/policy-topics/public-leadership-management/how-covid-19-has-changed-public-policy

Hindustan Times (2020, September 21). 'Committed to global order based on rules in post-Covid-19 world': Harsh Shringla on foreign policy priorities. Retrieved from https://www.hindustantimes.com/india-news/committed-to-global-order-based-on-rules-in-post-covid-19-world-harsh-shringla-on-foreign-policy-priorities/story-zC7ohdSW5Qy9S5XDRc6RwJ.html

Hossain, D. H. & Islam, M. S. (2020). *COVID-19 global pandemic and aspects of human security in South Asia: Implications and way forward*. New Delhi: Pentagon Press.

Kumaraswami, S. (2020, July 27). Relationship with India rock solid: Bangladesh. *Deccan Chronicle*. Retrieved from https://www.deccanchronicle.com/nation/in-other-news/270720/relationship-with-india-rock-solid-bangladesh.html

McCann, G. & Matenga, C. (2020). COVID-19 and Global Inequality. In P. Carmody, G. McCann, C. Colleran, & O'Halloran (Eds.), *COVID-19 in the Global South: Impacts and responses* (pp.161-171). Bristol University Press. Retrieved from https://www.jstor.org/stable/j.ctv18gfz7c.22

MOFA, Dhaka (2020a, May 2). Regional Cooperation: SAARC Initiatives on COVID-19. Retrieved from https://mofa.gov.bd/site/page/9ee3e51e-29dd-4619-9088-e82a63b32a05/Regional-Cooperation

MOFA, Dhaka (2020b, September 29). Joint Statement on the Sixth Meeting of the India-Bangladesh Joint Consultative Commission. Retrieved from https://mofa.gov.bd/site/page/947fae98-5490-4700-a2cd-7b304de3eaf2

Mustasilta, K. (2020). From bad to worse? The impact(s) of Covid-19 on conflict dynamics. (pp.1-8). European Union Institute for Security Studies (EUISS), Retrieved from https://www.jstor.org/stable/resrep25022

Noyon, A. U. (2020, July 5). Bangladesh-India trade relations under strain. *The Business Standard*. Retrieved from https://tbsnews.net/economy/trade/bangladesh-india-trade-relations-under-strain-102277

Ranjan, P. (2020, November 20). India's mask of economic liberalism is off. *The Hindu*. Retrieved from https://www.thehindu.com/opinion/lead/indias-mask-of-economic-liberalism-is-off/article33135677.ece

Rees, V. (2020, March 23). UK bans parallel exporting of crucial medicines to help COVID-19 patients. *European Pharmaceutical Review*. Retrieved from https://www.europeanpharmaceuticalreview.com/news/115637/uk-bans-parallel-exporting-of-crucial-medicines-to-help-covid-19-patients/

Sharfuddin, S. (2020). The world after Covid-19. *The Round Table*, 109 (3), pp. 247-257.

The Business Standard (2020a, August 18). Indian FS Harsh Vardhan arrives in Dhaka to boost ties. Retrieved from https://tbsnews.net/bangladesh/indian-fs-harsh-vardhan-arrives-dhaka-boost-ties-120973

The Business Standard (2020b, August 19). Bangladesh to get priority for Indian Covid-19 vaccine: Shringla. Retrieved from https://tbsnews.net/bangladesh/bangladesh-get-priority-indian-covid-19-vaccine-shringla-121516

The Daily Star (2020, August 20). Indian Foreign Secy's Visit: Dhaka, Delhi join hands on vaccine. Retrieved from https://www.thedailystar.net/frontpage/news/indian-foreign-secys-visit-dhaka-delhi-join-hands-vaccine-1947809

Toosi, N. (2020, April 3). 'Lord of the Flies: PPE Edition': U.S. cast as culprit in global scrum over coronavirus supplies. *Politico*. Retrieved from https://www.politico.com/news/2020/04/03/ppe-world-supplies-coronavirus-163955

11

LOOKING AHEAD:
STRENGTHENING THE PARTNERSHIP

The central argument of this book is that Bangladesh and India need each other for peace, prosperity, security, and development. It shows that Bangladesh-India ties have improved significantly since 2010. The long-standing maritime dispute resolution, the ratification of the Land Boundary Agreement, coastal shipping agreement, agreement on blue economy and maritime cooperation, growing development partnership, energy cooperation, security cooperation, cooperation over connectivity and increasing people-to-people contacts are hallmark developments in contemporary Bangladesh-India relations. Despite such improvements yet, water-sharing dispute, trade imbalance, border killings and NRC issue remain key challenges in Bangladesh-India relations. The domestic politics of India is creating more hurdles in water sharing and NRC issues, which require serious attention. This book also finds that the recent protectionist policy embraced by the Indian government will seriously impact Bangladesh-India trade relations. Against such a backdrop, this book contends that instead of focusing on narrowly defined short-term interests, Bangladesh and India need to work for their long term interests which requires visionary leadership, wisdom, and undoubtedly, reciprocal action. It is argued that nurturing a strong partnership in the areas of mutual concern and interest becomes essential to ensure the well-being of these two countries and beyond. This book suggests that it becomes necessary to take into account that following policy imperatives seriously strengthen the Bangladesh-India partnership.

First, a sustainable and warm political relationship between Bangladesh and India becomes necessary for the long term interests of these two countries. In this case, political regimes in both countries need to play a crucial role. For instance, one can argue that Bangladesh-India relations have become a model for others because of the role played by the Sheikh Hasina regime in Bangladesh and Manmohan Singh and later the Narendra Modi regime in India. Instead of narrowly defined regime interest, the political leadership on both sides need to understand the broader necessities and broader perspectives of the people of these two countries for shared prosperity and development based on a win-win situation.

Second, strengthening the existing development partnership becomes essential for the welfare and benefits of the people of both Bangladesh and India, as Chapter Three shows. In fact, trade and investment directly transform the lives of millions of people across boundaries. In addition, Bangladesh-India energy cooperation has positively impacted tens of thousands of people in Bangladesh. This book also notes that despite being close neighbours, Bangladesh and India could not utilise their investment potential for their mutual benefit for a long time. Bangladesh and India are the fastest-growing economies in the world with immense untapped potential. The business community can utilise this economic potential for their investments. Notably, Bangladesh is preparing special economic zones for Indian investors, which requires proactive actions from them. Indeed, forging agricultural and blue economy cooperation, and cooperation on knowledge sharing need to be prioritised in the Bangladesh-India partnership. This book also suggests that, in the post-pandemic world, there is no alternative to the promotion of Bangladesh-India economic cooperation at the bilateral, regional, and global levels instead of focusing on protectionist policies.

Third, this book argues that the role of India is critically essential in deepening Bangladesh-India relations. In this context, the *Indian Express* notes that India needs to recognise that 'each nation is an equal, irrespective of size, and has its agency. Inversely, as the biggest country in the region, India must show a large-heartedness and generosity that has been missing for too long, replaced by a blunt transactionalism' (*The Indian Express* Editorial, 2020). The daily also suggests that India's 'engagement with neighbours needs to be constant and large-hearted' (*The Indian Express* Editorial, 2020). It is argued that 'Dhaka, under her [Sheikh Hasina's] leadership, has proved herself to be New Delhi's most trusted ally in its fight against terror. Now it is India's turn to reciprocate with magnanimity' (Ghosh, 2017). Thus, it becomes important to change India's perceptions and policies towards Bangladesh. In this context, Mihir S. Sharma (2011) writes that 'Most importantly, New Delhi's mindset must change. India needs to go the extra mile, ensuring market access for Bangladesh'. *The Hindustan Times*, in its editorial (2020) also argues that 'Once derided as a basket case, Bangladesh is now the fastest growing economy in South Asia; it surpasses India on many development indicators, and has overtaken Pakistan's economy. The Indian vision of Bangladeshis...needs to be replaced with a realisation that migrants cross in both directions'. Another scholar, Rajiv Sikri, in his book, *Challenge and Strategy: Rethinking India's Foreign Policy* contends that 'From the perspective of India's Northeast Region, Bangladesh is India's most important neighbour, one that India simply cannot afford to ignore' (Sikri, 2009, p.58). Thus, India needs to nurture its partnership with Bangladesh based on mutual respect, benefit and reciprocity.

Fourth, the role of civil society needs to be proactive and constructive in deepening Bangladesh-India relations. More specifically, there is an increased need for concrete academic and media cooperation between Bangladesh and India. Unfortunately, the level of importance of Bangladesh-India relations at the practice level is not observed at the academic level. There is a paucity of both scholars and scholarship on Bangladesh-India ties which needs to be promoted. Consequently, it becomes crucial to introduce courses on Bangladesh Affairs at the Indian higher educational institutions and Indian Affairs at Bangladeshi higher educational institutions. There is also an increased need for promoting exchange programmes of students, teachers, researchers, and intellectuals. Additionally, increasing the number of scholarships to study in India and in Bangladesh on issues of mutual concern will be necessary. Thus, it becomes essential to simplify research and student visas. The Indian media needs to play a more active role in addressing the concerns of Bangladesh, i.e., the water sharing issue, border killings, NRC and trade imbalance.

This book argues that more editorials, open-editorials and front-page stories need to be written showing Bangladesh's contributions in addressing India's concerns, i.e., the security concerns, connectivity issue with India's Northeastern states, and the overall importance of Bangladesh for India and vice versa. The geostrategic significance of Bangladesh, the importance of the emerging development partnership between Bangladesh and India, the possibilities in Bangladesh-India connectivity, the importance of deepening people-to-people contacts, and the implications of better, improved Bangladesh-India relations to the tens of thousands of people across the borders, and most importantly, the necessity of demonstrating India's reciprocal action needs to be highlighted in the Indian media. If the Indian print media writes about Bangladesh's concerns regularly, one can expect a solution to the concerned issues which can result in a developed and sustainable Bangladesh-India partnership for the long-term benefit of the people of these two countries and beyond.

Fifth, nurturing people-to-people contact becomes important in deepening Bangladesh-India relations in the days to come. More specifically, for a sustainable partnership, it becomes essential to take people into confidence on both sides in general and Bangladesh in particular. The issue of water sharing has created disappointment and frustration among the people of Bangladesh. In fact, Bangladesh showed a positive gesture to address the demand for drinking water for the people of Tripura's Sabroom town. Thus, for the greater interests of the partnership, it is important for India to understand the people's perspective in Bangladesh and address the concerns of the country, especially the water sharing issue. Here, the strong political will of India becomes critically important. In addition, increasing the volume of cultural exchange programmes, including exchanges of students, teachers and musicians will be imperative in accelerating people-to-people contacts.

Finally, this book finds that there is a possibility of the rise of protectionism and less cooperation in the post-pandemic world. The coronavirus crisis showed the world about the apparent absence of global leadership when it was badly needed. Thus, it becomes imperative for both Bangladesh and India to support each other in the international forums on common causes including global health governance, climate change, and free trade. It is also argued that economic cooperation, peace, and stability would benefit all the countries in South Asia, including Bangladesh and India. In this context, India and Bangladesh need to constructively cooperate at the regional scale for a prosperous and peaceful South Asia in the post-COVID-19 world, which would ultimately benefit everyone. Additionally, if one looks at the national scale, the people in Bangladesh and India are interdependent and interconnected. Thus, a policy that is decided in New Delhi or Dhaka impacts the lives and livelihoods of many. For instance, the decision taken by the Indian government not to export onions to Bangladesh impacts the market largely, which directly impacts the lives of the Bangladeshi people. There is also a possibility of increasing intense food insecurity in South Asia in the post-pandemic world which requires cooperation over agriculture and food security. Thus, it is strongly suggested that India and Bangladesh need to promote free trade and cooperation at the bilateral, regional, and global levels in the interest of both the countries and beyond.

The contributions of this book are both theoretical and policy-oriented. From a policy perspective, its findings will be imperative for policymakers to deepen Bangladesh-India relations based on mutual trust, interest, and reciprocity. From a theoretical perspective, this book fills the existing knowledge gap in contemporary Bangladesh-India relations. More specifically, it is argued that the book contributes theoretically in eight specific areas. First, one should note that the Bangladesh-India development partnership has become an example of good neighbourly relations. But there is a paucity of scholarship on the Bangladesh-India development partnership, especially in the context of bilateral investments and energy cooperation. In this context, Chapter Three exactly fills the existing knowledge gap on the aspect of a development partnership between Bangladesh and India. Second, scholarship on security cooperation or challenges in South Asia predominantly focus on India-Pakistan rivalry while the Bangladesh-India security issue remains understudied. Sumit Ganguly *et al.* (2010, p.4), for instance, in their introduction note that '[t]he most compelling security issue in South Asia remains the Indo-Pakistan dispute over the state of Jammu and Kashmir'. Thus, it is important to understand Bangladesh-India security cooperation. Against this backdrop, Chapter Four of this book fills the existing knowledge gap on the Bangladesh-India security partnership. Third, after the LBA's ratification, the conventional wisdom is that tensions along the Bangladesh-India border are over. But the existing reality is that despite LBA ratification, challenges still remain in Bangladesh-India border management. There is no scholarship available covering the post-LBA Bangladesh-India border cooperation and challenges comprehensively. In this regard, Chapter Five makes a major contribution. It argues that instead of tensions and conflicts, the long Bangladesh-India border can be translated into possibilities that can immensely benefit the people across the borders. Fourth, the water-sharing issue remains a critical challenge in Bangladesh-India relations. There is no scholarly account on the question of why the Bangladesh-India water sharing dispute has not been resolved yet. This is precisely where Chapter Six makes a contribution. Fifth, the issue of connectivity is the hallmark in contemporary Bangladesh-India relations, though the subject remains understudied. Thus, the critical contribution of Chapter Seven is to fill this knowledge gap in the Bangladesh-India connectivity dimension. Sixth, existing literature on Bangladesh-India relations is dominated by state-centric analysis, in which the aspect of civil society is sidelined. In this context, Chapter Eight fills this knowledge gap precisely. Seventh, China is a key development partner of Bangladesh. The growing Bangladesh-China partnership is often seen critically from the academic and policy establishments of New Delhi. Against this backdrop, Chapter Nine contributes theoretically in the context of the China factor in Bangladesh-India relations. Finally, the conduct of a state's foreign policy and international relations would be impacted substantially in the post-pandemic world. In this context, Chapter Ten fills the existing knowledge gap in Bangladesh-India cooperation in the post-COVID-19 world. It is worthy to mention future research agendas. One of them would be to exclusively investigate the dynamics in Bangladesh-India relations in the post-COVID-19 era. The second research area could be to investigate the role of the epistemic community in Bangladesh-India relations. The third area would be to examine the role of mental borders in the Bangladesh-India border issue.

REFERENCES

Ganguly, S.; Liow, J. C. & Scobell, A. (2010). Introduction. In S. Ganguly, A. Scobell and J. C. Liow (Eds.), *The Routledge Handbook of Asian security studies* (pp. 1-8), Abingdon, Oxon: Routledge.

Ghosh, M. (2017, April 6). Hasina's visit could take India-Bangladesh ties to the next level if India plays its cards right. *Hindustan Times*. Retrieved from https://www.hindustantimes.com/analysis/hasina-s-visit-could-take-india-bangladesh-ties-to-the-next-level-if-india-plays-its-cards-right/story-WkW90oBLsVyDbUgJD7AGvI.html

Hindustan Times Editorial (2020, December 18). The Delhi-Dhaka bond: Sustain the partnership, reconcile domestic narratives, and manage China. Retrieved from https://www.hindustantimes.com/editorials/the-delhi-dhaka-bond-ht-editorial/story-pVlB1Yhp0J9DAHA2xyzWXJ.html

Sharma, M. S. (2011, July 5). The Delhi-Dhaka distance. *The Indian Express*. Retrieved from http://archive.indianexpress.com/news/the-delhidhaka-distance/812740/0

Sikri, R. (2009). *Challenge and strategy: Rethinking India's foreign policy*. New Delhi: Sage.

The Indian Express Editorial (2020, August 20). Repair and mend. Retrieved from https://indianexpress.com/article/opinion/editorials/repair-and-mend-6561757/

INDEX

Abdullah, Mohammad Mohiuddin, 123
Abraham, Itty, 167
Act East Policy, 173
Adani Power (Jharkhand) India, 58
Adarsh Swaika, 46
Advani, L.K., the then Indian Deputy Prime Minister, 28
Agartala to Chattogram port/Mongla port via Akhaura, 121
Agreement for Mutual Cooperation, 28
Agreement on Combating Terrorism, organised Crime and Illicit Drug Trafficking, 74
Agreement on Crude Oil, 20
Agreement on Cultural Cooperation, 20
Agreement on Mutual Legal Assistance in Criminal Matters, 74
Agreement on Transfer of Sentenced Persons, 74
Ahmad, Moen U, Army Chief, visited India, 29
Ahmad, Mozammil, 160
Ahmed, Imtiaz, 91, 102
Akhaura–Agartala Rail Link, 34
Alam, Jahangir, 92
Alam, Mahbubul, 125
Ali, S.M., 20
Ali, Syed Muazzem, 8, 56, 116
All Tripura Tiger Force, 71
Anam, Mahfuz, 46, 70, 74, 135
Ananda Bazar Patrika, 136
ANI, 59
Anti-dumping Duty (ADD), 60
Arms Smuggling, 91
Army-to-Army-Staff talks, 72
Asia Foundation, 110

Assam Accord, 124
Assam, 83, 92, 124, 145
Awami League, 26
Awareness Promoting, 95
AYUSH, 35
Azad, Abdus Samad, Bangladesh Foreign Minister, visited India, 18, 49

Bajpai, Kanti, 144
Bammi, Y.M., 67
Bandhan Express, 120
Banerjee, Mamata, 33-34, 85, 100, 104-06, 108
Bangabandhu Sheikh Mujib Shilpanagar (BSMSN), 157
Bangabandhu Sheikh Mujibur Rahman, 19
Bangladesh, 2-3, 28, 36, 56, 67, 120, 122, 134-35, 139, 157
 National Museum, 38
Bangladesh Bank, 77
Bangladesh Bhavan, 33
Bangladesh Economic Zones Authority, 157
Bangladesh Enterprise Institute (BEI), Dhaka, 147
Bangladesh Foundation for Regional Studies, 145
Bangladesh Nationalist Party (BNP), 24, 27-28, 106, 115, 126
Bangladesh Power Development Board (BPDB), 57
Bangladesh Power System Upgrade and Expansion Project, 156
Bangladesh vessel MB Premier, 122
Bangladesh, Executive Committee of the National Economic Council, 119
Bangladesh, India, Sri Lanka, and Thailand Economic Cooperation (BISTEC), 27

Bangladesh's
   Exports, 51
   Feni River, 105
   Imports, 53-54
   Petrobangla, 58
Bangladesh-China
   Bilateral Trade, 156
   Defence Cooperation, 158
   Economic Cooperation, 155
   Partnership, 160
   Plan of Action on Law Enforcement Training Cooperation, 158
Bangladeshi Export Basket to India, 62
Bangladesh-India, 2, 518-29, 22, 24, 29, 40, 59, 106
   Border, 84-85
      Border Killings, 87-88
      Border Tensions, 93
      Smuggling, 84, 89-92
      Women and Children Trafficking, 93
   Connectivity, 125, 127
   Cooperation on Power, 57
   Development Partnership, 45, 47-48
   Dhaka-Kolkata trail train, 118
   Framework Agreement on Cooperation for Development, Article I, 50
   Friendship Dialogue, 145
   IWT Cooperation, 120
   Rail Links
      Akhaura-Agartala, 119
      Chilahati-Haldibari, 119
      Khulna-Mongla, 119
   Security Cooperation, 67, 70, 78
   Smuggling, 90
   Trade Agreement, 50, 52
   Water Sharing Dispute
      Domestic Politics, 106
      Lack of India's Interest, 104
      Lack of Information/Knowledge of Water, 106
   Role of Media in Strengthening Relations between, 134
Bangladesh-India Friendship Society (BIFS), 145
Barucco, Armando, 167
Basu, Jyoti, 34
Baxter, Craig, 18
BBC, 124

BBIN Motor Vehicles Agreement, 122
bdnews24.com, 56, 158
Begum Khaleda Zia, 27, 117, 142
   visited India, 25, 28
Benapole-Petrapole Integrated Check Post, 119
Bhattacharjee, 137
Bhattacharjee, Joyeeta, 62, 137, 148
Bhutan, 48, 122
Big Brother, 23
BIMSTEC, 36, 173
Bindra, S.S, 67
Biswas, Bibhuti Bhusan, 10
Board of Investment, Bangladesh, 56
Booth, Ken, 69
Border Battle, 93
Border Cooperation Promoting, 94
Border Guards Bangladesh, 92
Border Security Force, 92
BRICS-BIMSTEC Outreach Summit, 32
BSF-BGB cooperation, 95

Carroll, Raymond, 133
CEAT Tyres, 56
Centre for Policy Dialogue (CPD), 147
Centre for Policy Research (CPR), 147
Chakma, 24
Chakravarty, Pinak Ranjan, 36, 116, 118
Changing Volume of Trade, 51-52
Chapainawabganj, 88
Chattogram Hill Tracts (CHT), 24, 26
Chattogram port/Mongla port to
   Agartala via Akhaura, 120
   Dawki via Tamabil, 120
   Srimantapur via Bibirbazar, 121
   Sutarkandi via Sheola, 120
Chaudhury, Dipanjan Roy, 76, 122, 125
China, 39, 154
China Council for the Promotion of International Trade (CCPIT), 155
China Factor in Bangladesh-India Ties, 153-62
China's Belt and Road Initiative (BRI), 156
China-Bangladesh Friend Year, 154
Chinese Investments
   in Bangladesh, 157
Chinese Navy Hospital Ship 'Peace Ark', 158

Index

Chowdhury, Iftekhar Ahmed, 153
Chowdhury, Zaglul Ahmed, 125
Christian Science Monitor, 39
Citizenship Amendment Act, 141
Civil Society, 130-33, 150, 180
Claudia Sadowski-Smith, 84
Closer Comprehensive Partnership of Cooperation, 154
Coastal Shipping Agreement 2015, 120
Combating Terrorism Cooperation on, 73-74
Commerce, Culture and Connectivity (3C Mantra), 117
Confederation of India Industry (CII), 145
Connectivity by Road, 117-19
Connectivity through Waterways, 120-21
Cooperation in Hydrocarbon Sector, 38
Coordinated Border Management Plan (CBMP), 94
Coordinated Patrol (CORPAT), 76-77
Cordner, L., 69
Cordner, Lee, 75
COVID Website, 170
COVID-19, 37, 136, 161, 166, 168-71
Creation of Research Platforms, 170
Creation of SAARC COVID 29 Emergency Fund, 170
Crime Free Zone, 94
Cyber Security Cooperation, 77

Daily Ittefaq, 107
Daily Star, 46
Dainik Inquilab, 27
Das, Riva Ganguly, 121
Das, Riva Ganguly, Indian High Commissioner to Bangladesh, 134
Dawki to Chattogram port/Mongla port via Tamabil, 121
Deb, Rouhin, 160
Deb, Biplab Kumar, 34
Debnath, M.L., 124
Defence Cooperation, 72
Dhaka Tribune, 3, 39, 87, 136, 162
Dhaka University (DU), 144
Dhaka-Kolkata Direct Bus Service, 115
Dhaka-Tongi-Joydebpur Railway Project, 35
Dinhata Camp, 86
Doraiswami, Vikram K., 108

Dowla, Arif, Managing Director, ACI Limited, Bangladesh, 60
Drugs Trafficking, 92
Dutta, Jyoti Prakash, 17

East Pakistan, 7-9
Economic Aspects, 2
Economic Diplomacy, 173
Energy Cooperation, 57
European University Institute, 169
Executive Committee of the National Economic Council (ECNEC), 56
Exercise Bongosagar, 77

Fahim, Sheikh Fazle, 157
Fake Currency Notes, 35
Farakka Barrage Disputes, 2, 24, 101
Farin, Noerita Mahmood, 54
Federation of Bangladesh Chambers of Commerce and Industry (FBCCI), 145
Federation of Chambers of Commerce and Industry (FICCI), 145
Feroz, A.S.M., 101
Firstpost, 72, 159
Foreign Direct Investment (FDI), 55
Framework Agreement on Cooperation for Development, 30
Framework of Understanding (FOU), 38
Free Trade, 4

Galwan Valley, 136
Gandhi, Indira, 9-10
    visited Bangladesh, 20
Gandhi, Sonia, visited Dhaka, 31
Ganga, 104
Ganga Water Sharing Issue, 12, 21, 24-25
Ganguly, Sumit, 182
General Deepak Kapoor, visited Bangladesh, 71
General H.M. Ershad, 22, 24
General Iqbal Karim Bhuiyan, Chief of Army Staff of the Bangladesh Army, 158
General Ziaur Rahman, 22-23
Geopolitical, 5
Geostrategic, 5
Ghosh, Partha S., 10, 143
Giri, V.V., Indian President, 19
Global Trade Alert, 169

Gokhale, Shri Vijay, Indian Foreign Secretary, 34
Gramsci, Antonio, 132
Gujral, I.K., the then Indian Foreign Minister, 34
Guleria, S.S., 91
Gumti River, 121

haats, 52, 62-63, 92
Haidar, Suhasini, 17
Haldibari camp, 86
Harun, Yousuf Abdullah, former FBCCI president, 146
Hasina, Sheikh, Bangladesh Prime Minister, 3, 26, 32, 34-35, 37, 39, 50, 58, 71, 74, 89, 106, 108, 119, 155, 162
Hero Honda, 56
High Contracting Parties, 20
Hooghly River, 101
Hoque, Mazibul, 118
Hossain and Rahman, 59
Huffington Post, 102
Human Trafficking, 35, 84
hundi system, 92
Hydro-diplomacy Culture, 109

Ichhamati, 88
IMF, 51
India-Bangladesh
    Facilitate Overland Transit Traffic between Bangladesh and Nepal, 30
    Protocol to the Agreement Concerning the Demarcation of the Land Boundary, 30
India, 2-3, 8, 39, 51, 67, 120, 122
India's Border Security Force (BSF), 84, 87-88, 95
India's Role, 1971 War, 8-10
India-Bangladesh Chamber of Commerce & Industry (IBCCI), 51, 145-46
India-Bangladesh Dialogue at Track II Level, 147
India-Bangladesh Friendship Pipeline, 35
India-Bangladesh Protocol (IBP), 121
India-locked, 3
Indian Chamber of Commerce (ICC), 145
Indian Coast Guard (ICG), 76
Indian Customs Rules, 2020, 61

Indian Investment in Bangladesh, 161
Indian Navy, 76
Indian Ocean Naval Symposium (IONS), 77
Indian Ocean Regional Institutions Cooperation, 77
Indian Ocean Rim Association (IORA), 77
Information Revolution, 132
Inland Water Transit and Trade, 120
Inland Water Transport (IWT) Links, 120
Institutional/Instrumental Development, 49-50
Integrated Health Platform for Disease Surveillance, 170
Internet Security Threat Report, 77
Investment, 55
Islam, M. Serajul, 125
Islam, Nurul, 53
Islam, Toriqul, 102
Islami, Jamaat E, 106

Jaishankar, S., Indian External Affairs Minister, 170, 172
Jamwal, N.S., Commandant, BSF, 90
Jane's Defence Weekly, 23
Jawaharlal Nehru University (JNU), 144
Jessore, Rights, 93
Jha, Nalini Kant, 10
Joint Boundary Working Groups, 17
Joint Consultative Commission (JCC), 35
Joint Economic Commission (JEC), 17
Joint River's Commission (JRC), 17, 101

Kabir, Arafat, 158
Karim, Masud, 93
Khan, Asaduzzaman, Home Minister of Bangladesh, visited India, 32
Khan, Morshed, Bangladesh Foreign Minister, 28
Khan, Shahab Enam, 137
Khasru, Syed Munir, 38
Khondaker Golam Moazzem, 61
Khoyraati (charity), 136
Kochanek, Stanley A., 26
Krishna, S.M., Indian External Affairs Minister, 94
Kumar, Nitish, Bihar Chief Minister, 100, 102

Index

Kumar, P.R., 159
Kurigram's Rowmari Border Point, 92
Kyunghan Lim, 75

Land Boundary Agreement (LBA), 83, 85-86, 138, 183
Larsen and Toubro Limited (L&T), 58
Least Developed Countries (LDCs), 50
Li Jiming, Chinese Ambassador to Bangladesh, 156, 162
Liberation War of Bangladesh, 1971, 2, 6, 10, 131, 154
Liberation War, 1
Line of Credit (LoC), 37, 56
Liton, Shakhawat, 103
Locke, John, 131
Lu Qian, 87

Mahbubani, Kishore, 170
Maitree Express, 118
Maldives, 122
Malik and Medcalf, 145
Maritime Cooperation, 75-76
McCann and Matenga, 174
Media Role, 131, 133-38
Medical Tourism, 5
Meghalaya, 83, 92, 145
Memorandum of Understanding (MoU), 30-32, 35, 37, 50-51, 70, 76-77, 105, 144
Menon, Shivshankar, 170
Merchant's Chamber of Commerce and Industry (MCCI), 51
Metropolitan Chamber of Commerce and Industry, Bangladesh, 145
Middle East, 76
Military Cooperation Narratives on, 71-72
Ministry of External Affairs, 127
    Annual Report, 29, 31-32, 118
Ministry of Liberation War Affairs, 8
Minorities, 2
Mizoram, 83, 145
Modi, Narendra, 34-35, 37-38, 58, 74, 89, 117, 119, 179
    Visited Bangladesh, 3, 31
Mohan, C. Raja, 6, 123
Momen, A.K. Abdul, Bangladesh Foreign Minister, 123, 136, 108, 162
Mostafizur Rahman, 148

Mukharji, Deb, 144
Mukharji, Shantanu, 160
Mukherjee, Pranab, the then Indian Union Finance Minister, 2
Mukhopadhyay, Asim, 110
Muni, S.D., 23
Munshi, Tipu, Bangladesh Commerce Minister, 116
Murshid, K.A.S., 3
Myanmar, 92

Nachiketa, 49
National Liberation Front of Tripura, 71
National Register of Citizens (NRC), 38-39, 159, 178, 180
National Register of Citizens of Assam, 141
National Thermal Power Corporation (NTPC), 57
Navy-to-Navy-Staff talks, 72
NDTV, 37, 75
Neighbourhood First, 173
Nepal, 47, 122, 159
New Age, 116, 119, 121, 125
Niblett, Robin, 168
Non-tariff barriers (NTB), 59
Nye, Joseph S., 168

ONG Videsh Ltd (OVL), 58
Online Training Capsules, 170

Parbattya Chattagram Jana Sanghati Samity, 25
Parvin, Sitara, 134
Passport and Visa, 20
Peace of Westphalia, 82
People-to-people Contacts, 3, 27, 123, 125, 132, 167, 181
Personal Protective Equipment (PPE), 169
Phulbari-Banglabandha Immigration Check Post, 119
Political Relations, 25
post-COVID-19 World, 5, 13, 173-74, 182
post-LBA Bangladesh-India Border Cooperation, 183
Power Grid Corporation of India Ltd (PGCIL), 57
Problems of Refugees, 2
Prothom Alo English, 70

Protocol on Inland Water Transit and Trade (PIWTT), 105, 119
Protocol on Trans-boundary Elephant Conservation, 38
Pukhrem, Shristi, 132

Rahman, Mofizur, 134
Rahmatullah, 115
Rajkhowa, Aravinda, ULFA Chief, 74
Ranjan, Amit, 84
Rapid Response Teams for COVID-19, 170
Rashiduzzaman, 93
Ray, Jayanta Kumar, 52, 102
Rear Admiral Aurangzeb Chowdhury, 76
Revised Trade Agreement, 28
Rizvi, Gowher, 107, 123
Rohingya Repatriation Diplomacy, 173
Role of Bangladeshi Media, 139-41
Roy, Jayprakash, 86
Roy, Pinaki, 103

SAARC, 5, 25, 28-29, 50, 122
Saran, Pankaj, former Indian High Commissioner in Dhaka, 127
Security Cooperation, 69
Sèna Kimm Gnangnon, 4
Shahriar, Saleh, 87
Shankar, Kalyani, 23
Sharma, Mihir S., 30
Shringla, 173
Shringla, Harsh Vardhan, Indian Foreign Secretary, 22, 36-37, 46, 58, 67, 94, 104, 117, 171
Sikri, Rajiv,
 Challenge and Strategy: Rethinking India's Foreign Policy, 180
Sikri, Veena, 117
Singh, Manmohan, the then Indian Prime Minister, 28, 100, 104, 179
 visited Bangladesh, 48, 68, 85
Singh, Rajkumar, 27, 34, 102
Singh, S. Swaran, 9
Singh, Shiv Sahay, 90
Sobhan, Farooq,
 The State of Terrorism in Bangladesh 2010-2011, 73
Sobhan, Farooq, 70, 109
Sobhan, Rehman, Chairman, Centre for Policy Dialogue, Dhaka, 126
Sokvibol Kea, 87
Sonar Bangla (golden land), 6
South Asia, 1, 51, 120, 144, 182
Special Economic Zone (SEZ), 32
Special Investment Zones, 56
Sri Lanka, 122, 159
Srimantapur to Chattogram port/Mongla port via Bibirbazar, 121
Standard Operating Procedure (SOP), 37, 121
State-to-State Basis Trade, 49
Strategic Satellites, 46
Subramanin, Uma, 124
Sujan, Nurul Islam, Bangladesh Railway Minister, 119
Sutarkandi to Chattogram port/Mongla port via Sheola, 121
Swaraj, Sushma, 33, 35, 56, 107, 116-17
Swaraj, Sushma, the then India's External Affairs Minister,
 visited Bangladesh, 31
Syed Sharfuddin, 173

Tagore, Rabindranath, 6
Taher, Abu, 86
Taken for Granted, 46
Tariffs and Non-tariff Barriers, 62
Tata Group, 56
Teesta Water Dispute, 100, 103-04, 107
Telecommunication, 20
Terrorism, 73
Thailand, 122
Thakkar, Himanshu, 106
The Asia Foundation, 60
The Business Standard, 105, 136, 161, 170-72
The Daily Janakantha, 33
The Daily Jugantar, 35
The Daily Kaler Kantha, 74
The Daily Prothom Alo, 31
The Daily Samakal, 31, 71, 85
The Daily Star Online, 108
The Daily Star, 5, 17, 35, 38, 46-47, 50, 54, 56-57, 60, 62, 70-71, 73, 77, 85-88, 90-91, 93, 95, 101, 103, 106-09, 116, 118-19, 122-23, 126, 132, 134-35, 142, 144, 146, 148, 154-55, 157-58, 162, 172
The Diplomat, 158

The Economic Times, 33, 74
The Financial Express, 60-62
The Hindu, 5, 17, 58, 68, 76, 89, 94, 107, 136
The Hindustan Times, 3, 68, 173, 180
The Independent, 158
The Indian Express, 3-5, 40, 74, 85, 107-08, 118, 179-80
The Statesman, 106
The Times of India, 68, 76-77, 124, 136
The World Bank, 60
Think Tanks, 146-48
Think West, 173
Third IORA Ministerial Blue Economy Conference, 77
Tin Bigha, 21
Tourism and Medical Tourism, 4
Trade, 48
    Agreement, 20
Treaty of Friendship and Peace, 20
Tripura, 83, 92, 145

UNB News, 121, 156
United Nations Human Rights Council, 39
United Nations, 9

Vajpayee, Atal Bihari, the then Indian Prime Minister, 26
    visited Bangladesh, 27
Vanish, 54
VAP Global, 54
Video Conference of Trade Officials, 170

Walt, Stephen M., 69, 168, 172
Water Conflict, 111
Water War, 111
West Bengal, 83, 142
West Pakistan, 7, 8, 9, 18
Wilson, Woodrow, 69
Win-win situation, 122
Win-win situation, 123
World Bank Group, 169

Xavier, Constantino, 159
Xi Jinping, China's President, 154-55

Zaman, Khandaker R., 121
Zamir, Muhammad, 101
Zhang Zuo, 156

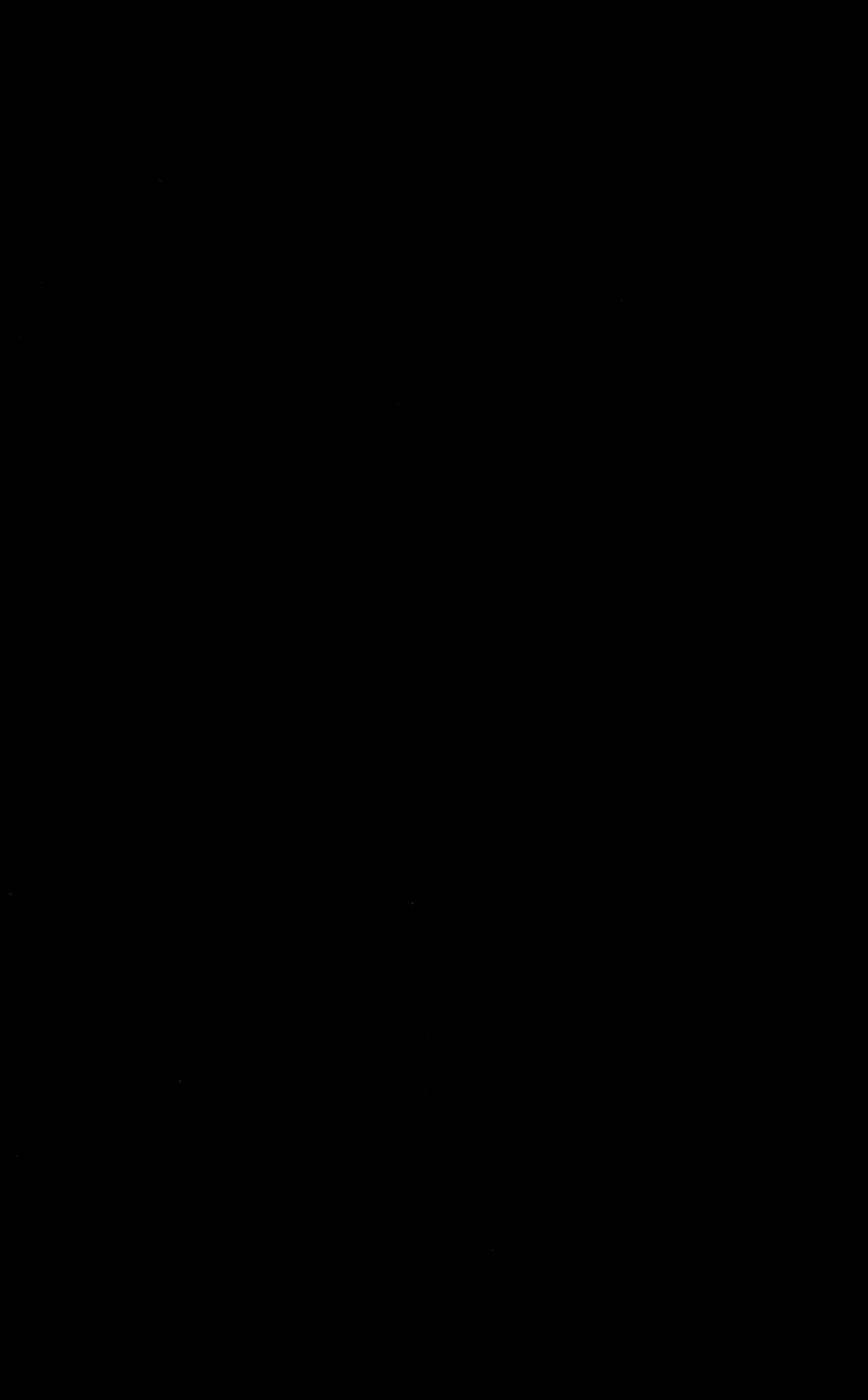